AF304879

The Real Story of the American Revolution

The Real Story of the American Revolution

Separating Myth From Reality

Mike Wells

First published in Great Britain in 2026 by
Pen & Sword History
An imprint of Pen & Sword Books Limited
Yorkshire – Philadelphia

ISBN 978 1 03611 080 2

A CIP catalogue record for this book is
available from the British Library.

Typeset by Mac Style
Printed in the UK by CPI Group (UK) Ltd, Croydon, CR0 4YY.

The Publisher's authorised representative in the EU for product
safety is Authorised Rep Compliance Ltd., Ground Floor,
71 Lower Baggot Street, Dublin D02 P593, Ireland.
www.arccompliance.com

For a complete list of Pen & Sword titles please contact:

PEN & SWORD BOOKS LIMITED
47 Church Street, Barnsley, South Yorkshire, S70 2AS, England
E-mail: enquiries@pen-and-sword.co.uk
Website: www.pen-and-sword.co.uk
or
PEN AND SWORD BOOKS
1950 Lawrence Road, Havertown, PA 19083, USA
E-mail: uspen-and-sword@casematepublishers.com
Website: www.penandswordbooks.com

Contents

Foreword

This is a small book about a big event which has been written about in many very big books and very well-researched articles by scholars to whom I am indebted. It does not even attempt to cover all aspects of the birth of modern America, nor to deal with the contributions of everyone involved. It does little to consider major elements that brought the end of British rule, such as the support various European powers gave to the revolution. Instead, it offers a critical overview and is an attempt to acknowledge alternative perceptions of some accepted narratives of events and to challenge some of the ways they have been interpreted. It brings back into focus some unpopular and less remembered views of those who were sceptical about taking opposition to Britain to the point of separation. It uses the words of those who were involved and engages with the costs, as well as the achievements, of conflict and change.

Introduction

The colonial and revolutionary past has a special place in the history of the US, so much so that it can be interpreted differently according to current preoccupations. This can be seen in both history books and fictional representations. It can also be seen in museums and reconstructions.

One of the most visited historical attractions in the US is the colonial town of Williamsburg, the former capital of Virginia. The real Williamsburg had sunk into decay by the early years of the twentieth century but historical enthusiasts, with very generous support from the great oil company Standard Oil and its founder John D. Rockefeller, reconstructed and remade the town during the 1920s and 1930s. It became a living museum of colonial America. At a time of economic depression, fear of Communism, the rise of political extremism and social tensions, Rockefeller aimed to reassure Americans of the wholesome traditions of the past and to stress American virtues.

In the pristine and well-maintained buildings could be found the roots of liberty in the Virginia assembly building, the House of Burgesses. Simple good taste and prosperity could be found in its mansions. Piety and clean living could be seen in its fine whitewashed church. Healthy industry could be seen in its workshops. The reconstructed – or perhaps constructed town was overlooked by the fine William and Mary College, a monument to the American Enlightenment.

It is hard not to enjoy visiting Williamsburg and being shown round by guides in immaculately reconstructed eighteenth-century costumes. There is a lot to see – artefacts, furniture, all sorts of buildings. The past comes to life. And there are plenty of pleasant cafes and restaurants for families to enjoy.

It seems a shame to be critical of such an attractive venue, but Williamsburg is not the past; it is a view of the past coloured by the desire of its creators to offer a view of colonial America. Interestingly, the church used by Black Americans was not reconstructed. It lay under a carpark until more recently excavated in an attempt to be more inclusive. What is celebrated in Williamsburg is sturdy enterprise by prosperous White males. Abused enslaved people, indentured labourers, the poor, the sick, abused women, beaten children, social conflict and the smells and filth of eighteenth-century life do not appear. The very limited franchise and the lack of real democracy do not figure strongly in the presentations about the House of Burgesses.

Well, why should all the downside of eighteenth-century life appear in what is essentially a museum or, more unkindly, a theme park? If visitors have a sense of being in the past, that awakens an interest in history, and does it matter if it is a rather one-sided view? Perhaps not, but illusions about the past can distort views of the present and 'golden ages' can be quite dangerous. The mentality of some sort of lost innocence or the need to restore virtues and qualities which did not exist can mislead and distort understanding of the past.

Russian nationalists who look back to a non-existent historical past of Great and Holy Russia as an excuse for a war of aggression have had a disastrous effect on modern policy making. The Hitler and Mussolini regimes looked back to eras of mythical greatness – Teutonic tribes living racially pure and virtuous lives, or the greatness of the Roman Empire. In Britain, nostalgia for simpler times of greater virtue have meant an odd idealisation of the era of the Second World War and the 1950s. The French Revolution justified violence in pursuit of a Republican virtue to be found in an unhistorical and mythical view of the ancient world.

In the US, it is still unsettling for many Americans to have established views about the past challenged. In a discussion about slavery in New England in the 1630s, a blog host was genuinely disconcerted when a historian presented evidence that the God-fearing Puritans had traded slaves.

Despite academic studies, the image of the colonial past as it appears in Williamsburg has a very strong emotional hold. Pious and freedom-loving colonists; brave and enterprising settlers; the development of a separate American identity which rejected the privilege and restrictions of Britain; the struggle for liberty; the heroics of colonists who took on and defeated the world's greatest maritime empire; the cruelty and stupidity of British rule; the excitement and purity of the new Republic; the greatness of the Constitution which still guides and defends American liberty; the fine leaders that emerged from rebellion and war. All these elements guided 'The Empire of Liberty', began the American story, set standards for later conduct, and formed the basis of greatness.

All nations need self-belief, and it would be ridiculous not to see some truth in this vision, but like Williamsburg, it is not the whole truth and as well as being the basis of US strengths, the Revolution was also the basis of some of the enduring problems and difficulties in US life. In addition, some of the participants have been rather neglected or, in some cases, overestimated. This is not resolved by some modern attempts at inclusion, for example having Hamilton portrayed in the musical by a Black actor or having information about George Washington's slave ownership at historical sites which generally commemorate his achievements.

Images of the American Revolution have not, on the whole, been as common in films as later stages of American history such as the Civil War and the American West. Two of the most popular were Hugh Hudson's 1985 movie *Revolution* and the 2000 *The Patriot* starring Mel Gibson. Both feature protagonists who are initially unwilling to participate in the Revolution but are forced to by circumstances. In *Revolution* Al Pacino is an illiterate trapper coerced by a patriotic mob to enlist and then driven to enthusiasm by the ill treatment of his son by sadistic British troops. In *The Patriot*, Gibson is a South Carolina planter who is unwilling to fight because of horrific experience in the wars against the French. He too is driven to enthusiasm by sadistic British actions which kill two of his sons. In both films there is general enthusiasm for the cause of liberty. Dissent is seen in *The Patriot* mainly in the form of a cowardly American loyalist who takes part in killing civilians. In *Revolution* it takes the form of an empty-headed loyalist mother and her silly daughters who want to catch well-born British husbands. In both movies the British troops are shown either as unthinking automata marching in line or as brutal sadists. In *Revolution* a sadistic sergeant beats and mutilates Al Pacino's son and relishes spearing colonial troops. In *The Patriot* a sadistic colonel locks a village community in a church and burns it down in the manner of Nazi troops. Both films have quite graphic violence with an exaggerated view of the possibilities of eighteenth-century firearms and a failure to depict fully the fog caused by gun smoke in eighteenth-century battles. The number of very young American soldiers is a reality not reflected in the movies. Native Americans appear as participants in *Revolution* albeit in small numbers but there is little depiction of African Americans. Where women are shown, they are either hysterical patriots or foolish and trivial loyalists. In *The Patriot* there are some slaves, but they are well dressed and loyal to the heroic Mel Gibson, one even saving a rather obnoxious racist White patriot to show his devotion to the cause which he hopes will free him. *The Patriot* is filmed in beautiful countryside suggesting a rural idyll. *Revolution* has more rain, mud and dirtier clothes and grubbier towns. Both celebrate heroism and in *Revolution*, Pacino's son rides off to set up a farm somewhere out west and there is stirring commentary from the hitherto rather inarticulate Pacino about liberty and opportunity.

In a lively and engaging 2000 movie for television, *The Crossing*, the very personable Jeff Daniels plays George Washington leading his troops over the Delaware to a victory against the Hessians (German troops used by the British). The online reviews were favourable, despite historical errors and omissions, and one said that every American patriotic person should see the movie. The authoritarianism of Washington, who in reality insisted on being addressed as 'Your Excellency', was less in evidence than the dedicated leader. Failures and brutality were not shown. This Washington would not have hanged a spy in New Jersey or supported the execution of a captured British officer at Yorktown in retaliation for loyalist atrocities. The filmed crossing took place in mild weather not the rain and bitter cold of the real crossing, in which any falling into the Delaware would have met with death. The army was older and better dressed than the real army. Alexander Hamilton (of rap musical fame) was shown as Washington's aide, whereas this promotion came later. And so on. However, what was important was that the film fitted in with very common and acceptable ideas and, even if the violence was overdone, the key point was that the heroic legend was maintained.

So here we have White males dominating the proceedings, a vile and demonised British enemy, and little focus on the internal strife between patriots and loyal colonists that was a major feature of the war. Little consideration of the extent of the role of other elements such as African Americans, Native Americans, foreign powers and women. The underlying myths are not unduly disturbed.

What follows is an attempt to probe an accepted narrative and to put some familiar events into a wider context. It is not new, and historians have repeatedly tried to undermine the heroic vision of the Revolution, sometimes creating interpretations that themselves veer into unreality, such as the view that the American War of Independence was fought solely to preserve slavery.

The aim is not to belittle what was a bitter and often heroic struggle against the world's greatest military power by forces with limited resources. It is, however, an attempt to look more realistically at what happened in the context of eighteenth-century life and attitudes.

The events and developments described confirm two 'laws' of history observed by the author over a long period of studying the past. The first was stated in a long-forgotten series of undergraduate lectures at Oxford by a visiting professor of American history. It is the law of unconscious hypocrisy. As stated in the lecture *'All men are hypocrites but not consciously so'*. At the time, dismissed by me and my fellow students as a platitude, now it appears a profound historical truth. It did not occur to some of the most highly educated and able men in America in the second half of the eighteenth century that it was utterly hypocritical to talk so much about 'freedom' while relying on enslaved people for economic survival and, in one notable case and in many others less famous, emotional and sexual comfort. A moment's thought will reveal any number of contemporary examples of a similar nature, such as over 400 delegates flying off to a conference to reduce the use of fossil fuel. The other law is that of unintended consequences. To achieve more prosperity, the colonists fought a long and debilitating war which ended in reducing that prosperity. Concerned about freedom from relatively modest taxes, they fought a costly war in which forced military service took away one of the key rights in the Declaration of Independence – life itself. Eager to rid themselves of a king who only intermittently imposed his policy on them, the colonists devised a form of government which gave them an elected monarch who, over the years, created a form of government which affected the lives of Americans more extensively than the founding fathers ever dreamed of. Resorting to war rarely delivers what was intended, and the American War of Independence was no exception.

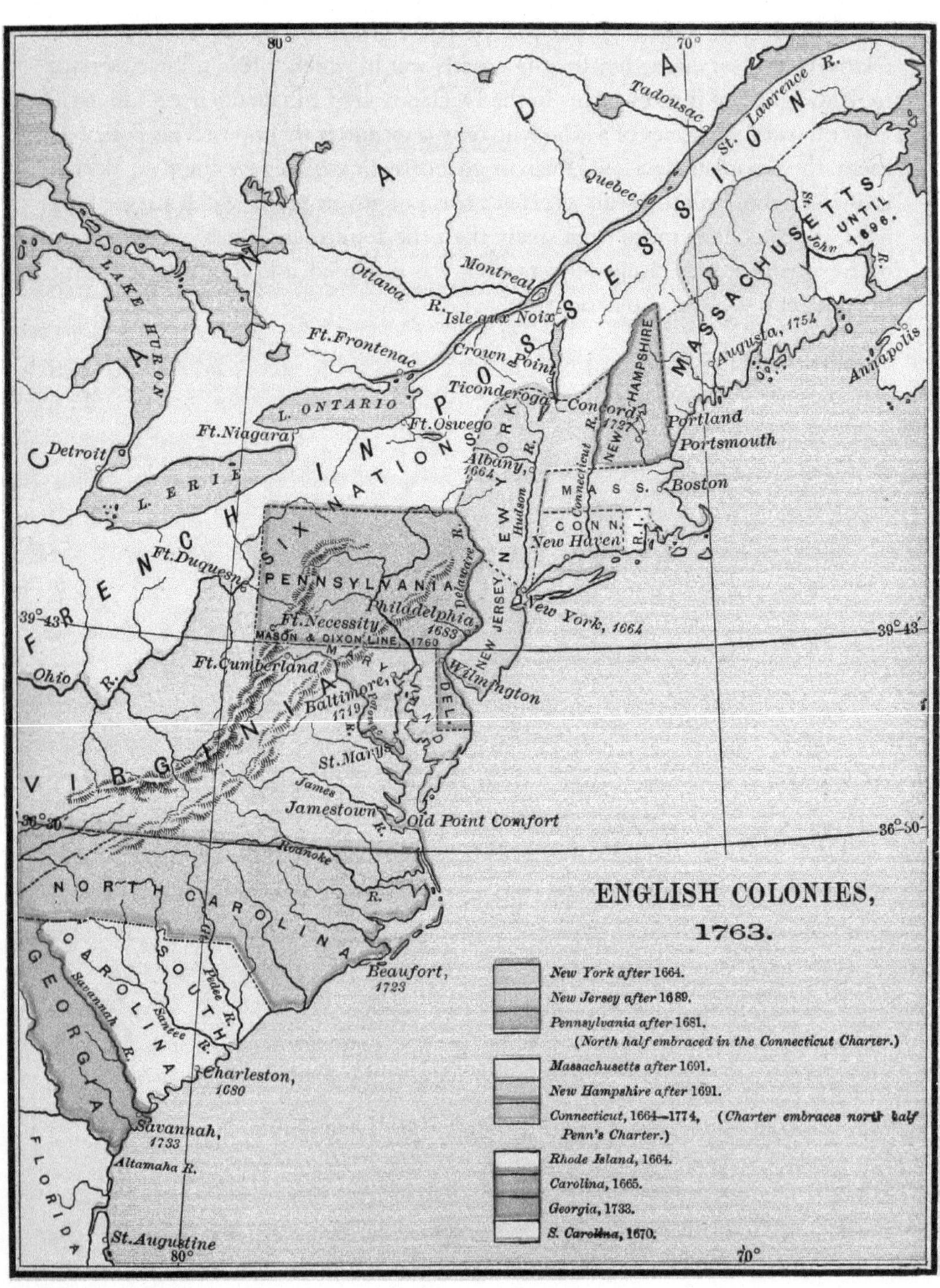

British North America in 1763.

Chapter 1

The American Colonies in 1763

One of the most remarkable aspects of the thirteen British colonies in America in 1763, that were to form the American Republic twenty years later, was the growth in population that had taken place in the previous fifty years. Often in history, great events have population change as their underlying cause. This was certainly true of the considerable growth of population which drove Britain's Industrial Revolution and the development of nation states and subsequent world wars. It will probably be seen as the key factor in changes in Britain in the twenty-first century. It was a major factor in the American Revolution, though rarely seen as such by many historians who prefer to see politics and ideology as the driving force. Colonial reconstructions such as Williamsburg reflect a static society, but a few figures will show that colonial America was in the grip of considerable demographic change. In 1700 there were 250,000 inhabitants. By 1763 this had risen to 1.54 million. The number of Black slaves exceeded the total population of fifty years before. The politically volatile colonies of Massachusetts and Virginia were experiencing dramatic population rise. Massachusetts had had only 55,000 people in 1700 but had over 200,000 in 1763. Virginia had jumped from 58,000 to 340,000. Not only had South Carolina's population grown from 6000 to 110,000, but by 1763 White people were in a minority.

An oddity is that when many books and websites give information about population, the Native American population – possibly some 600,000 – are not counted. Their population had declined as dramatically as the White and Black population had grown since 1600. Estimates are as high as six million in 1600. The arrival of Europeans was a disaster. A *Private Eye* cartoon of 2024 shows some Native Americans watching the arrival of the *Mayflower* with the ironic caption 'stop the boats'. Whatever the effects on Europe in the 2020s of migrants arriving in boats, it is nothing compared to the disease and destruction the European migrants of the seventeenth and eighteenth centuries had on the indigenous population. The final insult is to be omitted so much from population figures.

The growth of population meant that the colonies were a much younger society, more racially varied and more motivated to expand. It meant, as in most periods of population growth, more pressure on resources and eventually a growth of urban centres, though by 1763 over 90 per cent of colonial dwellers lived on farms.

More people provided markets for goods and also a larger work force. They provided people for military purposes, and they offered more of a target for taxation by the mother country. More people offered problems of control for the very limited resources of colonial government. More people read more books, talked about new ideas, looked for more opportunities, and wanted more land.

Divisions

The growth of population was obviously a key element in the American Revolution, but in terms of the size of the colonial areas the actual population was small. The entire White population could be fitted into modern day Liverpool. If they were miraculously swapped for the current population of Leeds-Bradford there would be spare accommodation. There are over seven times more people in modern greater London.

The word 'colony' as it was later understood does not really describe the British settlements on the eastern seaboard of North America by 1763. The people who had come from Britain saw themselves as British rather than colonial subjects in the manner of the Victorian Empire's colonised people. In terms of language and culture they were linked to the home country more than was possibly true of contemporary Ireland or Scotland. The colonies had been founded at different times between 1607 and 1713 by different groups and had developed in different ways. As the colonies later became 'states' it is tempting to see them as more unified and having more loyalty from their inhabitants than was the case. Nationality, as we know it, was not a strong feature of the eighteenth century. Most European states owed loyalty to a remote ruler whom few subjects had ever seen but who was the main unifying factor in very diverse societies. However, the main bond was not belonging to a nation, but to local communities. It is not possible to speak meaningfully of a French nation, for example, in 1763 as 'France' was a network of provinces and communities with different laws, currencies, languages, religions, cultures and economies. The same is even more true of 'Germany' which existed only as a historical concept and 'Italy', both of which had to wait until the middle of the nineteenth century to achieve some sort of meaningful unity. For most Europeans the state was not something to inspire patriotic passion, but an intrusion into a much smaller and more meaningful community life.

The colonists took with them European attitudes and concepts and 'America' was no more than a geographical concept. Though the term 'American' was in use by 1763, it did not mean much more than some modern use of the word 'African' – a broad term to include a variety of people without a common government or identity. In 1763 most of the British settlers thought of themselves as Britons with all that represented in the eighteenth century. The difference was that the huge area they lived in and the existence of many isolated self-sufficient communities, made local loyalties even more pronounced than in the home country. Self-regulating communities made up possibly 20 per cent of the colonies, and often groupings were religiously based, as one feature of the settlement was the desire of various groups to pursue their religion independently. Remnants of this can be seen in the Amish and Mennonite communities of Pennsylvania, living as far as is feasible a life cut off from modern USA. In 1763, especially after the upheaval of a major religious revival called the Great Awakening, it was even more true.

The isolation of many communities can be seen in the often limited or non-existent use of money and the variation in exchange. Paper money was not much used outside the relatively few substantial urban centres, and Spanish as well as British currency served. In many areas, a barter economy prevailed and even within states there was lack of uniformity.

As well as religious diversity – the continuance of which can be seen by the multiple churches in even small towns in the USA and the proliferation of 'pastors', a thousand of whom blessed Donald Trump's 2024 campaign in Georgia – there was linguistic diversity as immigrant communities of Germans, Dutch, Irish or Scottish maintained their own ways of communicating and their own culture. Divisions could also be seen in the different economic interests of various groups which determined their outlook. Perhaps the strongest difference was in the Southern colonies between the wealthier plantations of the coastal regions and the upcountry settlers. More broadly, there was a distinction between urban and rural, between different mercantile elements and farmers, and between free and unfree people. Divisions could often lead to conflicts and tensions which were an important element in colonial America, and which continued to play a large role in the Revolutionary period and beyond. This element of social disorder is an important theme of this book and its role will be considered later.

To consider one example, New Jersey was a particularly divided area. The historian Gary B. Nash has investigated conflicts which seem to anticipate the wider protests against British rule.[1] Land rights in the seventeenth century had been obtained by two different routes. The Dutch and English settlers had obtained what they thought of as legitimate land claims from the Dutch West India Company who had claims to the land. In 1664 English troops had gained control of the Dutch colony of New Netherland during a war between Britain and the Netherlands. The land had been granted to puritan settlers and legal documents showed negotiations with the Native Americans. Small farmers had established settlements and developed farms. However, there was an alternative claim. Two Scottish aristocrats had been granted all of northern New Jersey by Charles II's brother, the Duke of York. These English aristocrats went on to sell the grants of land to Scottish investors who organised themselves into a commercial company. The clashes, both legal and physical between the yeoman farmers and the Scottish investors and the people to whom they had sold lands, became intense and the English government took over New Jersey in 1701. In the 1740s a new generation of Scottish investors took up the claims, seeking to set up a sort of ideal community of enlightened feudal landlords developing New Jersey and improving the land. However, the farmers went into bitter opposition. There were threats to pull down the houses built by the incomers. The clashes were intensified by religious differences as the existing farmers were mainly nonconformists – Quakers, Baptists, Congregationalists and Presbyterians – while the incomers were mainly Anglicans. So the clashes pitted different religions, different classes and also had a political dimension as the Scots had the support of the English governor, defending a royal land grant. Minor clashes led to escalating protest. A farmer called Samuel Baldwin had cut down timber on land claimed by a wealthy landlord and had been jailed. In September 1745 a crowd of 150 farmers stormed the jail and set him free. Attempts sometime later to arrest the protestors resulted in a clash between a larger force of farmers who overcame the militiamen who had arrested some of the rioters. In July 1746 a crowd threatened to burn down the town of Perth Amboy. The actions went beyond protest and led to many areas being ungovernable by the authorities, with farmers electing their own militia, establishing their own courts and setting up a local tax system. This could be seen as a sort of dress rehearsal for the American Revolution but is better seen as an expression of the power of local communities in a divided colony. It revealed, too, the fragile nature of authority.

It was not an isolated incident. In the 1750s there were attacks on landlords in the Hudson Valley where the size of farms was unusually large for the northern colonies. Stress between the richer elements and increasingly large numbers of poorer people could also be seen in Boston. There was an institution called the Town Meeting, where artisans, seafarers and what one governor called 'the low sort of people' could have a say in urban government. An incident in 1747 sparked by the English Navy attempting to press gang Bostonians into service led to an angry crowd stoning the house where the Boston assembly met and burning a royal barge, defying the governor and the militia. The British naval commander Knowles threatened to bombard the city before being persuaded that it would be wiser to release the impressed men. Local communities, when moved by apparent injustices, could act together very effectively.

The possibility of instability and upheaval by poorer elements against richer elites and authority figures was a feature of a society with a growing population and significant divisions. It was also a feature of British and European life. France experienced rural and urban unrest even though the French state was quite well served by a strong army and urban police forces. Britain endured urban riots such as the Gordon Riots of 1780 in London, portrayed memorably in Charles Dickens's novel *Barnaby Rudge*, which saw temporary loss of control by the authorities. So social unrest was not in itself especially unusual. However, it was significant in that it could be exploited and those who led the protests against British rule after 1763 had a useful tool in existing social resentments and the precedent of local communal protest and violence.

The static and somewhat idyllic picture of colonial America is not consistent with these outbreaks of disorder and the class resentment they showed. Too many accounts of the American Revolution start with political protests in the period after 1765 and neglect the disorders already prevalent. In 1764, Philadelphia was the scene of a 1500-strong protest from White settlers from the frontier. These 'Paxton Boys' wanted more militia protection from the Indians, who they claimed were murdering them. When the largely Quaker assembly refused their demand for official reward for scalps, they went on a killing spree directed against local, perfectly peaceful Indians.

The prosperity for violent community action could be triggered by rent riots as in New York in 1766 or riots against smallpox inoculation in Virginia in 1768 and 1769 with no political motives. Bitter disputes over land deeds in upper New York led to the formation of a private community army called the 'Green Mountain Boys'. They waged a land war against settlers with rival claims, dressing as Indians, burning houses and haystacks and threatening to kill their enemies. By 1775 they controlled considerable areas of upper New York.

The violence of this irregular, communal force proved impossible to control by the New York authorities. There was a distinct class element involved. They captured a landowner, Dr Adams, and in an illegal trial tied the victim to a chair and hoisted him to the top of a tavern signpost, humiliated in full view of the local townsmen of Bennington.

The judgement of one historian is that Americans were willing to wage war in 1775 and declare their independence in 1776 because they had already participated in so many previous protests.[2]

The willingness of local groups to join together in protest and the difficulty that colonial authorities faced in dealing with these upheavals are part of colonial life. Where colonial government was seen to be failing, then community action filled the gap. In both North and South Carolina, a virtual alternative law and order system was set up by so called 'regulators', for instance. When disputes arose with Britain, these communities had already established a precedent for action because of an inherent characteristic of colonial life.

There had been a considerable influx of settlers into the American colonies in the late seventeenth and earlier- to mid-eighteenth centuries. However, the nature of immigrants remained the same and most were indentured servants. This aspect of contemporary Britain and indeed other European states is hard for us to appreciate but the distinction between employers and masters was an important one. Much employment bound those who worked into long term contractual arrangements which gave considerable power to the purchaser of service. Early settlement was characterised by masters taking their servants and apprentices with them as they might take their domestic animals or property. By 1763 the average age of colonists was remarkably young, and many were under tight control of those who employed them. This extended to families. The young Benjamin Franklin was apprenticed to his older brother in the printing trade and suffered from oppression, beatings and eventually had to flee. Escaped indentured workers and apprentices could be recaptured and punished in the manner of enslaved people. There is an interesting story of one apprentice, Ebenezer Fox, who was from a poor Massachusetts farming family and was sent off to work on a neighbouring farm at the age of 12. Excited by the talk of freedom, he and another boy, both indentured to work as virtual slaves, ran away to sea on the same day as the fighting broke out at Lexington and Concord in 1775, arriving in Providence Rhode Island. The short time spent as a sailor ended when Ebenezer returned home to Roxbury to be apprenticed to a barber. When his master was drafted into the Continental Army, like many others he had the option of sending a substitute, so Ebenezer was sent in his place as a boy soldier at the age of 16. He joined the Massachusetts militia suffering the usual hunger and cold. So much so that he got permission from his master to enlist as a sailor in 1780, where he took part in a battle with a British ship and was deafened for life. He was captured by the British after his ship had been attacked trying to plunder British vessels and suffered badly from being taken to a British prison ship. He was forced by illness and hunger to accept an offer to serve the British and sailed to Jamaica. There he escaped and made his way to the Spanish island of San Domingo. He found a place on an American vessel but narrowly escaped being taken on board a French ship. The American ship sailed to France where Ebenezer heard the news of the peace. In 1783 he came back to Boston, His only wealth was $80, which was part of the American vessel's prize money for raiding British ships. The Boston barber reclaimed both Ebenezer and the money and, at the age of 21, Ebenezer returned to forced labour. In 1783, Americans celebrated their freedom from oppression. Ebenezer had little to be cheerful about in the Republic of Liberty. He was poor, deaf, still suffering from the experiences in a war in which he had nearly died and had seen his shipmates perish from hunger and neglect. And he was unfree.

Fox wrote about his adventures in a published autobiography. Though relied on by historians, there is no easy way to corroborate what may be exaggerated, but other published memoirs by poorer people recount similar experiences.

Some historians see the age issue as so important that they view the American Revolution as being a revolt of a younger generation. It is true that apprentices were often at the forefront of protests and discontent, as in the famous Boston Tea Party. It is also true that recruitment of a regular revolutionary army depended heavily on teenagers. However, this may have been because they could be spared more easily, as masters needed to stay and run their farms and businesses or prevent their slaves from escaping. The domination by older people – parents, master craftsmen, employers, farmers – of a very young population is a warning against seeing colonial America as being a land of the free.

Free and Unfree

However, what makes talk of liberty most hollow by modern standards is the reliance on not just indentured labour, but on slavery. The early settlers were faced with a considerable problem. Heavy losses from disease and from encounters with the Indigenous peoples meant that there was a considerable need for labour. At first this was met by indentures of White men and women and by exploitation of family – wives and children. However, by the end of the seventeenth century, economic pressure to find workers for new lands brought under cultivation meant more and more reliance on slave labour in America, as in Britain's West Indian colonies. There was much talk about the rights and 'liberties' of settlers as Englishmen. However, 'liberties' had another meaning in the early modern period – of privileges and accepted custom. Most Europeans in the colonial periods saw it as a White privilege to use the labour of people they thought to be of an inferior race. However, such was the demands for labour that American landowners even paid for transported criminals from the homeland.

The records of the Middlesex assizes – a leading London court – give astonishing numbers of what were known as 'bonded labourers' in the period from 1615 to 1775 when the War of Independence prevented further trade in convicts. Maryland and Virginia were the main destinations, and quite a large number of vessels and captains were involved. Some of the records offer a disturbing picture of these voyages. In 1744, Captain Bond of the *Justicia* was tried for murdering his passengers, thirty convicts died on board the *Rappahannock* even before the vessel left Falmouth. Several of the ships had been used for transporting enslaved Africans. Indeed, the Americans did not draw a distinction. *The Maryland Gazette* of 14 November 1768 – at a time when there was widespread talk of 'liberty' – carried this announcement:

> *Just imported from Bristol in the ship Randolph, one hundred and fifteen convicts, men, women and lads. Among whom are several tradesmen to be sold on board the said ship now in Annapolis dock.*

Not all the White slaves were poorer people. One was a young nobleman sold into slavery by his uncle after a family dispute. He wrote about the conditions in Newcastle County, Delaware:

> *Besides the incessant toil, the nature of their labour is such that they are obliged to be continually exposed to the heats and colds. All the refreshment afforded is that of 'poue' a sort of bread made with Indian corn, heavy on the stomach and insipid on the palate.*

He writes of a woman shipped off by her husband to Pennsylvania after being kidnapped. She was forced to cook for the field workers and beaten when she wanted to ask for money from home:

> *It is a sort of barbarous policy of these planters to use their bonded labour ill just before the time of their services is due to expire. If any of them run away then if they are caught, which many are, they are punished for disobedience and forced to stay longer in servitude and have to pay their masters expenses for recapturing them.*

One indentured servant was punished for theft by being tied to a post, whipped, thrown in a dungeon for four days and sold, to another planter. He escaped but was caught and tied to a post in the market place until claimed by his original owner and then treated badly. Virginia set down thirty-nine lashes as a set punishment for escaping indentured labourers. In Maryland it was ten additional days' service, and in South Carolina ten lashes. All this indicates that bonded labour and personal servitude were entrenched in colonial America. The sufferings of imported Black labour, the hardships of convict labour and indentured service being often the only option for the poor seemed to find little resonance in American hearts.

Economic survival depended on finding justifications for exploiting different groups of people. This was often found in Biblical texts and legal doctrines of customary rights. The settlers had a right to own property and to make a living. With under two million people to carve out a future in huge areas of land, labour was sheer necessity. As with the disciplining of indentured labour, violence and punishment was just part of the eighteenth-century world. In a male-dominated environment enslaved people, indentured labour, women and children had a duty to obey. What was important was that economically active adult White males had the freedom to enforce the natural order without interference with their traditional rights. That view of freedom is so far away from a modern outlook, as to put an enormous gulf between the colonial period and ourselves, and for us to think in terms of outrageous hypocrisy. Washington came home to Mount Vernon, his Virginia plantation, after taking his army for their fight for liberty, to supervise his enslaved men and women. Thomas Jefferson who penned the inspiring words of the Declaration of Independence that *'We hold these truths to be self-evident that all men are created equal'* not only depended on slave labour for his tobacco growing at beautiful Monticello, his elegant Virginia home, but also for an enslaved woman, Sally Hemmings, for his sexual and emotional needs.

The whole issue of slavery in colonial America remains an elephant in the room, along with the other elements of social authoritarianism and control, mob violence and the use of child soldiers. Modern sensibilities and values do not always sit easily with many aspects of eighteenth-century life. The sanitised vision of colonial life in the Williamsburg reconstruction has little realism about any of these aspects. Visitors to historic Philadelphia can find a rather perfunctory notice board explaining that Washington was a slave owner. Guides to Mount Vernon point out the slave cabins, suitably tidied, without any criticism of Washington or his family. The author heard more than once on visits to sites that the view of slavery as an unremitting evil was not entirely true. At President Andrew Jackson's plantation in Kentucky, much was made by the guides of a slave who had been respected as a master of horse training as an indication that there was misunderstanding of the nature of slavery in pre-Civil War America. Abraham Lincoln's riposte to the defenders of slavery who argued for its benefits was that they should try it for themselves to enjoy what it had to offer came to mind.

Enslaved people, as well as loyalists, are not ignored in many histories of the American Revolution, but the emphasis on pre-revolutionary America is not generally on oppression by colonists, but rather on the oppression of colonists by Britain.

However, slavery was not a sort of footnote but absolutely fundamental to the development of colonial America and one of its defining characteristics. It does not figure largely in movies. Mel Gibson's heroic patriotic struggle is joined by an enslaved member of his household, even though, in reality, by far the most typical reaction to the Revolution among enslaved people was to attempt to escape. School and university courses are eager to include the contribution made by African Americans to the cause of freedom from British rule. However, examples are generally quite limited because relatively few were involved in actual fighting and by far the majority of African Americans who took part in the war did so on the British side. This was for the best of reasons – to attempt to gain freedom was far more fundamental than escaping from import duties on tea.

The earlier distinction had been between free and unfree, not between Black and White. However, with the greater reliance on Black labour, race became the major distinguishing feature between owners and owned. Because Black people were enslaved, degraded and controlled, the notion that they were inherently inferior developed. This was convenient as it justified keeping them in servitude. Even when slaves were the object of sexual advances or even affection by Whites, this did not lead to any major questioning of their racial inferiority or the 'natural' status of slavery.

Women

The very terms 'Pilgrim Fathers' and 'Founding Fathers' suggests a patriarchal society. It would be unsurprising given the European background of the White settlers if it had been anything else. Gender equality was not on the menu of the early colonists, as this law from Virginia in 1643 demonstrates – a package of gender and racial prejudice and desire for male control:

> *For the prevention of that abominable mixture and spurious issue which may increase in this dominion as well by Negroes, mulattoes and Indians intermarrying with English or other white women, be it enacted that whosoever English or other white man or woman being free, intermarry (thus) shall be removed From this dominion forever. If any English woman shall have a bastard child by any negro or mulatto, she shall pay a sum of fifteen pounds.*

Had attitudes changed much by the mid-eighteenth century? In 1771 an announcement was made in a Boston newspaper[3]:

> *I have lately removed my living and my wife Ruth Kingman refuses to remove and live with me as she ought to do. I warm all persons not to trust her and I forbid all persons to trade with her or purchase any of my goods from her or pay any debt she may contract.*

This was in the most socially and economically progressive parts of America. In more remote rural areas, on the frontier or on the plantations of South Carolina, there was even less sense of equality. It was not, however, a matter of believing that women could not work at all sorts of trades or should play no part in economic life. That would have been impossible in the early settlement when labour was so scarce. Women did work and there was an economic partnership with men, even if it was one-sided. Newspaper adverts in Boston reveal urban work in the form of independent business, many inherited from departed husbands. Most were linked to women's domestic roles such as cleaning, washing, and nursing but there were taverns and coffee shops. There were also independent wage earners, and the range of trades went beyond the purely domestic and included tailoring carpentry. There was no concept that 'the angel of the hearth' should not soil her hands by manual work, except in the small minority of families who could afford a life of tea-supping leisure. Well over 95 per cent of women worked.

However, those women who worked for wages earned less than a third of the not very generous rates of pay enjoyed by men. So much so that women often preferred the very restrictive arrangement whereby they signed indentures and were contracted to semi-slave status in return for food and lodging. Adverts offering this sort of employment often made it clear that both Black and White women were acceptable. The distinction between slave and free was blurred.

The early colonists had depended heavily on the family unit with low population and scattered settlements, and the role of women in what was often subsistence farming was crucial. Their status was below that of the head of the household and above that of the children. Her role in household management was vital and the tasks diverse and demanding. In the South, a much higher death rate had meant less emphasis on the family unit, but in New England, where many lived longer, it was central. By 1700 this difference had eroded. More survived in the South and more died in the North. This tended to extend the importance of the family throughout the colonies.

By 1763 there had been important changes and there were more diverse immigrants – Scots, Dutch, German and large numbers of Africans. The South was more reliant on slave labour; the North had developed more trade and commerce. There were also some more urban centres and the marriage age had increased to around 23. But the past still had a strong hold. The family remained central to colonial life, and there were fewer opportunities for women outside it than in contemporary England. Colonial laws continued to reinforce male authority. Despite some changes, inheritance favoured males, with widows and female children treated unequally. Indeed, things had gone backwards in some respects. Widows often had less power over inherited property than in the seventeenth century. It is true that domestic economic activities were more diverse, particularly in spinning. The rapid expansion of domestic textiles meant that in Massachusetts a third of households had spinning wheels by 1760. Women were able to set up trading networks for cloth and also butter and cheese, but work was tied to the home. In the southern colonies more women oversaw slaves and even owned them, but again this was tied to the farm or plantation.

One major change also kept women homebound. Though women had been responsible before the eighteenth century for child rearing, the view of women's responsibility for instruction and upbringing was that by the age of 2 or 3, children fended for themselves more. Religious enthusiasm after the late eighteenth century and changing views of childhood meant that women were given or took up more responsibility for the education and training of children to an older age – 6 or 7. Relatively fewer women could write but most could read, so they took up responsibility for the teaching of reading. After independence, this trend became much more pronounced as a cult that was called Republican Motherhood took hold, but by 1763 women's domestic responsibilities had increased, and opportunities outside the home were restricted.

As there were more people and the economy grew, there were moves to allow more women to run businesses, and legal changes in most colonies recognised '*sole femme traders*'. The religious revival of the 1740s gave women more outlet for independent responsibility. However, in broader political terms women had limited rights. Legally, they faced discrimination; socially, men dominated through the all-pervasive importance in a pre-industrial situation with only a few well populated urban centres. By 1763 women had become economically more diverse and there is no downplaying their importance in settlement and their bravery in frontier life. However, there was a massive contradiction between talk of liberty and equality and the position of women. The colonial experience which might have been supposed to offer more independence and freedom than was available in the home country had boosted the importance of the family, and the family unit was, despite the vital role played by women, dominated by a hierarchy which favoured men. The much later political defeats of Hillary Clinton and Kamala Harris as presidential candidates may show the long shadows thrown by the colonial past.

Wealth

The American colonies were subject to regulation and control from Britain as part of a system known as Mercantilism, developed in the seventeenth century. The idea was that raw materials from colonies would be transported solely in British ships, taken to Britain for processing and re-export, and in return the primary producing colonists would receive British exports, manufactured products and other goods and foodstuffs. The legislation that controlled this was in the form of five Navigation Acts which were passed between 1651 and 1696.

It seems obvious that as the population increased and the colonies developed, in the form of five Navigation Acts which were passed there would be resentment about these controls and that economic factors would be a key reason for independence. However, the economic realities were more complex.

Firstly, the different parts of America had different economic activities and needs. Broadly, there were four regions: New England (Massachusetts, Rhode Island, Connecticut and New Hampshire); the Middle Colonies (New York, New Jersey, Pennsylvania and Delaware); the Upper South or Chesapeake region (Maryland, Virginia and the part of North Caroline round Cape Fear); and the Lower South (most of North Carolina, South Carolina and Georgia). However, there were important divisions in these regions – between urban centres like Boston and New York and the rural areas, and between coastal regions and inland regions, especially in the south.

The trade and economic contact between these regions was often less important than the trade done by each region with England or the West Indies and Canada. The colonies did not make up a coherent economic whole.

However, there were some characteristics that were common to all regions. The first was population growth and its importance. Overall, between 1650 and 1760 the population doubled every twenty-three years. This did not mean that cities grew disproportionately. The percentage of people living in cities as opposed to the countryside actually fell in the eighteenth century. The colonies were overwhelmingly rural. The economic situation remained the same. The colonies had land and natural resources in abundance but were short of labour and capital. The main market for the colonies' produce remained England. It was a rising English population who wanted furs, fish, forest products, wheat, corn, rice, indigo and tobacco exported from the main ports of Boston, New York, Philadelphia and Charleston. In return, the colonists wanted manufactured goods, tea and alcohol.

The colonies did not manufacture all that much. The iron workshops produced more than Britain, but most raw materials were processed in England for either domestic sale or re-export. This may have been 'colonial' and some found it restrictive, but in fact the American colonies enjoyed the highest level of prosperity per capita of anywhere in the world, including Britain where standards of living were lower by 50 per cent. The per capita income of the colonists did not rise much in the eighteenth century but was still high by world standards. A change in the terms of trade also meant that colonists' money bought more imported goods by 1763 than it had twenty years earlier. The sale of 100 bushels of wheat was worth 150 yards of imported cloth in 1740 and 250 by the 1760s. The gap between the value of imports and exports was not huge and there was actually a surplus in the south. The British did not enforce the navigation laws very strictly and American merchants were able to use their own vessels to trade and develop not only direct trade with England but also a profitable coastal trade,

The fact is that the relationship with England in 1763 had proved profitable for the Americans. English forces stationed in the colonies to fight the French and Indians in the so-called French and Indian war of 1754 to 1763 had brought money into the colonial economy. The English government gave some subsidies to the colonists – for example for forest products. A growing English population offered markets for the considerable number of exports. British ships protected trade and British soldiers helped to defeat the French and their Indian allies and protected the colonists from foreign powers.

Contrary to some assumptions, there were few purely self-sufficient family farms in the North, as some trade was vital to obtain goods the farmers could not produce. Neither was New England the most prosperous part of British America. The soil there was relatively poor, and it was the intensive cash crop farming of tobacco and rice which made the south the richest region. Being part of the British Empire had meant that the trade in New York had trebled after 1750 and that of Philadelphia had doubled. England supplied capital and the migrants often brought skills and some money into the colonies.

Though the use of enslaved labour was much more important to the plantations of the south, most of the colonial countryside depended on family, servants, and unfree labour of various sorts, rather than wage earners who were only common in the cities. Though there were increasing tensions in the years after 1763, there was plenty of reason for many Americans to see themselves as English, to offer loyalty to the crown and, as we will see, be concerned about worsening relations with Britain. The costs of independence will be considered later. However, there is little doubt that economically, at least in the short run, the colonists would have been better off not breaking relations with Britain.

Education and culture

The predominantly rural nature of colonial life meant that education was dominated by the family. It was largely a case of 'home schooling' with substantial emphasis on religion in the early days of the colonisation. Often parents used other families to help to educate their young. Learning about farming and domestic manufacture was a key part, but literacy was important. What was remarkable was the high literacy rate by 1770 of 80 per cent of men and 50 per cent of women among the White population. This was achieved without much public education. As well as family-based education, there were apprenticeships. Agreements or indentures bound masters to supply education in reading and writing as well as teaching the trade in return for young labour, Though not always provided, this was an important route to literacy. The mainstay though was individual teachers. As early as the 1640s, Massachusetts authorities had stipulated that settlements over fifty families should provide a teacher in reading and writing and those over a hundred should provide an instructor in 'Grammar'. In the south and middle colonies, individuals set up teaching establishments which were more common in the larger urban areas but also existed as 'field schools' in the Carolinas. There were religious-based schools funded by organisations like the Society for the Propagation of the Gospel. In Pennsylvania the Quakers were active in promoting learning. Public schools as such, such as the Grammar School at William and Mary College in Virginia, were rarer. There were more limited opportunities for what was to become 'High School' education until the 1830s, but there was medical training and university education in some key institutions, like Harvard which was founded as early as 1638. It has been suggested that the diversity of educational provision reflected the diversity of society in colonial America.

There was considerable interest in the printed word and educational manuals encouraged reading, such as Fisher's manual of 1748 – *The Instructor or American Young Man's Best Companion*. The evidence for literacy is not always easy to find – letters and diaries, books owned or bequeathed and booksellers or newspapers have been used but the signatures on legal documents (rather than just a cross) reveal that possibly ability to write was as high as 90 per cent by the end of the Revolutionary War, Levels of literacy were higher in the North than the South, in urban rather than rural areas, and among men more than women. However, literacy levels were higher by 1770 in the colonies than in most of Europe. There was an interest in promoting literacy. New England had begun it but Jefferson had drafted a bill 'for a more general diffusion of knowledge' for Virginia in the 1770s as a means of preventing tyranny. Greater education was seen to be political weapon. The benefits of education were of course limited to the 60 per cent of Virginia's population who were not enslaved. It did, however, include girls and one of the greatest changes was the rise in female literacy in the eighteenth century, even if this lagged behind that of men. School teaching became an accepted role for women. Enlightened owners also made provision for teaching their slaves to read and write, not with any liberation in mind but to make to make them more useful workers.

Increased literacy had a knock-on effect in the interest in newspapers and almanacs and in the study of religious texts and the drafting of political manifestos. At the higher level it promoted what has been called 'The American Enlightenment'. This was mainly based on the study of British and European thinkers, though there were American scientists and thinkers, most famously the polymath Benjamin Franklin and the political theorist Thomas Jefferson. The reporting of major events after 1763 had a major effect on generating support for the Revolution and keyworks like Paine's *Common Sense* was widely read (if not as widely as has often been assumed).

Printing had been established in New England early in the colonies' history in 1638 – the Cambridge press was linked to Harvard College founded that year. Though linked to religion, the press turned out all sorts of secular documents – legal documents, almanacs, and schoolbooks as well as sermons. In the south, printing did not appear until the 1730s. When printing spread to Boston after 1675, news was often included in such publications as obituaries and almanacs to show divine intervention into contemporary affairs. These documents were prototype newspapers, but the first well-established newspaper as such was *The Boston News-Letter* of 1704 followed by *The Boston Gazette* of 1719. *The Virginia Gazette* appeared in 1736. On the eve of the Revolution there were thirty-seven newspapers. (In England some twenty-one newspapers had been founded by 1750 for a larger population.) This meant a lot of reporting. In what became an established tradition in the US, the newspapers were often produced by the printers, The standard format was four pages of London-derived news, local news and advertisements. Given the other sources of information as well as these newssheets, a literate population was remarkably well informed. This has been seen as a major factor in bringing about a revolution, but the printed material could also include opposition to protests and pro-British sentiments. The growth of literacy and press may also explain the divisions in the colonies and the basis for later virtual civil war. However, the interest in political ideas and the rapid spread of news were a significant result of the development of printing.

An important figure whose fame and influence grew as a result of this growth of printing was Benjamin Franklin, who is often taken to exemplify the growth of the American Enlightenment and political consciousness in the period before the Revolution.

Franklin's early life shows the rise of a talented figure to prominence from a difficult upbringing and a thirst for reading and knowledge that was part of the American experience. Born in 1706 in Boston, he received only a basic education before being put to work in the family soap and candle business at the age of 10. Finding the work unpleasant, he dreamed of a life at sea, not unnaturally in the busy port. To control him, his father apprenticed him to his brother James, one of the family's ten sons. This typical indenture bound the 11-year-old to a ten-year apprenticeship in the printing business. Though better for a bookish boy than soap making, the conditions were harsh. There was no pay until the age of 20 and escape would be a criminal offence. Typical for the time, the printing business was linked to the production of a newspaper called *The New England Courant*. James refused to let Benjamin write but he slipped in letters purporting to be from a woman called Silence Dogood. The hoax letters became popular and even elicited offers of marriage. The brother was not amused and when Benjain confessed, he beat him. James fell foul of the religious authorities for some of his articles and Ben ran the newspaper while his brother was in jail but was still beaten for his pains. At 17 he escaped to New York and by the age of 24 had established himself as a master printer in Philadelphia. Living with a common law wife, Deborah Read, he made a name for himself as a journalist and writer. The best known of his publications was *Poor Richard's Almanac*. Sexually promiscuous and unfaithful despite an unprepossessing appearance, he achieved fame as a man of letters and of science

By 1748, Franklin had made enough money to retire from business and concentrate on science and inventing. His inventions included the Franklin stove and the lightning rod. He demonstrated that lightning and electricity are identical with his famous kite experiment. Franklin also became more active in politics. He was clerk of the Pennsylvania Assembly (1736–1751), a member of the Assembly (1750–1764), and deputy postmaster for the colonies (1753–1774), reorganising the postal service to make it efficient and profitable.

Franklin was also involved in many public projects, including founding the American Philosophical Society, a subscription library and, in 1751, an academy which later became the University of Pennsylvania.

From 1757 to 1774, Franklin lived mainly in London where he was the colonial representative for Pennsylvania, Georgia, New Jersey and Massachusetts. His attempts to reconcile the British government with the colonies proved fruitless. On his return to America, the War of Independence had already broken out and he threw himself into the struggle. In 1776, he helped to draft, and was then a signatory to, the Declaration of Independence. His illegitimate son William, royal governor of New Jersey between 1762 and 1776, remained loyal to Britain, causing a rift that lasted for the rest of Franklin's life.

Later that year, Franklin and two others were appointed to represent America in France. Franklin negotiated the Franco-American Alliance which provided for military cooperation between the two countries against Britain and ensured significant French subsidies to America. In 1783, as American ambassador to France, Franklin signed the Treaty of Paris, ending the American War of Independence. He was extremely popular and well known in France, but in 1785 returned to America. He continued to be deeply involved in politics, helping to draft the Constitution.

Franklin died in Philadelphia on 17 April 1790 and remains one of the most honoured and affectionately remembered founding fathers. Yet there is also a darker side. In the late 1760s Franklin linked up with land speculators who claimed from Britain the rights of 2 million acres along the Ohio River. When the colonial secretary encouraged them to increase their claims, thinking this would lead to rejection by the Privy Council, they joined British bankers and aristocratic businessmen to claim 20 million acres and wanted to create a new province in modern day West Virginia and eastern Kentucky which Franklin named Vandalia. There were distinct financial motives for supporting a revolution which might well endorse such land grabs. This was a long way from the homespun proverbs of 'Little Richard' and the profundities of the Declaration of Independence but just as typical of the outlook of the American elites.

As Americans were more literate and on the whole wealthier than Europeans, it was not surprising that, at least in urban centres, there was a growth in interest in cultural pursuits. The obvious model was Britain. Fashion, lifestyle, literature, music, knowledge and philosophy owed most to Britain as would be expected, since Americans in terms of being freeborn were subjects of the British crown. Even the most devoted lovers of Americana of the colonial period find it difficult to enthuse about the hymn tunes, parlour songs and dance music that were 'American' as opposed to renditions of European composers like Handel. Nothing very specifically 'American' emerged musically until composers from a Jewish immigrant background in the twentieth century, like Copland, Bernstein, Gershwin and Weill who wrote cowboy music and musicals celebrating US city life and culture. The hymn tunes of William Billings are more authentically American but of very limited musical appeal today. 'American' colonial art remained linked to craft and the homely values of plain colonial homes. More sophisticated painting and sculpture followed British and European models. Unlike the French Revolution, the American Revolution produced little that was distinctive in the way of art, music or literature. The poetic odes that represented 'high culture' even from distinctive figures like Phyllis Wheatley are derivative and offer little to the modern general reader, as opposed to the historian. The ideals of the Revolution are firmly rooted in ideas outside America: the English John Locke for the rights of resistance; the Swiss Jean-Jacques Rousseau for contractual theories of government; the French Montesquieu for the separation of powers; the German Kant for the separation of Church and State. The most influential writer in support of opposition to monarchy and independence was British-born Tom Paine. The lengthy outpourings, sermons and exegeses of Puritan and Anglican Divines that were often the staple study of higher education have mercifully passed into history.

Politics and Government

To see the colonies as dominated by cruel use of labour, or by a greed for land at the expense of Indian neighbours would be a distortion. There was a vigorous intellectual life, a considerable religious revival and participation in elected assemblies. Some of these offered limited democracy and participation. In the south there was the political domination of an economic elite of planters. However, the Town Meetings did have more popular participation, and local protest indicated a wider and wilder political awareness.

The Crown had taken increasing control of colonial settlement, though there were still two private colonies deriving from their original proprietor – Pennsylvania from the Quaker Penn family and Maryland from the Catholic Calvert family. Most of the colonies were governed by a Crown-appointed governor and officials. However, early on the colonies had developed forms of representative assemblies elected by free, White men. These assemblies had different names and different procedures; the qualifications for election to them varied and the requirements to be a representative also varied. By modern standards these were not democratic, as mostly the qualifications were based on wealth. This was not surprising, as the costs of attending meetings could only be met by men of some substance. Also, wealth and status were linked. The freemen, merchants and landowners needed men to speak for them who could gain respect and had sound reputations. Though reasonable wealth was a given, it was made clear that character was important as they were to consider matters of 'the general good'. The constituencies had been established in the seventeenth century and Britain did not allow an expansion to take into account population growth and the settlement of new lands on the frontier. Thus, the White freemen were not all that well represented. Some frontier areas had no-one to speak for them, though the average in all the colonies was one representative in colonial assemblies for every 1187 inhabitants – substantially less than in eighteenth-century Britain. Americans, however, could not choose their rulers, either in terms of the British ministers or the representatives of royal rule in the colonies. Poorer White men did not have the opportunity to vote or stand in elections. In New York there was a requirement to own £40 worth of lands. In Delaware men had to own 50 acres. New Hampshire was a little less severe, but £50 worth of personal property was set as a qualification. The numbers of voters did increase with the general prosperity. but there were limits to the opportunity to take part in the political life of the Assembly.

Despite the supposedly more egalitarian nature of American society, deference and status were important. It was often made clear that leading and established figures would be appropriate to represent constituencies in a way not too different from class-ridden England.

This trend can be seen in the relatively small number of elections to the various Assembly that were actually contested. In Virginia, for instance, between 1728 and 1775 there were meaningful contests for only a third of the constituencies, and in most colonies the trend was for the same people, or at least the same families, to be chosen year on year.

All this might suggest that, in fact, the demand for 'no taxation without representation', a famous slogan used by opponents of British rule, could easily be applied to the colonies themselves. Many areas had no representation and no chance to choose a spokesman for their point of view about local taxation. Those without the required property qualification had no representation but were still liable for taxation. Women were not generally voters or representatives. The unfree had no voice and different ethnic groups living in the thirteen colonies were not part of political life.

However, in some respects America was more democratic in the sense that a wide range of people could participate in a broad political process. The representatives in the assemblies were expected to consult their constituents and be responsive to their wishes. They were not always delegates, elected to follow their own ideas, but were seen as the voice of their local areas. For the English authorities this was sometimes too democratic. The Deputy Governor of Virginia railed at members of the House of Burgesses in the early eighteenth century:

> *All your proceedings have been calculated to answer the notions of the ignorant populace, the giddy views of the illiterate vulgar.*

The illiterate vulgar did get a say. In Rhode Island a Town Meeting could put forward a proposal which could be circulated to other Town Meetings and then to the Assembly of the colony. When the Massachusetts Assembly was considering an Excise Bill in 1754 which would have put a duty on home distilled spirits, it was decided that 'it is the desire of the House that they call the several towns together that they might know the minds of their constituents'. Sometimes governors urged their assemblies to consult the wider public, as in New York in 1749 when the governor suspended the assembly to give the representatives *'time, cooly, to consult with your constituents'*. The public could make their feelings plain as they did in 1755 when the Virginia Burgesses (or Representatives) proposed giving themselves a pay rise, but public clamour made them change their minds. It was not unknown for representatives who ignored their constituents to not be re-elected. The freemen of Boston held a public meeting to make it clear to their representatives in 1745 that they were going to give *'such instructions upon particular matters as we any time shall judge proper'*.

The prevalence of public meetings – some spontaneous and some regular as in Town Meetings – added an element of popular political influence not seen in the home country. These had emerged out of the necessity of the early settlers to work together and to consult on key policies. As the population grew, these meetings were more difficult. People had to travel and give up time from the day-to-day essential farming activities, so they chose representatives. Gradually, systems for electing these spokesmen evolved, but something of the early American group meetings persisted.

As has been shown, local protests and local groups formed for protection against supposed injustice were also a legacy of the way the colonies developed and were an informal but effective way of people to exert influence. This was politics in a wider sense. After 1763, the popular protests grew in importance, but they were not created by British taxes, they were already part of colonial political life.

Americans considered themselves as British subjects and there were few in 1763 who envisaged a new country. For the increasing number of prosperous plantation owners in the south and merchants and manufacturers, the expression of success lay in taking up English manners. Fashionable families in Boston, New York and Philadelphia had moved away from the hardships of early settlement into comfortable mansions, furnished to European standards with English fashions and of course tea drinking. The overall standard of living was the highest on earth. There were fortunes to be made in trade, in the production of cash crops like tobacco and rice and in a more limited way in manufacturing. A third of the ships in the British Navy were made in New England using plentiful forest products. Though the urban population was small, it led to greater literacy, more reading and a growth in learning associated with what has been called 'the American Enlightenment'.

The Frontier

Population pressure and an overwhelming desire for new land drove many to expand the frontiers. George Washington noted that this frontier availability affected the way land was farmed:

> *The aim of the farmers in this country … is not to make the most they can from the land, which is, or has been cheap, but the most of the labor, which is dear, the consequence of which has been, much ground has been scratched over and none cultivated or improved as it ought to have been.*

This in turn encouraged a move westward. Washington and many of the Virginia elite of landowners had invested in western land and were affected when Britain restricted western movement to preserve peace with the Indians. It was, however, as difficult to control determined migration in 1763 as America found it in the twenty-first century. The irony of a country of migrants seeing further migration as one of the major threats is lost on many Americans today. It was the Native Americans who faced the greatest threat from a growing White population anxious to gain land while ever increasing numbers of Africans who were forced to immigrate became ever more essential to the continuing growth and supremacy of the southern economy – though cotton was still to come. Suppressing the native population and oppressing the enslaved population had led White Americans to have, ironically, a more equal society in terms of wealth distribution and unprecedented per capita prosperity. When opposition to British rule grew, the assumption was that an end to restrictions and payments would pave the way for a more prosperous, independent America. Recent calculations challenge this. However, as the Brexit vote showed in Britain, the economic facts and the perceived economic reality, heavily influenced by emotions and resentments, are not always the same.

What set America apart from the European life its richer inhabitants so admired was the availability of land and the huge desire to expand to own it. Many of the elite, like George Washington, speculated in land and had a vested interest in being free to expand the frontier. That had led to the enthusiastic support for a war against the French and their Indian allies who stood in the way of establishing 'an Empire of Liberty'. British restrictions after 1763 on expansion were a major cause of the breach between the colonists and the home country.

The rush to expand westwards once the British had begun to defeat the French and their Indian allies was an indication of the changing dynamic of the colonies. More and more, people moved to the frontier. Vermont, uninhabited by colonists in 1750, had a population of 20,000 by the 1760s. People from New England and Pennsylvania moved into western Massachusetts. Pennsylvania saw extensive movements west. The so-called backcountry of Virginia, as it was called, saw a movement of population. In the Carolinas there was a distinctly different settler population from the planters of the coastal regions – Germans, Swiss, French Huguenots and Scots-Irish as well as English.

Settlement was often accompanied by violent disputes. Land grants were often bought up by speculators and there were clashes with other settlers with different claims or squatters. There were also widespread clashes with the Indians. A pattern of violence emerged as there was little control over settler attacks. Large-scale fighting was common. In South Carolina the extension of the frontier brought the type of lawlessness later associated with the Wild West, with bandits dominating whole areas. This led to vigilante groups and atrocities and destruction on both sides. This spread to North Carolina. The self-help law enforcers were called Regulators and they themselves clashed with authorities trying to establish more conventional law and order. By 1763 many colonists were on the move.

Religion

There was not only physical movement, but spiritual restlessness. America by 1763 was still feeling the impact of a religious revival called the Great Awakening. This took the form of evangelical preachers inciting large scale religious enthusiasm. Preaching urged individuals to commit themselves to God and affirm their Christian beliefs individually. This individual commitment was more important than membership of a religious organisation and attending conventional meetings. It involved soul searching and renewal of faith to find assurance of salvation. It began in 1733 with an inspirational Massachusetts preacher called Jonathan Edwards. But the arrival of the charismatic English preacher George Whitefield was a key element. He drew huge crowds, especially in Boston. Other evangelists emerged to emulate these dynamic figures. The reborn Christians were known as 'the New Light'. For some this burned more brightly than others, and some meetings turned into over emotional displays of uncontrolled shouting and writhing about. In one meeting, the preacher James Davenport urged a new life by people casting off their clothes as symbols of their old sinful lives. Even for the re-born it was too much when he took off his breeches and wanted to burn them. The movement was multi-denomination and depended a lot on whether the existing ministers – whether Presbyterian or Anglican – bought into the rebirth and worked with the preachers. Some did, but others saw the travelling disciples as simply anarchic and uncontrolled, likely to undermine rather than reinforce established Churches. For the revivalists, the old Lutheran idea of the Church as the body of believers rather than an institution was key. Some wanted to include Black people and Indians in the mission, something likely to undermine the basis of society in the southern colonies and to threaten frontier expansion.

Often said to have brought Americans together, the religious revival also divided them, with traditionalists seeing the fervent preaching and emotionalism of the religious revival as a threat to stability. It has, nonetheless, been claimed as a major factor in the American Revolution. By challenging existing hierarchies and also presenting a struggle against Good and Evil, between those who saw the light and those who remained 'mired in sin', it is said to have encouraged rebellion against the established political authority. This is unlikely and there is limited evidence of a direct connection between the revolutionary agitation and the religious revival. In Virginia, for instance, those who opposed and those who supported rebellion had both participated in the Great Awakening.

The appeal was strong in the individualistic backcountry settlers from strong, Protestant European backgrounds, but many of these opposed the war with Britain. It is unlikely that the Boston mobs who protested against British policies were strongly influenced by memories of Whitefield's preaching and devotion.

However, there is one striking example that is often used. Before the Massachusetts troops moved northwards into Quebec in an expedition in 1775, they dug up Whitefield's body and took bits of his mouldering clothing to bring them good luck. This bizarre episode probably has more to do with traditional anti-Catholic feeling, very common in Massachusetts, than revivalist fervour being an inspiration for revolution. Sadly, for the religious visionaries, the existence of the great preacher's relics did not prove efficacious, and the expedition failed.

How to sum up? By 1763 it is generally agreed that the colonists, at least from Britain, saw themselves primarily as British subjects. On one of the most heated days for riots against British taxes in 1765, the people of Boston had celebrated the Prince of Wales's birthday. In general, despite restrictions, the colonies had prospered. Modern economists see the separation from Britain bringing more economic loss than benefit. The political position was odd. The colonists were subject to policies made by the British royal government and passed by the British parliament but had no direct representation. They were under governors in a way that British people were not, but they had local elected assemblies with representatives who were expected to put forward their views. Unlike British people, the Americans had the chance for local meetings to express themselves politically, as well as formal colonial assemblies. The spread of prosperity meant that more were qualified to vote than was the case in the home country. However, this was not democracy. Large sections of the colonial population were excluded from direct and formal participation in politics – the poor, the indentured labourers, Black people, most women. However, there was a wider sort of political activity that was more democratic in communal protest movements, difficult for authorities to control and often tolerated.

On the frontier there was more liberty from authority, and some have seen 'a rude democracy' or at least freedom to pursue lives and take communal action. This led to whole areas being outside control and virtually self-regulating. Settlers simply opted out from any authority.

New currents of thought were emerging. The European Enlightenment influenced a minority of the American elites. The Great Awakening affected many more people. However, both were derived a lot from England.

It has been tempting to see the frontier expansion or an interest in enlightened ideas or religious enthusiasm as moulding a new society more likely to break from England and have an 'American' identity. However, in 1763 the bonds with England were still strong, and to see 'the new world' as a freedom-loving, egalitarian society inevitably likely to seek liberty and independence is to look at history through the wrong end of the telescope. The benefits of being part of Britain and its empire, huge reliance on unfree labour, and the prevalence of widespread divisions casts some doubt on traditional narratives of an inevitable progression to freedom.

Notes

1. Gary B. Nash, *The Unknown American Revolution*, Cape, 2005.
2. Ray Raphael, *The American Revolution, A People's History*, The New Press, 2001.
3. Maggie Parfitt, Massachusetts Historical Society, May 2024.

Chapter 2

Conflicts 1763–1770

Visitors to US historical sites often have highly-informed guides from the National Park Service who speak with refreshing directness and authority. This invaluable historical institution has published a short guide for the visitors to the various places associated with the American Revolution.[1] It summarises a well-accepted narrative.

The story begins with a dispute over taxes. The British and the colonists had taken part in a war from 1754 to 1763 against the French and their Indian allies. This had resulted in a British victory and the acquisition of French lands in North America. It was part of a wider European war called the Seven Years War fought between 1756 and 1763. This had strained Britain's finances. To protect its new lands in the face of a major war against the Indians, known as Pontiac's Rebellion, for the first time Britain had to keep forces in America. To pay for this, the British government of King George III imposed new taxes on the colonies as a whole. This measure was known as the Sugar Act of March 1764. In a famous justification the British premier, George Grenville, explained that the new duties were 'for defraying the expense of defending, protecting and securing' America.

Another tax was announced but was deferred until parliament authorised it in March 1765. This was a stamp duty. Various items had to have a stamp attached to them which had to be purchased from the British revenue officials. These included newspapers, the popular almanacs, pamphlets, legal documents, customs documents, playing cards and dice. The stamps had to be paid for not in paper money but in hard currency, of which there was a shortage. The collection of customs duties and the new tax was to be tightened up and defaulters subject to Admiralty courts in which there were no juries. Naval officers took part in the collection of revenue.

The arguments against these taxes were partly practical – they would restrict trade – but also political. There was talk of the colonies' 'inherent right' to impose their own taxes. Opposition to the stamp act in the words of the guide 'turned exclusively' on the political issue of rights. Freedom from taxation without the consent of their representatives was 'the undoubted right' of Englishmen whether in England itself or in America.

Indignation led to a special congress in which delegates from different states met to protest. This was called the Stamp Act Congress. This declared that the Stamp Act 'subverted the rights and liberties of the Colonies'.

Writers in the colonies refuted the British argument that the colonists were represented in parliament by members who spoke for the good of all British subjects. It was irrelevant that the colonists did not vote for them as few British people actually voted at this time. Richard Bland of Virginia wrote that it was ridiculous to think that men who are excluded from voting for members of parliament can be represented in that parliament.

The issue of taxation had therefore become a wider political issue about representation and rights. When petitions outlining these high-level theories of government and consent failed, the colonists moved to more direct action. A crowd in Boston forced the resignation of the tax collector Andrew Oliver and by November the Stamp Act could no longer be enforced. There was also a limited boycott of British goods.

A change of government in Britain led to the abandonment of the Stamp Act but a Declaratory Act made it clear that Britain did have the right to impose taxes. Then 'rather than leave bad enough alone', there were more taxes in 1767 imposed by the Chancellor of the Exchequer, Charles Townshend. A range of articles was listed including glass, paper, lead, paint and tea. The taxes would be used to pay royal officials to collect taxes and dues and were passed without the consent of the colonists. A double blow.

Colonists were rallied by a series of imaginary letters by a lawyer from Philadelphia called John Dickinson. These *Letters from a Farmer in Pennsylvania* challenged the distinction between customs dues and internal taxes and argued that all forms of taxation should be with the consent of the governed. Once again there were popular disturbances and 'a mob' attacked officials and tore down the home of the Deputy Governor in Boston.

Dickinson disapproved of this sort of action and was still openly loyal to the king but advocated what came to be known as non-importation. A boycott of British imports and a reliance on 'our ingenuity, industry and frugality' to fill the gap. This showed a unity of purpose among the different colonies and in 1770 all the duties except that on imported tea were removed.

The colonies dropped their boycott and normality seemed to be restored but there was the unresolved issue of the rights of the colonists and increasing mistrust of the king, his ministers and parliament as news of repression in Ireland and the campaign against the radical writer and political agitator John Wilkes in Britain reached America. The main problem, however, came with the dispatch of British troops to Boston in 1768. In 1770 there was a serious incident in which British soldiers fired on a hostile crowd in Boston – the so-called Boston Massacre – and also a clash between colonists and Britain when HMS Gaspee was seized and destroyed after its captain had been overzealous in trying to prevent smuggling.

The narrative of the ten years from 1763 to 1773 is a growing sense in the colonies of political rights, deepening popular protests, provocative acts by Britain and unresolved issues around the central problem of taxation and representation. Central was the slogan 'No taxation without representation' and also the emergence of influential writers like Dickinson and activists like Sam Adams and James Otis in Massachusetts and Patrick Henry in Virginia, whose supposed speech in 1775 with the words '*Give me Liberty or give me Death*' was so influential. Though the events of these years did not result in a mass movement for independence, they laid the groundwork for it and were a precursor to the more acute disagreements and eventual outbreak of war in the years from 1773 to 1776 which will be considered in the next chapter.

This is not an unreasonable narrative and is, by and large, what is accepted in many history courses, but there are some possible issues. First, there is a lot of stress on political ideas and issues about taxation which may skew the reality. Secondly, the motivations of British governments are not always fully explained; and thirdly, the popular element is not explored in the context of previous discontent in the colonies. Lastly, and perhaps most importantly, the reservations and concerns of those who did not approve of opposition and protest are not always given their due. When war came, it was not a question of patriotic and freedom loving patriots against old fashioned and repressive imperialism. It was also a civil war in which the colonists were quite deeply divided. It also took place in a society where violence and oppression of different groups were endemic and not a society which was necessarily driven by high-minded enlightened pamphlets and political ideas. The space given to these pamphlets and writings is disproportionate to the space given to popular protests. When writing history, it is tempting to look more at published materials written by an educated elite than to look at events which have left behind less evidence. Identities of those who took part in crowd actions are not widely known, but well-established critics of British rule are easily identified. Debates within colonial assemblies were not generally published, so dissenting voices have often disappeared from view. But pamphlets are a rich and readily available source, giving somewhat skewed emphasis to writing such as that of Dickinson.

The moral high ground was not exclusively held by the protesting colonists of the 1760s. After the end of the French and Indian War in 1763 there was a royal proclamation about the new lands which restricted settlement in the lands of the Indians west of the Appalachians. The tone may seem quite refreshing to modern readers:

And whereas great Frauds and Abuses have been committed in purchasing Lands of the Indians, to the great Prejudice of our Interests. and to the great Dissatisfaction of the said Indians: In order, therefore, to prevent such Irregularities for the future, and to the end that the Indians may be convinced of our Justice and determined Resolution to remove all reasonable Cause of Discontent, We do. with the Advice of our Privy Council strictly enjoin and require. that no private Person do presume to make any purchase from the said Indians of any Lands reserved to the said Indians, within those parts of our Colonies.

This was part of a general settlement which established new colonies in Quebec and West and East Florida. It granted lands to those who had fought in the war. It was also a response to a major outbreak of fighting between the Indian tribes and the British known as Pontiac's Rebellion in which hundreds had died. Though it seemed to be aimed at small, independent settlers, much of the land was bought and settled illegally by speculators. These included some leading figures in the American Revolution, men like George Washington, Patrick Henry and Henry Laurens. The Proclamation Act was resented, and settlement went ahead anyway, as it proved difficult for British troops to stop it. Washington, then a slave-owning Virginia planter, had invested in this land. In 1767 he expressed an opinion that the Proclamation Line was simply '...*a temporary expedient to quiet the minds of the Indians*'.

This proved correct in the long run. Illegal settlement was too hard to stop and there was a steady erosion of Indian rights, leading to another war in 1774. The Creek Indians had a special word – *Ecunnaunuxulgee* – or 'People greedily grasping after the lands of the red people'. Very conscious of their own rights, the American patriots were less concerned with the rights of others.

Washington certainly took a high moral term in a letter to George III in 1765 which seems rather a long way from concerns to grab as much Indian land as possible:

May it please your Majesty,

TO permit an unworthy, but loyal subject to approach your Majesty's throne in this manner, as your ministers will not let me do it in any other; declaring that I will lose my life in the protection and defence of your royal person and family, and also of my country.

There seems, may it please your Majesty, to be a mighty contest between Great-Britain and North America! Without any sort of dispute this evil originated in, by, and through a base, vile and wicked ministry, and an ignorant and corrupt parliament, who have arrogated powers to themselves in no wise appertaining. To exhibit this most clearly, it appears, – first, that the Parliament of Great-Britain are chosen to represent the people of that land only; therefore, of course, cannot represent your good and loyal subjects of America.

Secondly, That as your Majesty is sovereign of America, distinct from the power and authority of the parliament of Great-Britain, no body, or set of men, but your assemblies or parliaments here, (which are constitutionally fixed by charters of your royal predecessors) can lay any tax, tallage or impositions whatsoever within this your dominion of America.

Thirdly, That the pretence of your parliament of Great Britain to tax your American subjects, is an absolute insult upon your Majesty's understanding, and a robbery of your sole right to govern them, in as much as if this vile institution be left to take place, your majesty and your parliament will be tenants in common.

The issue here is firmly one of principle; but there is no questioning of the authority of the monarch. Indeed the final part is grovelling in no uncertain terms. Like many of the American elite – landowners and local big wigs like Washington as well as leading merchants – natural deference and obedience meant devotion to the established order. It was not the king but wicked ministers and MPs who were to blame. There is even a forerunner of modern conspiracy theories, in suggesting that George III's chief minister, Lord Bute, was conspiring with the Jacobites for a Stuart restoration. The Lord in this letter is definitely on the side of the Americans.

Perhaps resentments over taxation came to subsume resentments over the Proclamation Act and more material concerns of land speculation. Or perhaps it was better to fight on the moral high ground to restore the situation where the elites could wind the clock back to the situation at the end of the war. British lives and British money had secured for the colonists huge opportunities for expansion. Before 1763 there had been limited interference in what was a profitable relationship, resulting in Americans having a higher per capita income than British people and more political influence over their local assemblies.

When Britain had attempted to tax imports, such as the Molasses Act in 1733 putting a 9d duty[2] on the vital molasses needed for the flourishing New England distillery trade, the collection proved impossible, as local officials were under too much pressure to collect taxes. Smuggling was a national industry. The Navigation Acts attempted to restrict colonial manufactures and trade to ensure British goods and merchants had a monopoly. But these were not well enforced and local manufacture, though officially forbidden, had been established. Slave labour and a growing British economy offered great opportunities for riches. The whole policy of Britain has been called 'salutary neglect', though was not seen by contemporaries like this. The colonists thought of themselves as British and that they should enjoy the rights and privileges of British people. Quite what these were was vague, since the bulk of British people were excluded from the political process, were ruled by aristocratic cliques and suffered very harsh laws to protect the property of their betters. The 1723 law called The Black Act made poaching with a weapon an offence liable to be punishable by death. Lesser poaching offences, even catching rabbits on private land, could result in transportation to the colonies. Those without property or wealth had rather limited rights. Local communities in the home country were dominated by privileged social elites depending on deference. Liberty meant freedom from state interference and the right to jury trial. However, a harsh penal code fell heavily on the poor while the state was essentially a means of control or for promoting the economic interests of the elites by wars to gain trade and colonies.

The changing economic context was a major factor in the developing discontents in the colonies after 1763, as well as ideological and high-minded concern for political principles. British policies took place against a background of change in America, which made them seem irksome, and the reactions to them were coloured by developments in trade.

The growth in trade over the Atlantic did offer unprecedented opportunities, but like all trade-based economic growth, it was subject to fluctuation. The late 1740s had been a time of considerable prosperity in the colonies. But the early 1750s had seen a downturn. The war period saw a recovery with high levels of economic activity between 1756 and 1762, but the end of the war saw a depression which coincided with a period of political conflict. The late 1760s saw both an economic revival and a return to less conflict between Britain and the colonists. The resumption of conflict in the period after 1773 coincided with a slump in trade.

The problem had begun before 1763 with English suppliers of imported goods offering greater credit to encourage American importers. To make sure that they did not have too much stock, English businessmen cut deals with smaller merchants and retail outlets, and not just the larger businesses that usually handled imports. British firms employed local agents to deal with all sorts of importers and offered direct auctions. Lower prices hit the profits of established American companies.

The war period interrupted this trend. The demands for goods grew. The presence of large forces in America helped boost sales, and the war boosted trade in timber products, iron and shipping.

From 1763 the economic picture grew bleaker. There were no longer profits from British spending. Instead, there were stocks of unsold goods as the demands dried up and British firms worked harder to cut deals and undercut traditional importers. There were complaints from larger merchants that British salesmen were extending credit for shopkeepers to buy cut price goods. There was some economic diversification, as American businesses set up their own manufacturers in all sorts of products. However, these did not compensate in the losses in traditional British imports.

There was economic resentment among some merchants of British policies before the provocative taxation of the 1760s. The Currency Act often gets less prominence in historical accounts than the Sugar Act and the Stamp Act, but was significant in provoking unease.

The assumption that most countries used regular national currencies in the eighteenth century is false. The use of money was more restricted than is generally supposed. The colonists used all sorts of things when buying goods, including Indian shell money (wampum), stamps, animal skins, and foreign coins as a means of exchange. At times, to respond to immediate needs, colonial legislatures issued their own paper money. It might be thought that was dangerous and difficult for trade, but the system, or lack of it, did just about function. However, there was the problem in traders being paid in currencies which lacked sufficient backing. The Currency Act did not affect the key trading areas in New England, as paper money had been restricted there in 1751. The Southern colonies had produced paper money to pay for their contribution to the French and Indian war. This was mainly in Virginia, and Britain had been requesting the Assembly to act since 1759 to restrict currency production. The Act was applied not just to the south where the problem lay, but to the whole of the colonies – an example of a tendency following the end of the French war in 1763, for Britain to legislate for the whole of the colonies. It required all currency issued by the colonial assemblies to be taken out of circulation. It benefited English merchants who did not want debts incurred in sterling to be paid in local currency worth less. The southern planters were particularly opposed to the act.

The Sugar Act was a greater cause for unrest for both economic and political reasons. It reduced the existing duty on molasses from 9d to 3d but increased arrangements for actually collecting the tax, which mainly affected New England. It applied duties on molasses and a range of other imports to the colonies as a whole – as with the Currency Act a tendency to see the American possessions as a whole, rather than separate units. It employed outside agents rather than relying on local officials. It also set up an Admiralty Court in Halifax, Nova Scotia, as a body to hear cases. As a military court, this meant that its hearings were without juries. who would have acquitted those accused of evading or not paying dues.

An initial reaction was to boycott some imports and use economic pressure to force British ministers to change their minds. The whole policy of non-importation was revived when Britain put more duties on in 1767. This was very much presented as a patriotic exercise. Imported tea was discouraged. Various treatises were produced to show that tea was unhealthy and un-American. So-called sewing and spinning 'bees' were instituted by women to produce homespun products and, where possible, goods produced in America were urged on consumers. Though the ladies were enthusiastically patriotic, the clothes made were for the lower orders and not for the middle-class ladies who spun so industriously. They continued to wear the imported finery. Protest had its limits.

However, to go back to the economic situation, the non-importation was not quite the disinterested, politically-led activity that it appeared to be. It was in the context of merchants being undercut by direct trade arrangements and goods stockpiled. Reduction of imports would help clear the backlog and affect continuation of the agreements being made. Profits in any case came first. The Boston boycott lasted only a year in 1768 and the very lucrative trade with the British West Indies was not included.

Economic events in the south helped to fuel resentment of British policies. Southern planters had come to depend heavily on credit to expand into new lands and to buy even more slaves. This had come, to a large extent, from Scottish firms. They too had diversified away from just the larger owners to get more favourable terms from smaller tobacco producers. Larger planters faced some problems getting capital, and in 1762 the Scottish businessmen cut back generally on credit. The Currency Act came at a bad time, as it restricted the ability to pay debts with more available but less valuable paper money.

This is not to suggest that higher-minded points of principle were not important, and as in Washington's appeal to George III they offered powerful arguments, but they do not tell the whole story.

This is particularly true when looking at the popular actions. The actions of the people of Boston made the implementation of the Stamp Act in all colonies too difficult. The re-emergence of unrest led to the abandonment of duties on trade, with the single exception of tea. This duty was paid, largely because it was of limited importance as so much tea was smuggled. Only the most dedicated opponents of British rule wanted to continue resistance to this.

In 2008, a group of artists and writers published *A Guide to Democracy in America*,[3] concerned with recent revelations of abuses by US forces. A comforting article quoted Jefferson *'the boisterous sea of liberty is never without a wave'* and pursuing this maritime theme referred to Boston, a bustling seaport which laid the ground for democracy to grow. Like seaports, generally it bred tolerance and acceptance of individuality. Visitors to Boston follow the Liberty Trail of revolutionary sites and the city is obviously pound of its libertarian past.

The resistance to the Stamp Act and then to the Townshend Duties seems to indicate a passion for liberty. However, it is not clear whether this was entirely the motivation for the people who took part in disturbances in the port.

The demonstrations against the Stamp Act did not come out of nowhere. They were orchestrated by a group of lesser merchants and craftsmen called 'the Loyal Nine', with links to more prestigious and richer merchants' groups. They gained the support of key men who could mobilise the poorer elements in the city's Northend and Southend. Rioting was not a new phenomenon in the city. It was almost nationalised in the form of Pope's Day celebrations, the traditional Fifth of November celebrations, which were an expression of anti-Catholic feeling more than a celebration of the safety of James I's parliament being saved by the thwarting of the Gunpowder Plot in 1605. There were recognised leaders of popular demonstrations, often involving a degree of rowdiness. As seen in chapter one, popular violence was as much a feature of colonial America as puritan piety or hard-working farming and trading. The Bostonians had a particular reputation for what one contemporary called 'a mobbish turn'. During the riots against impressment in 1747, the governor had to use the armed militia against the crowds. Popular unrest was often stirred by a radical newspaper called *The Independent Adviser*. The Town Meetings were often characterised by hostility to authority, and the elite merchants and wealthier Bostonians had wanted to ban them. There had been clashes over the Writs of Assistance, giving customs officials more power over the considerable amount of illegal smuggling that the liberty-loving people of Boston indulged in. The radical press and pamphlets blamed the wealthier elements for supporting the collection of customs fees and also for supporting the Currency Acts.

Boston had suffered from a Great Fire in 1760 and a smallpox epidemic in 1764. Economic downturn added to the discontent with British measures – fifty Boston merchants urged non-importation in August 1764, but economic protests had limited effects. The Stamp Act provoked a petition against the threat to liberty. Interestingly there was quite a lot of discussion about exactly what was being threatened. There was no objection to taxation as such or even to a Stamp Act, as the Massachusetts General Court had imposed such a tax internally in 1755. What was at stake was 'liberties'; the accepted practice of colonies taxing themselves. The original petition did not speak initially of 'liberty' but 'liberties'. In the sense of English legal and political wording, 'liberties' were discussed as another way of writing about 'privileges'. In other words, maintaining existing rights and exemptions, not 'freedom'.

By June 1765 the people of Boston were aware of the Virginia Resolves passed by the House of Burgesses in Virginia. These have often been seen as a key moment. The Journal of the House of Burgesses recorded the resolves on May 30, 1765 but refers to amendments which have been lost.

[1] *Resolved That the first adventurers and settlers of this his Majesty's Colony and Dominion of Virginia brought with them and transmitted to their posterity, and all other his Majesty's subjects since inhabiting in this his Majesty's said colony, all the Liberties, Privileges, Franchises and Immunities, that have at any time been held, enjoyed and possessed by the people of Great Britain.*

[2] *Resolved That by two Royal Charters, granted by King James the First the colonists are declared entitled to all Liberties, Privileges and Immunities of Denizens and natural Subjects to all intents & purposes, as if they had been abiding & born within the realm of England.*

[3] *Resolved That the taxation of the people by themselves, or by persons chosen by themselves to represent them, who can only know what taxes the people are able to bear, or the easiest method of raising them, and must themselves be affected by every tax laid on the people, is the only security against a burthensome taxation, and the distinguishing characteristic of British freedom, without which the ancient constitution cannot exist.*

[4] *Resolved That his Majesty's liege people of this his most ancient and loyal colony have without interruption enjoyed the inestimable right of being governed by such laws, respecting their internal polity and taxation, as are derived from their own consent, with the approbation of their Sovereign or his substitute; and that the same hath never been forfeited or yielded up but hath been constantly recognized by the Kings & People of Great Britain.*

Patrick Henry was a young lawyer who is immortalised by a speech he made in 1775 to the Virginia Assembly when war was imminent. *Is life so dear, or peace so sweet, as to be purchased at the price of chains and slavery? Forbid it, Almighty God! I know not what course others may take; but as for me, give me liberty or give me death!* So here was an iconic figure as early as 1765 urging resistance. The problem is that records are incomplete, and his stirring words may have been written later and not said by him. Back in 1765, the proceedings in the House of Burgesses in Williamsburg were observed by a French visitor.

His entry for 30 May 1765 brings us up with a jolt. '*Arrived at Williamsburg at 12 where I saw three negroes hanging at the gallows for having robbed Mr Walthe of 300 pounds*'. The debate about liberty took place a short distance from this grisly scene. The gallows and its victims do not figure in the sanitised recreation of Williamsburg today.

Henry's passionate speech is recorded:

One of the members stood up and said that in former times Tarquin and Julius had their Brutus, King Charles had his Cromwell and he had no doubt that some good American would standup for his country.

This was not acceptable to the Speaker who warned Henry that this was treason and that 'he was sorry to see that not one of the members of the House was loyal enough to stop him'. The firebrand Henry now backtracked, '*if he had offended the Speaker or any member he was ready to ask his pardon and would show his loyalty to His Majesty King George III at the expense of the last drop of his blood*'. It was the heat of his passion for liberty that led him to say something more than he attended.

The following day, 31 May, the diary recorded that the whole House agreed with recording the resolves but 'differed much with regards the content'. Some wanted to resolve that anyone saying that parliament had the right to levy the tax should be seen as a traitor, but the governor dissolved the Assembly before a vote.

The Virginia debates seemed to have shown some passionate feelings but also a reluctance to go too far and some caution, even by a radical like Henry. In the event, Virginia did not send delegates to a special Stamp Act Congress suggested by Massachusetts. Rhode Island had suggested action but the congress, which represented nine of the colonies, offered a criticism of the Stamp Act on essentially conservative grounds that it was 'unconstitutional'. In other words, it was undermining existing rights and privileges. There was no formal constitution, so the argument was really that established practice and precedent was being broken. Underlying this might have been the concept that British actions had broken an informal contract between governed and government. This idea of a contract had been set out by European Enlightenment political theorists of the late seventeenth and eighteenth centuries. Or it may have been that 'unconstitutional' was a powerful and emotive way of saying that established privileges had been swept aside by Britain. So for radicals it was something new and politically controversial that was being argued, but for conservatives it was a matter of reasserting the old ways of doing things.

Whatever the legal and political niceties, the agitation led to more violent actions in Boston than in the other colonies. More radical opponents had a ready-made weapon in the organized mobs of the poorer areas and their leaders. Usually intent on fighting each other, it was a small step to divert the energies usually spent on the Pope's Day disturbances to protest about the Stamp Act.

The legal and constitutional issues and desire to be free from unpopular economic restrictions and to assert 'liberty' may have motivated some. However, the crowds who began attacks on officials in August mainly showed their resentment at the wealth of the homes of the people they picked out for attack. As in the riots against impressment, it was the poorer community, with the encouragement of groups of businessmen, that showed traditional solidarity and hostility to authority.

Was all this 'democracy'?

The right to protest is now seen as a key feature of democracy. Public meetings against the Stamp Act were held in Boston in June 1765. The Virginia Resolves were common knowledge and there was outrage about British policy expressed in the Massachusetts General Court. Other colonies were written to and separate petitions encouraged against the measure. Invitations were sent for a special Stamp Act Congress. But there was a difference between respectable citizens petitioning and actually taking more direct action. New Hampshire, Virginia, North Carolina and Georgia did not send delegates. And most histories forget about the loyal Canadian-British colonists in Quebec whose inhabitants are rarely included in this story. Those delegates who did come to this assembly were far from being revolutionary and were mostly cautious.

These were men who needed the law. There was no legal means to void a British act of parliament, and the legal way forward was to petition and to claim that in fact Americans were victims of innovation – that the new taxes were 'unconstitutional', whatever that meant, since there was no formal constitution governing relations between the colonies and Britain.

It was difficult to see how a duty on newspapers, almanacs, deeds, warrants, leases, bills of sale, bonds and customs dues and a few odd items like playing cards could have the effects claimed by the people of Braintree (Massachusetts, not Essex) in their instructions to their representatives:

> *… in a short space of time (the Stamp Act) would drain the county of cash, strip multitudes of the poorer people of all of their property and reduce them to absolute beggary' even if stamps had to be paid for in hard currency.*

Though there were political issues, such as the resentment about lack of representation to approve the taxation and the use of Admiralty Courts without juries to enforce customs payments, the effect on ordinary people seems to have been exaggerated. In Boston, the driving forces for a wave of popular agitation and violence seems to have come from one of the many political clubs that supported a general agitation led by 'The Sons of Liberty'. The so called 'Loyal Nine' were a group of small businessmen – John Avery was a junior partner in a distillery; Benjamin Ede ran a privateering business; Thomas Chase was a distiller. Other were master craftsmen, small scale manufacturers or relatively small property owners. They had links with wealthier clubs in the city, some of which had members deeply hostile to British rule. However, it was important for these propertied people to work indirectly. Popular organisations existed in the poorer regions of Boston and the highlight of their year was 5 November when parades against the Pope, whose effigy was carried through the streets, often led to violence and clashes between the Northend mob, organised by a shipwright called Henry Swift, and their rivals in bigotry – the Southend rowdies – led by a fireman named Ebenezer Macintosh.

The competing groups came together on 14 August in a familiar manner with a parade and effigies – not only of the Pope this time but also of two Stamp Duty officials. This took place at Boston's famous Liberty Tree and was the subject of as much interest as the traditional Guy Fawkes demonstrations. Fifty craftsmen came as a body to watch Swift's men carry the effigy of the chief stamp tax officer, Andrew Oliver. Schoolchildren were sent to watch this display of hatred as part of their civic education. A large crowd dismantled the office of the Stamp Duty Collector, stamping the bricks with a mock stamp. Oliver's effigy was then beheaded in front of his house. But then matters took an uglier turn. Oliver was a wealthy man, while the people from Northend and Southend who united in this crowd action were definitely not. Class antagonism was evident when Oliver's house was vandalised, and the liberty lovers drank his wine. An attempt by Deputy Governor, Thomas Hutchinson, to restore order was prevented. Oliver wisely resigned, and there were threats to destroy Hutchinson's house.

Once the feelings had been stirred, then it was difficult to stop popular feeling. Other officials were targeted, and Hutchinson's house was damaged. But was this over constitutional liberty?

Hutchinson had been involved in a contentious land dispute and had also supported the unpopular currency reform. Both sailors and merchants resented trade restrictions. The crowd was described as 'boys and children', probably indentured servants and apprentices acting on behalf of their masters. There was a good deal of drinking and property was not only vandalised but there were also thefts. There was a good deal of hostility when a minister preached against disorder.

All this indicated that the attempts to use popular power by certain sections of the Boston elites had got out of hand. The ruling council, the justices of the peace and militia officers condemned the violence of 26 August but not that of 14 August, and a show of force backed now by 'gentlemen volunteers' put the lower orders back in the box. Though without shots being fired. Mackintosh was arrested but conveniently released for lack of evidence.

He and Henry Swift were virtually bribed by the radical merchants not to make the usual Fifth of November celebrations the occasion of another outburst of violence, by being wined and dined and given special uniforms.

Protests spread though other communities in Massachusetts in the autumn. Over 2000 people rioted at Newburyport and, in the quiet and respectable towns of the Boston hinterland, unusual crowd activity made the collection of stamp duty impossible.

The port and the courts began to operate as normal without stamps being bought and attached because officials were too fearful of violence and intimidation. An undertone of resistance continued into the new year with a burning of stamps, after a mock trial of the offending objects in a somewhat bizarre episode showing supposed respect for laws while deeply undermining it. The stamps, absurdly, were found '*guilty of a breach of Magna Carta and a design to subvert the British Constitution and alienate the affairs of his Majesty's loyal and dutiful servants.*'

In one even more disturbing incident, a sea captain called Thacher had actually had his customs clearance officially stamped. The offending document was seized, carried round Boston on a pole and then ritually executed.

There were similar disturbances throughout Massachusetts, and the limited resources available to the British colonial authorities to collect the taxes and to keep order led to an inevitable climb down. Given the alliance of traditional elites with the 'mobbish sort' and the lack of force available, the Stamp Act was repealed on 18 March 1766.

Samuel Adams was one of the most determined and vociferous opponents of British policy. Embittered by his wealthy father's financial failures and himself an unsuccessful businessman, Adams worked in the brewing industry but involved himself in radical politics. He saw the need for businessmen to gain popular support. He himself was Harvard educated and deeply interested in political and moral concerns. He appreciated that the mass of people was not so politically aware but saw a supposed change. He wrote that '*The people of lower ranks have become more attentive to their liberties and were determined to defend them*'. This was one interpretation of the continuation of the disorders usually seen in anti-Catholic demonstrations and the plunder of the richer people whose wealth was resented. Of the few rioters whose identities are known, did James Freeman, who was a habitual rioter and had been convicted of multiple disorders, really care too much about Magna Carta? Did Magnus Mode, a sailor who was convicted of theft of property, commit robbery for the cause of liberty?

The violence had concerned many of the more substantial property owners and businessmen of Boston. This can be seen in the contradictory mixture of affirmation of loyalty to the monarch and in protests and support for disruptive popular action. It really was a case of having one's cake and eating it. Social status and wealth depended a lot on Britain. Britain had protected the colonists against France and against Indians; Britain had even encouraged a sense of unity among the colonies, albeit unwittingly, by applying policy to the colonies as a whole. The sums involved in the disputes over taxes were relatively small. The duty on molasses had been reduced from 9d to 3d. By comparison with Britain, taxation was low. The Stamp Act, though irksome, was not new and had been imposed in Massachusetts already. It was unlikely to have brought about the general state of misery claimed. The emergence of unchecked mob violence created more danger and disruption than anything Britain had done, and it also set a precedent which had dangerous consequences.

The violence accelerated when Britain imposed the Townshend duties – again not life changing given the widespread acceptance of smuggling. The protests of 1765 and 1766 set a precedent but this time there was more personal violence.

The tentative moves of 1765 to non-importation of British goods were much more developed after 1767. The boycott was accompanied by a wave of vigilante acts against those who disobeyed. Community disapproval could take obnoxious forms of informers and punishment. The homes of importers were daubed with 'Hillsborough paint', described by the historian Gary Nash as 'a nasty recipe of body wastes'. In the small town of Newburyport, a carpenter accused of informing on his criminous neighbours to the authorities, some of the many local smugglers, was put into stocks on top of a sharp stone, pelted with stones and gravel, stripped and left tied up in a warehouse.

Another informer was tarred and feathered. This form of humiliating and painful punishment, dating back to the Middle Ages, became increasingly common. The most famous incident was that of a financial official, John Malcolm, in January 1774, the subject of a famous depiction of violence, but the practice was established earlier. In 1766 a sea captain fell foul of the people of Norfolk, Virginia, for supposedly informing the British authorities of smuggling. Led by the town mayor, he was covered with tar and fathers and thrown into the sea. After 1767 the practice was adopted as a deliberate policy of terror against tax collectors. Throughout New England, tar and feathers soon became the 'popular Punishment for modern delinquents'. By March 1770, at least thirteen individuals had been feathered in the American colonies: eight in Massachusetts, two in New York, one in Virginia, one in Pennsylvania, and one in Connecticut. In all of these instances, the tar brush was reserved exclusively for customs inspectors and informers, those persons responsible for enforcing the Townshend duties on certain imported goods. Indeed, American patriots used tar and feathers to wage a war of intimidation against British tax collectors. Usually, the victims were tarred over their clothes. The object was humiliation. The perpetrators were the usual servants and apprentices. More deadly attacks followed after the withdrawal of the Townshend Duties. Examples in 1775 saw deaths result from hanging or severe burns. Malcolm sent the British parliament a box with his scalded skin and was rewarded with a pension. By the 1770s, not only people but also houses and horses were tarred and feathered.

By 1770 a situation had developed in which it had become acceptable to resist unpopular but essentially lawful measures by communal violence. This was not new, and it was to be an important part of the early stages of the war with Britain. It was encouraged and coordinated by radical political figures in relations with popular leaders and 'street captains' in a way that was later seen in France during the French Revolution. Though opposition was expressed in terms of 'liberty' and defence of rights, the motivations were not solely idealistic. It established some unfortunate precedents in American life where the 'democracy' consisted of communities expressing their will independently of actual law and regular authorities. The tarring and feathering could be seen as a direct ancestor of the lynchings which characterised much of southern life after the Civil War and well into the twentieth century. The very term 'lynch law' derives from the independent Green Mountain community of the Revolutionary periods. The rioters of 7 January 2021, backed by elements within the US elites trying to restore Donald Trump, are just as much the direct heirs of the Revolutionary period as respected presidential figures depicted on Mount Rushmore.

The protests were in a large measure successful and, like the Stamp Act, most of the duties of 1767 were removed, with the token exception of tea. This was limited in its effect because perhaps three quarters of imported tea was smuggled. This meant that not even firebrands like Samuel Adams could get much indignation worked up among the people, especially as the economic situation was brighter.

No underlying issue had been resolved, though, and the presence of a British garrison in Boston offered the constant threat of friction in the way that a British army presence in Northern Ireland did in more recent times. With a restless population having enjoyed a taste for disorder, and the existence of radical opponents, the chances of an incident with British troops who were far from home, underpaid and conscious of hostility with locals were high.

It came with the so-called Boston Massacre of 1770. The subject of a famous print by Paul Revere and exploited by Sam Adams, this incident might have been expected to have provoked more opposition than was actually the case. This is an example of history being written by the victors, as the very term 'Boston Massacre', still in general use, represents a huge and lasting success for the anti-British writers of 1770 who coined the term. Loyalists described the events as an 'Unhappy Disturbance'. The Massachusetts Historical Society has preserved an account written by Francis Maseres which does make a point about language. It is worth quoting. This is the whole of what the Boston Narrative calls the Horrid Massacre.

How far it deserves that appellation, let the unprejudiced reader judge. For my part, I cannot but think it a very gross abuse of language and highly injurious to the unhappy officer and soldiers who were concerned in this affair to call it by the same term that has hitherto been used to describe such wanton, unnecessary and premeditated acts as the slaughter of the Protestants in France in 1572 and of the Protestants in Ireland in 1641; to which a resistance of twelve soldiers against more than a hundred people armed with sticks and bludgeons in defence of a post which it was their duty to defend, seems to me to bear no resemblance.

Writings hostile to Britain, like the *Short Narrative of the Horrid Massacre in Boston*, of course offer a very different view:

The troops were not sent here for any benefit to the town or province, and that we had no good to expect from such conservators of the peace. It was not expected however, that such an outrage and massacre, as happened here.

A neutral diarist called John Rowe recorded the event:

Party of the 29th under the Command of Capt Preston fird on the People they killed five – wounded Several Others – particularly Mr. Edw Payne in his Right Arm, – Capt. Preston Bears a good Character – he was taken in the night & Committed also Seven more of the 29th – the Inhabitants are greatly enraged and not without Reason –

6 March Tuesday.
Most all the Town in Uproar& Confusion. The Govr.& Council met. The Cryer went abo.to warn a Town Meeting at Eleven of Clock. The inhabitants met at Fanewill Hall. They chose a Respectable committee to wait on his Honor the Lieut. Governor to desire that the troops might be removed from the town. Returned for answer that the 29th Regiment should go to the Castle.

Unusually, an enquiry was held into the events and the testimony of witnesses recorded. The background is reasonably well established. There had been a quarrel between some soldiers and a group of ropemakers. It was not unusual for soldiers to supplement their incomes by casual work when off duty. A small group went into a rope works run by a Mr Gray and one of his workers asked if the soldiers wanted work. When they said yes, he said '*Well go and clean my shit-house*'.

The soldiers returned later in the morning with some friends armed with clubs, not their muskets, and were ready for a fight. But the rope workers beat them off. Then a larger group of soldiers, accompanied, interestingly by 'a negro drummer' turned up and there was more fighting until the soldiers again were driven away.

This was on Friday, 2 March. News spread thorough the town and among the soldiers. By Monday there was some eagerness among the younger and rougher elements in the city for more clashes, and the soldiers too were ready for a fight. After a clash, officers managed to get the soldiers away while the youths catcalled, and a few threw snowballs. One youth rang the fire alarm bell which brought more people out into the street. One of the youngsters testified that some of the people assembled were near the Customs House guarded by a sentry. The crowd dared the soldier, '*Fire, fire and be damned*'. The sentry knocked at the door of the Customs House and Cain, rather inconclusively, describes someone, probably a servant, opening the door. Then a squad of thirteen soldiers, led by Captain Preston and armed with muskets and fixed bayonets turned up. A sailor called Wyat testified that they shouted, '*Where are the damned cowards, where are the liberty boys?*' The soldiers drew up to protect the sentry and the Customs House and Wyat recalled that the officer ordered the troops to fire. He cursed '*Damn your bloods, fire be the consequences what they will*'. Three people fell and others were wounded. He then yelled again '*Damne ye, rascals, why did ye fire for?*'

This account, suspect because of the exact words quoted and the contradictory testimony of others, is challenged by the account by Francis Maseres and also by the 'Horrid Massacre'. He cites evidence given at the trial and writes:

> *A large stick, or, a piece of ice, that was thrown at the grenadier on the right of the party, struck him with violence and made him stagger, upon which both he and the soldier next him fired their pieces without any order from Captain Preston for that purpose and soon after the rest of the party did the same; by which three men were killed on the spot, and eight wounded, of whom two have since died of their wounds. Presently after the last gun was fired off, Captain Preston sprung before the soldiers, and waving his sword stick, said, 'Damn ye, rascals, what did ye fire?'*

This account talks of attempts by Preston to stop the crowd provoking the soldiers and his assuring the people that they would not fire, and also a lot of hostile actions by the crowd.

The 'Horrid Massacre' insists that shots were fired, not by the soldiers guarding the Customs House, but from within the building. The trial in which, oddly, Preston was defended by one of the most active opponents of British policy, John Adams, as a professional lawyer, acquitted Preston, but two of the soldiers were found guilty of murder and branded with an M on their thumbs.

A highly emotive engraving by Paul Revere shows Preston commanding the soldiers to fire. Those killed received an elaborate funeral. They included, in the words of the 'Horrid Massacre':

Crispus Attucks, a mulatto, killed on the spot,
two balls entering his breast.

The presence of a person of colour has engendered a great deal of writing about the contribution of Black people to the cause of liberty, though whether this sailor was simply part of an excitable crowd that got out of control may be discussed. The presence of a Black drummer earlier on in the disturbances on the British side, however, has not been much remarked on.

The whole episode has been seen as an example of British misgovernment, sometimes wrongly described as a brutal reaction to children throwing snowballs. It has been taken out of context, of a spate of clashes between soldiers and workmen. Its significance has been overstated. One view is that this was 'Tiananmen Square in miniature' or the equivalent to Nazi atrocities. It is commonly seen as 'uniting the colonies' and paving the way to Revolution. The alternative view is that it was a propaganda device used by radicals to stir up apathetic public opinion. As is common, the loyalist view and the concerns about the unruly behaviour of the Boston populace have not received their full attention. As will become clear in the following chapters, these increasingly violent and divisive episodes led not only to a Revolution but to a civil war. To compare an incident which took place months after British troops arrived in Boston, which did not lead to large scale protests and which resulted in a trial of the soldiers – something that did not happen until years later in the case of 'Bloody Sunday' in Northern Ireland, to the horrific killings in China in 1989 or to Mai Lai in Vietnam or to the Nazi atrocity at Babi Yaga – is to strain credibility. It obviously affected relations between Britain and the colonies, but did not unite colonial opinion or prevent the development of improved relations which followed the repeal of the Townshend Duties. It did give rise to more opportunities for radicals to produce anti-British propaganda and was, as the loyalist source indicated, 'an Unhappy Disturbance'.

Notes

1. Charlene Mires, Pauline Maier, Don Higginbottom, Gary B. Nash and Goerdon Wood, *The American Revolution*, Official National Park Service Handbook, US Department of the Interior, 2005.
2. 'd' stands for pennies – there were 240 pence to the pre-decimal pound.
3. *A Guide to Democracy in America*, Creative Time Books, 2008.

Chapter 3

The Tea Party and its Consequences
1773–1775

Much of the discussion about the events which led to war in 1775 and the Declaration of Independence in 1776 deal either implicitly or explicitly with 'blame' or 'responsibility'. However, as so often in the past, actions and decisions result from a choice of options which is often much more limited than appears. 'Blame' is not very helpful when possible actions are not unlimited and leaders and their people are often boxed in by circumstances.

In 1775, as fighting broke out between colonists and British forces, a group of Bristol merchants wrote to George III:

> *It is with an affliction not to be expressed and with the most anxious apprehensions for ourselves and our Posterity that we behold the growing distractions in America threaten, unless prevented by the timely interposition of your Majesty's Wisdom and Goodness, nothing less than a lasting and ruinous Civil War, We are apprehensive that if the present measures are adhered to, a total alienation of the affections of our fellow subjects in the colonies will ensue, to which affection much more than to a dread of any power, we have been hitherto indebted for the inestimable benefits which we have derived from those establishments. We can foresee no good effects to the commerce or revenues of this kingdom at a future period from any victories which may be obtained by your majesty's army over desolated provinces and [...] people.*

They were not alone in expressing concern about the rift that had developed since 1763. The eminent economist, Adam Smith, had argued for giving the Americans what they asked for – representation in the British parliament. This would have solved a major issue that American opposition leaders had developed – that regulation of trade, restrictions on colonisation and taxation were somehow illegal or unconstitutional because the people of the colonies were not represented.

One possible solution, in hindsight, would have been to return to the pre-1763 situation of 'salutary neglect' or, indeed, never to have abandoned it. That is to have made minimal demands on the colonies financially, to accept that they should be treated individually and to have seen the commercial benefits of trade as being worth foregoing any plans to tax or to reform the colonies, for instance by preventing paper money or restricting clashes with the Indians.

The other possible solution would have been to permit formal independence, to remove the royal governors and to rely on economic links and shared kinship to ensure peaceful relations between independent countries.

Looked at in this way, British policy after 1763 may become difficult to understand. The British and the colonists had worked together harmoniously to defeat the French and their allies and the victory in the war had seemed mutually beneficial. Why not let sleeping dogs lie and just continue the status quo?

However, Grenville explained the position in a speech to the British parliament which offered a coherent view and was not merely arrogant or unrealistic.

That this kingdom has the sovereign, the supreme legislative power over America, is granted. It cannot be denied; and taxation is a part of that sovereign power. It is one branch of the legislation. It is, it has been exercised, over those who are not, who were never represented. It is exercised over the India Company, the merchants of London, and the proprietors of the stocks, and over great manufacturing towns. It was exercised over the county... of Chester... before they sent any representatives to parliament.... Protection and obedience are reciprocal. Great Britain protects America, America is bound to yield obedience. If not, tell me when the Americans were emancipated? When they want the protection of this kingdom, they are always very ready to ask it. That protection has always been afforded them in the most full and ample manner. The nation has run itself into an immense debt to give them this protection; and now they are called upon to contribute a small share towards the public expense.

The logic was impeccable; the understanding of the American reaction was almost entirely lacking. The war had brought Britain into closer contact with America. British forces could not just withdraw because of the need to protect new territory. The problems of ongoing conflict with the Indians could not just be ignored. The political support for taxing America for its own defence could not be wished away. There was a general consensus in parliament and government that it was necessary to enforce laws, control smuggling, raise revenue and tighten control over colonies which were so economically important, and which had been expanded in a costly war. Earlier British ministries, such as that of Lord Bute, were planning to do this, and proposals for a Stamp Act had been discussed for the previous ten years. No British government could return to salutary neglect.

The experience of resistance to taxation in Britain and a greater understanding of the colonies might have shown the dangers and ministers did not foresee the depth of feeling. Should they, therefore, in order to facilitate the policy of reform – logical but dangerous – have accepted American representation? This is an intriguing idea but this would have involved a wholesale reform of parliament which was based on completely different principles. A great many people were not represented in the eighteenth-century parliament. There was a property qualification for voters for the two MPs elected for each county. In towns, most MPs were either chosen by the ruling borough corporation, a self-electing body of wealthier citizens, or by very small number of voters in boroughs later known as 'rotten boroughs'. In extreme cases, like Old Sarum in Wiltshire, a handful of voters were left when the mediaeval town decayed, and most people left for nearby Salisbury. However, the ancient and once thriving borough still returned two MPs until 1832. Many towns sent no MPs. Many boroughs were controlled by important local men or by the Crown or ministers. There were some more democratic boroughs with a wider electorate, for example Westminster, but mostly elections were not contested or contests involved seeing which candidate could bribe the most voters. For American participation to be meaningful, the whole of the system would have needed massive reform, something that had not been wholly completed by 1914 when no women and only one man in ten voted, despite reform bills passed since 1832. Also, Americans would not have been able to participate in the House of Lords which remained an equal partner.

Should ministers have accepted that feeling in America was too strong and abandoned any attempts to tax them or prevent smuggling and illegal activity? In practice, they did make concessions which were not made in other parts of the Empire. Most duties were scrapped, the Proclamation Line was in practice not enforced, and the Stamp Act was not pursued. However, to accept the principle that Britain had no right to tax and had no real power was difficult, given that Britain needed to be able to control other colonies. No other colonial power at the time could have made such concessions. When faced with major disturbances as will be shown, Britain could not just ignore deliberate flouting of its authority without accepting virtual independence.

So why not? The answer is not difficult. There was no precedent for simply abandoning sovereignty. Britain was a hugely powerful military state. Rebellion was a dangerous and infectious political disease. An independent America would be vulnerable to Britain's European competitors and enemies. It took years of costly and bitter warfare to bring Britain to a position where there was enough political support and lack of alternative to accept independence for its Empire in the twentieth century. The idea of self-governing dominions had emerged in the eighteenth century.

Looked at like this, it becomes less a question of blame for the ongoing conflict than how it could really have been avoided. The British ministers were very different personalities – the fussy, pedantic and obstinate Grenville was different from Townshend and the more intelligent Lord North – but the range of options each faced was not unlimited. So what of the colonies? Could the opposition leaders have avoided a costly and dangerous war?

The most significant of the colonial opponents to British policy was Samuel Adams. Adams often gets quite limited treatment but he was a key figure. He made his reputation as a speaker in Boston's Town Meeting, a political name for himself, and gained a seat in the Massachusetts Assembly in July 1765. His strong religious views were linked to an understanding of British Enlightenment political theory which had underpinned Britain's Glorious Revolution, which overthrew the Catholic and authoritarian King James II in 1688 and replaced him with the Dutch ruler William of Orange, and his wife Mary, the daughter of Charles II. A Protestant rule was established, which gave an important role to an elected parliament. In practice, with a small electorate, Britain was ruled by leading aristocratic families, but there was much talk of liberty. Theorists like John Locke wrote influentially about rights of resistance when monarchical rule became tyrannous. These political theories had an influence on men like Adams and formed the justification for slogans like 'No Taxation without Representation' and were discussed in political clubs in Boston and other urban centres.

In 1772 Adams gave this report to the Boston Town Meeting in his capacity as chairman of the Committee, which corresponded with other colonies:

These are some of the first principles of natural law and justice, and the great barriers of all free states and of the British Constitution in particular. It is utterly irreconcilable to these principles and to many other fundamental maxims of the common law, common sense, and reason that a British House of Commons should have a right at pleasure to give and grant the property of the Colonists The words of the Massachusetts charter are these: '[That colonists], shall have and enjoy all liberties and immunities of free and natural subjects …. as if they and every one of them were born within this our realm of England.'

Now what liberty can there be where property is taken away without consent? Can it be said with any color of truth and justice, that this continent of three thousand miles in length, and of a breadth as yet unexplored, in which, however, it is supposed there are five millions of people, has the least voice, vote, or influence in the British Parliament? Have they all together any more weight or power to return a single member to that House of Commons who have not inadvertently, but deliberately, assumed a power to dispose of their lives, liberties, and properties, than to choose an Emperor of China? Had the Colonists a right to return members to the British Parliament, it would only be hurtful; as, from their local situation and circumstances, it is impossible they should ever be truly and properly represented there. if the breath of a British House of Commons can originate an act for taking away all our money, our lands will go next or be subject to rack rents from haughty and relentless landlords, who will ride at ease, while we are trodden in the dirt. The Colonists have been branded with the odious names of traitors and rebels only for complaining of their grievances. How long such treatment will or ought to be borne, is submitted.

It is difficult to know where to start with all this. 'Natural law' is quite a vague concept, and 'common sense' is quite subjective. Quite what the 'British Constitution' means is not explained. The argument deals with the original Massachusetts charter. If 'liberties and immunities' means being free of taxes which one does not agree with, then that was certainly not a right held by most people in England. Also, most people in England, either at the time of the charter or in 1772, did not vote for a member of parliament. Though it could be argued that taxation is theft, no responsible thinker supported this proposition. The concept was popularised by the French writer Frederic Bastiac in 1850 who claimed 'taxation is plunder'. But it is only in this rather extreme sense that Britain was taking away property. Where a million people comes from is not clear. But the key admission here is that even if Americans did elect MPs to Westminster, then it would only be hurtful. The claim that Britain was planning to inflict rack rents and tread colonists into the dirt has no foundation. Without even mentioning that natural law and justice were not being applied to enslaved people, those who did not qualify to vote for state assemblies or to women, this is not a strongly logical report, and it was not its intention. The logical consequence of this inflammatory propaganda was to promote independence, though this is not stated, and the actual effect was to stir up discontent. Perhaps it accounts for other leading figures being more honoured and remembered as the great men of the Revolution than Adams – men like Benjamin Franklin, Thomas Jefferson and George Washington. Adams may have more in common with present day conspiracy theorists.

For Adams and other 'firebrands' the resistance to Britain, fuelled by the unhappy experience of his father, became obsessional. He was eager to spread his ideas through Massachusetts and then, by Committees of Correspondence, throughout the colonies. In modern terms, he was a master propagandist. His experience in Boston politics at street level also led him to enlist the support of the lower orders, though he professed to disapprove of violence.

A lot about the claims made by him and his fellow enthusiasts is specious. He claimed loyalty to Britain but opposition to policies. But 'No Taxation without Representation' was really meaningless. It would have been impossible for a substantial group of elected MPs to travel to London to take part in debates.

It was hard enough to find people in the individual states who could afford to leave their farms or businesses to attend assemblies. And even then, there was no certainty that their oratory would have changed minds, as the majority of British MPs supported taxing America. The other alternative would be that Britain would leave taxation to the local assemblies and give up any right to taxing the colonies either though trade or directly. This would have been to give up any rights to rule America and would have been tantamount to independence. There was no guarantee that the state representatives, heavily influenced by their constituents' wishes, would have voted money to support British taxpayers.

As for pious claims that he disapproved of violence, this is somewhat ingenuous. As with a lot of political leaders, who stir up opposition and appeal to popular outrage and then deny that they are responsible for the violence that follows, there is an element of hypocrisy at work.

So there was an element of dishonesty for all the rhetoric of liberty and ideas about rights. What was really being proposed, given the circumstances, was just 'No Taxation' – always a popular policy. To justify this, Britain was cast as a tyrant and said to be going against a 'constitution'. But this was a constitution that existed only in colonial propaganda. It was similar to ideas in seventeenth-century England, that in a golden age Englishmen had been free and the Normans had come in 1066 and imposed a tyranny. At no time in the past was there an agreed constitution which said that Americans needed representation before being taxed as English people in English colonies by an English government. But simple unwillingness to pay, even if it was for their own defence, and to stop smuggling would not have been enough. It needed a sort of religious zeal about an issue of principle and a moral cause which Adams was adept at providing.

It became increasingly possible for those who wanted to resist British measures and insist on American rights and liberties to get support. Taxation resistance in Britain, for example to the unpopular excise duties added in the eighteenth century, was just based on unwillingness to pay. In America it was elevated to a matter of principle and related to other issues, such as shortage of physical money. Alliance between radicals and the populace was possible because of a tradition of communal protest. The very presence of British troops was bound sooner or later to lead to an incident such as the Boston Massacre. Attempts by Britain at law enforcement led to disputes such as the suspension of the New York Assembly in 1767 and the burning of the British revenue ship the *Gaspee* in 1772, which kept disputes alive after the main taxes and dues had been rescinded. A relatively small group of activists could keep resentment going until more issues arose.

However, Adams's view and the outbreaks of mob violence and ongoing illegality such as smuggling, did not win universal support among the colonists. By 1770 both the colonists and the British government were locked into an impossible situation. It had become a widespread belief that there was something unacceptable about taxes and dues being imposed without any discussion or representation. However, what was not acceptable either was more and more popular protest, attacks on those the crowd saw as collaborators and disruption of normal activities. For most Americans in 1760 the option of independence was, even if remotely likely, just not on the agenda. But the fact remained, 'No Taxation without Representation' which was seen and talked about everywhere, amounted to virtual independence.

By 1770 the choices were to get on with normal economic activity and try to ignore the tensions; to continue with agitation to stop irksome activities by customs officers and to deter Britain from any more attempts at increasing control; or to support and defend British policy and oppose further mob action and political protest as being against the colonists' interest of prosperous trade and reliance on British forces for defence. In the end, the differences between these positions proved irreconcilable and the American colonies embarked on a civil war as well as a rebellion.

In the words of a much later British leader, Harold Macmillan, to an American president, Kennedy, what decided matters were *events, dear boy, events*. From 1773, a series of events led to an outcome that only a minority in 1770 had wished for. The range of options became dangerously reduced.

The great opportunity for those seeking more opposition arose over an unlikely issue – tea. The most famous protest in American history, in December 1773, took place over that most English of things – tea. The protest also has a famous and misleading name, the Boston Tea Party. Colonists dressed as Indians threw overboard a consignment of tea in Boston Harbour in a protest about tea duty. The reaction of the British government and the king to this 'tea party' was so severe that it could be seen that American independence can be traced back to this incident. It is the American Revolution's equivalent to the storming of the Bastille. After Britain closed the port of Boston and shut down the Massachusetts Assembly, there was no going back. Tensions rose to such a point that in 1775 fighting broke out and in 1776 the colonies declared independence.

There are many depictions of the incident, some from close to the time, but the actual term 'Tea Party' was not used before or during the Revolution. The more accurate and less fanciful term 'the destruction of the tea' was general until the early 1800s. Depictions often show the men throwing relatively small crates of tea into Boston Harbour whilst wearing Indian feathers and headdresses. Often this is depicted in fine daytime weather. The mood is often seen as joyful. A jape. A thumbing of Bostonian noses against the unpopular British tax on tea. Tourists today visit Griffins Wharf and are shown what happened on 16 December 1773 by costumed guides as part of the city's Freedom trail. The impression is of cheering crowds and united support. Unlucky History students grappling with the origins of the colourful and dramatic incident find a complicated story. Much easier to see it as a patriotic and spontaneous protest against overbearing tax policies in defence of freedom. This is how it is commonly portrayed.

A visitor attraction in Boston Harbour offered in 2019 the chance to revisit the night of 16 December 1773 when American colonists rose up against the 'tyranny' of the British. Visitors can hiss and boo the British oppressors and put on feathers to dress up as Mohawks. They can also throw lightweight bales of tea into the harbour. All this is advertised as the way that history should be taught. A website for patriotic young people has (erroneously) Samuel Adams, John Hancock and a large group of men disguised as Indians boarding the British ships to oppose tyranny.

In 2009, a group of conservative Republicans began the Tea Party movement in protest against the Federal government bale out of banks in the Financial Crisis. One of its founders claimed *We realized that government spending without the will of the people is a form of taxation without representation*. In the election of 2024, 'Tea Partyists' took up conservative viewpoints towards abortion, immigration, 'big government' and welfare. The events in Boston have cast a long shadow and have been an inspiration for political attitudes quite a long way removed from the grievances of the original protesters. But they shared one thing. They assumed they spoke for all Americans. The children's books often make the same assumptions about the protestors. It was 'the American colonists', not some of the people of Boston led by some of the political activists. The other common assumption is that tea was associated with tyranny and oppression. For the Tea Party supporters, the people who disapproved of illegal and wasteful actions and also threats of violence and intimidation seem to be lost to history.

The origins of the tea protest are quite complex and often poorly grasped. The British government of Lord North had moved away from the policies of the 1760s and did not aim to recover the expenses of the war by increasing taxes on the colonies. The only remaining tax from the Townshend era was on tea. It had ceased to be a popular cause of concern simply because so few actually paid it. Americans had resumed drinking tea on a large scale – it was almost a national drug. However, most of the tea was smuggled in and drinking it did not mean accepting an English tax without representation. Putting a boycott on English tea would not have made much difference because between 75–90 per cent of tea was brought in by smuggling, or perhaps to put it more kindly by unlicensed imports which fell outside the reach of customs officials. People were anxious to have their tea and there was a flourishing body of importers and sellers. Offshore depots, such as on the Dutch island of Sint Eustatius (still a Netherlands possession in the Leeward Islands) were used. British customs vessels could not police such a long coastline and even the most law-abiding citizens were happy to drink 'illegal' tea. The situation was similar to the period of salutary neglect, when Britain seemed to accept colonial traders and manufacturers not observing the Navigation Acts. To have tried to suppress the trade would have launched too much protest, and retreats from the Stamp Act and most of the Townshend duties was not something that Lord North wanted to repeat with tea, which was not a major element in British finances. However, his government decided on a bale out. The great East India Company, which could be compared to the later US corporate giants like Lehman Brothers, was in serious trouble. Because it was so important to Britain and virtually ran British India – that is Bengal – and had so many influential investors, it could not be allowed to go under. Its main product was tea – also in huge demand in Britain and in the European market. Thirteen million pounds of tea, brought by the company from India and China, came into England and the duty on it amounted to 6 per cent of the revenue of the country.

By 1772, the credit of the East India Company had run out. It owed £300,000 to the Bank of England and could not borrow on the market. It owed £1 million in customs duties on tea brought to England. While the duty was unpaid, the tea lay in bonded warehouses as a wasting asset.

The government came up with what they thought was a solution which would benefit everyone. The Tea Act of May 1773 allowed the East India Company to export the tea directly to the colonies without paying duty. When the tea got to America, it would be subject to a 3d import duty on each pound, left over from the Townshend import duties. When the other duties had been removed, the duty on tea had been reduced from 9d.[1] Freed from export duty, the Company tea would be cheaper than smuggled tea. The American market was very large – up to two million pounds of tea were consumed annually. The tea drinkers of the colonies could satisfy their urge to drink tea more cheaply, the Company would gain and be able to pay its debts and Britain would gain some more money.

Another idea in the act was that the duty on tea would be used to pay British officials who would actually have an incentive to collect the duty. It would stop the growth of smuggling which was seen as generally undesirable and impeding legitimate trade.

To facilitate this revival of the tea trade, the tea brought in would be marketed by specially nominated traders. In Boston there were the two sons of the governor

– Thomas and Elisha Hutchinson – the wealthy importer Benjamin Faneuil, and Hutchinson's nephew Richard Clarke. Thus, a small group of loyalists called consignees would benefit, while the wider range of merchants would be severely hit by cheaper tea. The assumption was that this cut price tea would be bought by the mass of people even if it did include a small amount of duty. One of the staple consumer products would be cheaper, so the tax would not be burdensome or take valuable hard currency.

Of all the causes of revolution, this must be the most innocuous. There was no real 'tyranny', in the sense of government oppressing the people. There were no great losses in war, as with the Russian Revolution, coming after the slaughter of the First World War, no mass poverty and feudal burdens as in France in 1789. Government action did not mean heavy tax exactions. It is regrettable but perhaps understandable that actually reducing the tax burden was not seen by Lord North as likely to provoke such a strong reaction. The tax on tea was not introduced in 1773 and had been paid without a lot of protest since 1770.

However, the new act stirred up the 'no taxation without representation' arguments as more tax would be paid even if the tea were cheaper and more was consumed. The situation was ready made for the Boston radicals. The merchants were already concerned about the direct deals done by British exporters and manufacturers which excluded traditional merchants. The East India Company had made this worse by dealing with small groups who did not usually trade in tea. The fact that these were wealthy men stirred up popular resentment. Colonial rights were being undermined by the rich and powerful. Then here was the fact that the ships carrying tea were bound for all the major ports. This would carry the agitation through the colonies and not just Boston. This was a major opportunity. Finally, the long voyage to the colonies gave time to prepare agitation and here was the sense of the colonies facing a hostile invasion fleet – even if he ships carried not armed men but a popular drink. There is another and more disturbing element. By focusing on tea, the radicals had an easy way of identifying those not fully committed to opposition to Britain. Community pressure could be brought to bear on those buying the wrong sort of tea; and even the drinking of tea might set someone outside the accepted norm. The issue brought about pressure and intolerance in the name of liberty.

The intimidation, not usually celebrated as part of the 'tea party', began on 2 November when Governor Hutchinson's nephew, Richard Clarke, was summoned to the Liberty Tree in Boston. The people gathered here demanded that he and the four others selected to sell the East India Company tea should resign as 'consignees'. There was an attempted attack on his warehouse, driven off by his men. The threats continued after Sam Adams called a public meeting on 5 November. Three consignees gave way and fled the city. On 17 November a mob ransacked Clarke's house and he, too, fled.

This sort of manipulated popular action had been seen in relation to the Stamp Act and there was an obvious determination to act when the *Dartmouth* arrived carrying 114 chests of tea on 28 November.

At this point a complicated rule kicked in. If the tea had not been unloaded, within twenty days after inspection, by customs officers and the duty paid, the goods could be seized and sold at auction. Customs officials had inspected the cargo, so there was a difficult situation. If the ships were unloaded, then the duty would have had to be paid and there would probably have been riots. If the tea stayed on board, then it could be sold at auction and so reached the people against the wishes of the Patriots.

The next demand was the *Dartmouth*, now joined by two other ships, the *Eleanor* and the *Beaver* at anchor in Griffins Wharf, should return to England with the tea.

The emotional temperature was raised by news that the activists at Lexington, later to be famous but then a small obscure town outside Boston, had gathered its tea and burnt it. In a way, this might have suggested that unloading the tea would not have been significant. If the majority of people supported opposition, then all that they would have had to do is to have refused to buy the tea. However, it was not likely that there would be unanimity. Not everyone cared about the tea tax and some opposed a return to mob action. The people whom Adams and his allies claimed to speak for were not unanimous about taking violent action.

The issue could have been postponed if the ships had returned, but Governor Hutchinson refused to allow the captains the necessary permission to leave port before the tea was unloaded.

The impasse was broken by direct action after a well-attended protest meeting at Old South Church. This was not spontaneous. On a cold December night some thirty young men, mostly apprentices or servants of the Boston Sons of Liberty, merchants and professionals, boarded the ships. The leading organisers, Sam Adams and the merchant John Hancock, certainly did not take part directly. The thirty youngsters were joined by a group of over fifty more. In contrast to some popular notions a number of corrective points can be made:

- This all took place in a dark and cold night with the spectators carrying torches.
- The protestors wore ragged clothes, hoods and blankets and some smeared their faces. They did not disguise themselves in full Indian costumes with headdresses.
- They were described as 'people of the lowest sort' and were young.
- This was a planned action not a spontaneous jape.

- Adams sent messages to other Sons of Liberty in New York and Philadelphia praising the action.
- The easy hurling of quite small chests into the sea often shown is false. The 342 chests each weighed 400lb and the water in the wharf was shallow.
- Not usually shown are the large mounds of tea in huge piles. The great waste of a valuable commodity was all too apparent. 92,000 lb of tea was ruined with a value of £9659 – a considerable amount which may be equivalent to £1 million in today's money. (This is often simplified to suggest it was a million in 1773.)
- The work was heavy and demanding. The 'Indians' were under orders not to cause damage to the ships or to other cargo and the ships were swept after the destruction.
- Many were shocked at the deliberate destruction of property and there were calls throughout 1774 for compensation to be paid to owners. Even when British leaders responded strongly, not everyone blamed them, given the destruction of property and the poor reputation that Boston would have as a trade centre which could undermine its wealth.

However, the biggest omission is to see the Boston Massacre in isolation, as there were some ten incidents in 1773. Threats and violence were not just employed in Boston, but there were different scenarios in other ports, and it would be misleading to see Boston as being typical.

The news of this act of pointless vandalism (for some) or powerful political protest (for others) led to the firmest (or most provocative, depending on your point of view) reaction.

The reaction of the British government is not normally seen in a wider context. Since November 1772 the opposition groups in Boston had revived the idea of linking up with other groups in the colonies by Committees of Correspondence, This amounted to a concerted attempt to end British rule, even if this was not openly admitted, The other elements are the more widespread actions taken to prevent the landing of the tea. There were up to ten 'tea parties' and a considerable amount of intimidation. There was more than a sort of patriotic prank in Boston.

Captain Ayres of the *Polly* had 697 chests of tea (larger than the Boston consignment) moored at Chester on the Delaware River a few miles away from Philadelphia. He received this threat on Christmas Day 1773.

What think you Captain of a halter round your neck, ten gallons of liquid tar decanted on your Pate with the feathers of a dozen wild geese to enliven your appearance?

Though Philadelphia was the most English of the colonial cities, there had been agitation about the tea for three months. A group of influential merchants led by William Bradford, a coffee house owner, were concerned about the monopoly of imports from the company and its use of a new group of importers. They organised a public meeting and put pressure on the consignees to resign and for the river pilots to refuse to bring the *Polly* down the river. They also managed a peaceful resolution by bringing Captain Ayres to the State House and persuading him to return to England, encouraged no doubt by the 8000 strong crowd that had gathered outside. Though a milder 'party' than that of Boston, it nevertheless had elements of threat, crowd pressure and interference with legitimate trade.

In Charleston, South Carolina, the Sons of Liberty were also busy with exaggerated claims that unless the tea were prevented from landing it would mean that '*our posterity would be reduced to slavery*'. A topic of which the White people of South Carolina had considerable knowledge given the large population of enslaved people in the colony. The captain of the ship *London* was threatened with the burning of his vessel. However, the Sons of Liberty were less successful, and the tea was unloaded and placed in a warehouse. The following year, however, the activist Christopher Gadsden and his supporters were successful when the captain of the *Britannia* was forced to jump overboard, and his tea cargo was thrown into the sea.

In New York the tea controversy revived anti-British feeling, which had died down since 1770. In New York the radicals prepared for the landing of the *Nancy* with its tea cargo. One proposal, fortunately not adopted, was to prevent the landing and kill the governor and the council. The *Nancy* was delayed and did not arrive at New Jersey until April; it was forcibly prevented from entering New York. Another vessel, the *London* was boarded by a crowd in a sort of homage to the Boston Tea Party and the cargo was dumped into the river. A cheerful crowd escorted the captain of the *Nancy* to New Jersey and departure. The captain of the *London* was hunted, unsuccessfully, by a more violent and vengeful mob.

By 1774 there was increasing violence. In Annapolis, a crowd insisted that the importer, Anthony Stewart, burn a cargo of tea. The tea had been unloaded and placed in a warehouse. Unless duty were paid, the ship carrying it could not unload cargo and passengers, including indentures servants who would have to return to England. To avoid this, Stewart paid the duty and now faced threats. A crowd, urged on by a fanatical Son of Liberty called Dr Charles Warfield, surrounded his house where his wife was expecting a child and insisted that not only the tea, but also the ship should be burnt. The burning took place where Stewart's wife could see it and Stewart was forced to initiate the destruction.

Incidents of destruction continued in other places in 1774 – Edenton, Wilmington and Greenwich, with local committees assuming more and more influence. The 'Boston Tea Party' is almost a shorthand term for an increasing opposition involving crowds of people and incited by radicals growing more strident in their opposition.

However, there is another neglected aspect – the growing concern about disorder and economic disruption. In the narrative there seems a steady progression towards independence, but there was also a growing fear of anarchy. Men like Adams, Gadsden and Warfield did not speak for all of the educated and propertied opinion. And not all colonies pursued opposition with the zeal of the Bostonians.

The historian, Mary Beth Norton, in her study *1774*[2] writes about the seventh vessel carrying tea in late 1773 – The *William* – which was wrecked off Cape Cod in mid-December. The Boston radicals expected that the locals would do their patriotic duty and destroy the tea. In fact, a local justice of the peace supervised the unloading of the tea and a Salem sea captain took the tea to safe warehouse in Castle William. Despite pressure from opponents, the tea was bought and sold in the Cape Cod area. There were divisions in the area between the 'Indians', who wanted destruction, and those who put their desire for cheap tea before politics and those who disapproved of mob action, These mirrored more widespread divisions about tea and, by implication, how far to take opposition to Britain.

When agitation increased in 1774 with calls for a Solemn League and Covenant for a total boycott of trade and with unrealistic claims that here '*was no alternative between the horrors of slavery and the carnage and destruction of civil war*' and demands that those who refused the boycott should be named, shamed and punished, a minister – Jeremy Belknap of Dover New Hampshire – produced a loyalist argument. The counter view to the opposition to Britain is less often encountered in the general disapproval of the measures taken by Britain in the aftermath of the Tea Party, but is worth considering.

Tyranny in one shape is as odious to me as tyranny in another was the theme of the sermon. Belknap righty pointed out a key contradiction. The committees, which were becoming so powerful, had not been selected to impose total boycotts and the people had not been consulted. Yet the whole argument was based on the need for representation. Radicals were '*imposing their own private opinions upon other people*' as 'private men', without any elected status, and imposing threats stigmatising their critics as 'Enemies to their Country'. This was no more acceptable than acts of the British parliament being imposed. Communal pressure and threats in the name of liberty were just another form of tyranny.

Not all Americans saw the British reaction as unjustified. This became more pronounced as a view when incidents of mob violence increased. In March 1774, the Marblehead smallpox hospital, owned by the town's leaders, was destroyed by an angry mob fearful that the hospital, by inoculating people, would spread smallpox in the town. It seemed that once mob action had begun, it might spread to challenge all sorts of authority. (Hysterical 'anti-vaxers' appear early in American history.)

Not all people in the colonies shared Boston's anger about British measures. When Britain closed the port of Boston in response to the Tea Party, one customs officer in Philadelphia reported that 'the sober sort of people' thought that the mother country had brought in a 'wide and sober measure'. The planters of South Carolina were concerned about the destruction of property and thought that the East India Company should be compensated. Benjamin Franklin's son, William, the Governor of New Jersey, tried hard to support legal proceedings to compensate merchants for the property lost. Through 1774, elements of a nascent civil war can be seen in the efforts of patriots and committees to suppress concerns and to remain loyal to Britain. Patriotic violence was not always a matter of political principle. A famous example is the tarring and feathering of the British official John Malcolm in January 1774. This did not arise because of enlightenment ideas of representation but over a street quarrel. Malcolm had got into an altercation with a Bostonian called George Hewes, over Malcolm's rough treatment of a boy in the street. Coincidentally, Malcolm was an excise officer. Hewes raised a crowd, and Bostonians congregated at Malcom's home, eventually dragging him outside. He was thrown into a cart and driven through the city streets. The crowd had Malcom stripped and covered first with tar and then feathers, giving him a 'modern jacket'. The riotous parade continued through the city, stopping periodically to demand Malcolm renounce British authority, which he refused to do. The mob drove on past the Liberty Tree, where they threatened to hang Malcolm. They put a rope around his neck, tied him to the gallows, and beat him with clubs. Malcolm, severely injured, was eventually driven back to his home and unceremoniously rolled off the cart.

So, in a broader context, the Boston Tea Party was not a one-off incident, but part of a growing tendency to opposition, crowd pressure and violence. Expectations of a restoration of order and authority were not just the angry reactions of British MPs, ministers and the king but also quite widely held in the colonies where Sons of Liberty or local 'Indians' or 'Mohawks' did not have the support of more than a third of the population or have equal support in all colonies.

Britain made its disapproval clear. The Boston Port Act closed the port of Boston (though not the other ports involved) and suspended the Massachusetts

Assembly. Boston was closed until compensation for destroyed tea and damage to property had been paid. The Massachusetts Government Act changed the charter of 1691 by having the upper house of the assembly appointed by the British crown, not selected by the lower house. The governor was given the power to remove judges, elected juries and to restrict Town Meetings to one a year. General Thomas Gage was chosen as governor, effectively instituting military rule. The Administration of Juries Act allowed officials accused of murder in pursuit of their duties to be tried in England not by local courts. A new Quartering Act made provision for more troops to be stationed by giving powers to requisition vacant houses. This applied to all colonies.

The so called 'Intolerable Acts', a later appellation, did lead to more resistance and could arguably have been seen as a considerable error of judgement. However, what were the options open to the British government in the face of a renewal of the elements of the Stamp Act agitation – correspondence, committees, economic warfare, a degree of violence and coercion and exaggerated claims about the damage done by Britain? A degree of appeasement and recognition of concerns by removing measures had not yielded much. It was not a matter of confronting all colonies and all of the people – there were substantial elements which did not approve of disorder.

The options were to make another retreat and repeal the Tea Act; or try to isolate the radicals in Massachusetts and assert British control while not extending measures to areas less affected by discontent; or a substantial reinforcement of British power, given the obvious weakness of British authorities during the protests of late 1773. Options one and three were not really realistic. Flagrant breach of the law and destruction of property could not be ignored unless Britain was ready to accept a *de facto* loss of authority over some of its most valuable possessions and admit to fundamental weakness as an Imperial power, losing face both at home and in other parts of the Empire and in Europe. Option three would have been a sledgehammer to crack a nut. There had not been the same degree of protest in other ports where tea had been sent. Boston was known to be a hotbed of radicalism in a way that New York, Philadelphia and Charleston were not. Costly deployment of large forces to control civic disobedience would not have achieved much and military occupation of such a huge area was, as later events proved, impossible.

But as the old saying has it, 'the middle path rarely leads to Rome'. The measures taken were not enough to suppress opposition and would be likely to feed it. Because troops were deployed elsewhere on the frontier, and in securing newly acquired lands in Canada, the power available to General Gage was limited. The type of dialogue and propaganda to win over 'the sober sort' and isolate the radicals were probably beyond the ministers of George III. Also, sentiment in Britain, which depended on commerce and stability of trade, was strongly opposed to the events in Boston. However, taking a tough line without the means to enforce it is always a hazardous policy, however limited the alternatives are.

So with radicals with a good organisation, dedicated leaders, strong propaganda, and with resentful foreign powers looking on with some pleasure at the growing difficulties, England faced the prospect of growing problems and then decided to add to them.

Westward expansion would have been a safety valve. Those intrepid and resourceful people who looked for a new start in the west would not have been deeply moved by issues of representation or the price of tea. Britain had tried to avoid the consequences of westward movement in terms of costly wars with the Indians in 1763, but had gradually given way to pressure and lack of genuine concern for the wellbeing of the indigenous people. Restrictions had not been enforced, and new deals had been made with the tribes, But in 1774 came the Quebec Act, something that is sometimes seen as rather a side issue compared with the mighty political and constitutional issues.

The Quebec Act introduced in May 1774 was, however, one of the major causes of discontent and perhaps more significant in creating opposition to Britain than the Coercive Acts. The Act provided for the fourteenth colony – Canadian Quebec – to have a regular civil government. It had some notable features, the first being toleration for the Catholic French population. The second was that there would be no elected assembly – on the curious grounds that a largely Roman Catholic colony was excluded by Britain's laws against Catholic voting. The Act set up English courts and most importantly extended the boundary of the new colony southwards to the Ohio, cutting off expansion by settlers from Virginia and Pennsylvania. The Act revived the attempt made in 1763 to protect Indian rights from American colonists as the colony had a substantial protected area for Indians and there were prohibitions on colonial incursions.

The Act caused a perfect storm because of the religious toleration. A flood of anti-Catholic pamphlets, speeches and sermons resulted. There were concerns about a Catholic take over, even though the total Catholic population was only 35,000. New England Town Meetings condemned a pro-Papal, pro-French British policy undermining the security and values of the Protestant colonies. The patriot leaders used anti-Catholic prejudice to bolster the status of the local revolutionary committees which had little legal authority. Not only were these bodies now seen to be saving American liberty but also American religion. The impact of the Great Awakening referred to in Chapter One was probably seen more strongly in this negative intolerance than in the more positive light of encouraging healthy individualism and a desire or freedom claimed in some studies.

The anti-Catholic bias in Britain itself, which prevented Quebec from having an elected assembly, was seized on, in a curious twist of logic, as evidence of a desire to deprive all the colonies of their assemblies and establish a tyranny. But most of all, there were complaints that the extension of the border deprived Americans of their birthright to expand westwards. This was particularly irksome to the settlers, hunters and land investors of Virginia and Pennsylvania who had showed themselves less concerned with tea. British policy was very concerned with the Indian issue. The violent upheaval of Pontiac's Rebellion had led to the Proclamation Line of 1763, restricting American incursions into Indian territory. Britain had been impressed by the power of the Indian fighters during the French War and the fate of General Braddock, ambushed and defeated in 1755 by French and Indian fighters. However, though Britain had been appalled by the violence and unlawful behaviour of backcountry hunters and settlers, despite efforts to keep them out of Indian territory, in practice it proved impossible to hold them back.

The high level of settler violence, which even extended to attacking British troops and supply trains, led to increasing conflict with the Indians and the danger of a full-scale war. In 1770, Britain was warned that if it persisted there would be a large-scale conflict between Virginia and the Six Nations, a well-established alliance of the six major tribes. Unable to regulate the backcountry via the colonial authorities, the British government intended to make incursion and settlement of the Ohio valley difficult through the Quebec Act. Settlers who moved into Quebec after 1775 would find themselves under the jurisdiction of British courts, not Virginia or Pennsylvania juries. They would find no opportunities to settle and be elected to an assembly or juries. They would find high import duties on key items such as liquor. They would find French civil law a barrier to making legal claims to settled territory.

The type of violence and its effects was shown in the spring of 1774 when backcountry thugs killed the family of a Shawnee king, which led to reprisals and a bloody campaign of Virginian militia attacking Indian villages.

As the Quebec Act came into force in May 1775, when fighting had already begun between colonists and British forces, it is not possible to say whether it would have provided the protection for the Native Americans or whether frontier violence could have been curbed.

It is perhaps not surprising that narratives of 'the struggle for freedom' do not dwell on the act. Opposition was fuelled less by a desire for liberty than traditional colonial anti-Catholic prejudice and hysterical claims of a Popish Plot. The freedom to go westwards was not, in this period, the freedom for enterprising and vigorous settler families in covered wagons fulfilling the nation's 'manifest destiny'. It was freedom for more land seizures, violation of Indian hunting rights and property, and indiscriminate violence likely to provoke major war and genocidal reprisals. The Park Service guide, to give one instance of an accepted narrative of causes of the Revolution, deals in quite a detailed way with the Coercive legislation but passes over Quebec, even though it was seen as a major cause of the Revolution. Religious intolerance and backcountry racial violence do not always figure strongly in many standard accounts.

The British government had to deal with immediate problems – the danger of a repeat of the large-scale Indian wars and the need to settle the government of its recently acquitted Canadian colony, as well as the disturbances over tea. Whether they were wise to attempt the Quebec Act at the same time as the Coercive Acts, when they had only limited resources to control an increasingly agitated population, is another matter. How far the opposition to these measures was based on concerns for liberty in a modern sense is also open to interpretation.

Notes

1. There were 240 pennies indicated by the abbreviation 'd' in each pound sterling (£) in 1773. Roughly one pound in 1773 was worth £2400 in modern terms so a 3d duty was broadly equivalent to £30. In 1770, a labourer might earn 7s (shillings) or 84d a week
2. Mary Beth Norton, *1774*, Knopf, 2020.

Chapter 4

The Road to Independence 1773–1776

Events in the colonies were of the utmost importance to the whole history of the world in the period between the famous Tea Party in December 1773 and the Declaration of Independence in July 1776. Historians do not usually consider 'what if?' scenarios, but sometimes it is irresistible. What if the British government had decided that it was unrealistic to control increasingly unruly colonists and that a return to salutary neglect, while relying on economic links and mutual prosperity to maintain a loose relationship, was more sensible. What if, in the light of this, an ongoing westward expansion and the advantages of a strong trade with an increasingly populous and industrialised Britain, had strengthened the power of the possible third of the colonists who were loyal, and the possible third who were indifferent to the fears and theories of the patriots had held sway? A boom in cotton would have led the slave colonies to prosper even further. The expansion westwards would have relieved the strain of inequality. There would have been no war of independence, just a gradual move to *de facto* autonomy, The French would not have had a reason to intervene and would have avoided the heavy costs that helped to bring about the French Revolution. The French radicals would not have had the model of American liberty. No American Revolution. No French Revolution. No United States, just a loose association of colonies each dealing with the mother country. No union to defend in 1861 and no civil war. By the late nineteenth century, even great slave owning states like Brazil and Russia had abandoned slavery. The British Empire would not have been weakened by the loss of America. The United States would not have emerged as a great power.

Well, this might make a good novel, but it is based on a more unlikely premise than even more radical depictions of 'might have beens', like Bernadine Evaristo's novel *Blonde Roots*, postulating an African establishment of White slavery. The biggest stumbling block for a 'Sliding Doors' type of novel is the very first 'what if?'. How could Britain, the world's foremost military and economic power which had emerged so strongly from the Seven Years War, possibly accept the sort of rebellion that was incipient by 1773 and developed rapidly in 1774 and 1775? Also, how could an increasingly strident and self-righteous opposition just go quietly back into the box after the successes of the 1760s and the excitement of the Tea Party?

The traditional view is that the reluctant move of the colonists to declare full independence made 1776 the key year. This is seen in the US national holiday of 4 July (even though the Declaration of Independence was signed on 2 July). It is seen in the idea of the 'spirit of 76'. The signers of the Declaration are the 'fathers'. John Hancock, the first to sign, is synonymous with 'name' ('Put your John Hancock here!'). Thomas Jefferson who drew up the first draft is honoured by a huge memorial in Washington DC. With the possible exception of Lincoln's Gettysburg address, the Declaration is the most important document in American history and is widely reproduced, framed and displayed.

However, it is arguable that the Declaration only recognised an independence established earlier. Also, that independence was inherent in the demands and ideas circulating in the 1760s.

So much of the path to independence is tied up with the reaction to the British responses to the Tea Party, that it is worth looking a little more closely at this. The impression is given in many narratives that an intemperate response by Britain unified the colonists behind resistance, and poisoned relations between Britain and America. A study of the cabinet discussions in London reveals a more complex situation.

The first thing to note is that illegal activity over customs duties was not new. In 1771, a noted incident occurred near Chester on the Delaware River. A British customs vessel had intercepted a snuggling boat containing tea and wine. Before the contents could be impounded, the boat and its crew were attacked by smugglers dressed as Indians, the boat was destroyed, the officials injured and forced to swim for safety and the smuggled goods taken away.

Smuggling was not some picturesque jape but a major industry, and smuggling gangs working in collusion with established merchants, and Dutch and North German companies were often violent if challenged. Smuggling had turned into a large-scale defiance of law and established authority. A modern parallel might be Latin American gangs who operate above the law and intimidate attempts to suppress them.

So when the Tea Party so openly and brazenly challenged authority, it was inevitable that there was a reaction. One problem was that the British Army and Navy could have intervened but were prevented legally. Under the Mutiny Act, which defined the use of the British military, this would only have been possible if they had been asked to do so by the civil power. This would have meant that the Boston authorities and assembly would have needed to accept the governor's wishes and authorise the protection of the cargo and the ships. This was not given, so Admiral Montagu and Colonel Leslie, the British commanders, were powerless. In any case, Montagu feared that action would have *endangered the lives of many innocent people*. To remedy this the British government needed to change the terms of the Charter and replace the upper house of the assembly with men nominated by the Crown who would not be unwilling to call for military support.

The closure of the Port of Boston was a means of getting the mercantile community to recompense the owners of the tea for its destruction. The other measure discussed by the cabinet was the arrest and removal of the ringleaders, including John and Sam Adams, for trial for High Treason in London. This would indeed have been an extreme and possibly decisive reaction, but the British cabinet lawyers prevented it. The evidence for the collusion was not strong enough and the legal basis for such a trial was weak. Had Adams been taken off in irons and then executed for treason by the prevailing method of hanging and mutilation, then there would have been no doubt that the measures were disproportionate.

The other measures included strengthening the Boston garrison. However, General Gage did not recommend overkill. He told the cabinet that four regiments would be enough and expected that resolute action would meet with little resistance – the colonists 'will undoubtedly be very meek'. The cabinet and the king saw the Tea Party as part of what George III called 'an increased in pretentions to independence'. But, there was no certainty that massive repression was the answer.

Other measures established quartering for an increased military presence which sometimes is represented by uncouth British soldiery turfing honest citizens out of house and home. In fact, the act referred only to uninhabited houses, barns and outbuildings, and quartering in inns was paid for. The unruly Town Meetings were prohibited but not fully as the meetings to elect assembly members and juries were permitted. The aim was to control growing agitation, not to impose a sort of tyranny.

Whatever the truth about the concern for legality in cabinet discussions, the effect of the measures went beyond their intentions. Lord North and his colonial secretary, Lord Dartmouth, overestimated the importance of Boston as the only serious source of opposition. North stated that '*Boston is the ringleader of all violence and opposition to the execution of the laws of this country. It has to answer for its own violence and for having incited other places to unrest*'.

In fact, there is evidence that the greater reliance on smuggled goods in the middle colonies led to pressure on Boston to take more decisive action. The other colonies had been more active in boycotting English imported tea and buying tea from Dutch merchants. Foreign merchants had campaigned for boycotts and resistance, but the Boston merchants before 1773 had put profit and consumer demand first and Boston used more English tea even with its

3d duty. There was some pressure on Bostonians not to be left behind rather than all of the impetus coming from Boston for boycotting.

British policy may have been based on suppressing lawlessness in Boston as the key to pacification, but this was a miscalculation and growing discontent focused on the Coercive Acts and the Quebec Act. The latter had been planned which was nothing to do with the Boston Tea Party and had been planned the previous year.

The events of 1774 were crucial to the American Revolution and hinge on the reaction to the British measures. The closure of the Port of Boston produced sympathy from the other colonies but they did not commit to a colony-wide boycott of British trade. The suspension of the assembly caused more concern when news reached the colonies in August. Possibly the greatest concern was the increased military presence in Boston.

There were a number of parallel developments. The first was the increase in committees. The initial committee of correspondence had originated in Boston in 1772, and its aim was to share grievances and ideas with other towns in Massachusetts. The resentment about British policy increased the spread and importance of the committees in other colonies and less isolation. The second major development was the convening in Philadelphia of a Continental Congress, enforced by the committees. This, in turn, led to more committees to enforce a boycott of trade and also other congresses, particularly in Massachusetts. By the end of the year, the colonies had developed committees and an Intercontinental Congress, which had the features of an alternative government to that of the British government, parliament, the king, the royal governors and the usual elected assemblies. When the new bodies started preparing for conflict by gathering arms, the situation became revolutionary. By December 1774 it was only a matter of time before some sort of armed clash broke out.

The narrative thrust of this scenario is powerful. In 2016 the American journal *The History Teacher* proudly published a student contribution which expressed a fairly widely accepted overview. The paper focused on the role of the Committees of Correspondence, and its conclusions are well worth consideration.

There committees were not new, as similar groups had taken a leading part in enforcing non-importation protests during the Stamp Act agitation, threatening and ostracising those who would not comply. However, they had fallen away after the repeal of the act. The committees revived after November 1772 were led by activists in Boston.

The Boston Committee was chosen by the voters, freeholders and other inhabitants to record grievances to be submitted to the Crown. However, instead of a petition, a document of grievances was sent to 290 towns in Massachusetts with a clear message – the people were being held in slavery by Britain and had a moral responsibility to repudiate tyranny. The network of committees was established when 144 towns drafted replies. More committees were formed after the Gaspee Incident. The *Gaspee*, an official customs ship had been burnt by a crowd of Rhode Islanders, and the British response was highly unpopular, This was because independent judges had been appointed to investigate, thus bypassing the normal law officers and courts. This 'tyranny' prompted more correspondence, with Virginia establishing committees, and by 1773 twelve colonies had joined the network. The publication of the restrictions on the government of Massachusetts in 1774 was another impetus for the committees which took centre stage in political protest. They urged a boycott of British trade; they took the lead in organising an Intercontinental Congress which met in Philadelphia in September in which half the delegates had been on committees. The committees and congress amounted to a clear infrastructure, paving the way for countering British oppression and creating unity. And eventual independence.

There is something wholesome and reassuring in seeing the Revolution develop through committees and a congress rather than through conspiratorial groups or dynamic individuals. Committees are usually elected. They imply the sharing of views and sustained discussion. A committee of correspondence is even more of 'a good thing' with ideas being written and read and an exchange of proposals made. As for a congress, that is even more praiseworthy, with elected representatives, discussions, deliberations and actions which are the result of a free exchange of views. Modern US democracy is exercised through a congress – a coming together of representatives of the nation. Who could object to these developments to resist tyranny and the exercise of Imperial power on a people against their will?

In addition, the respectable, well-educated committee members and congress delegates expressed their loyalty to the Crown, asked for grievances to be met and did not even declare independence. If this was a revolution it was a moderate one, based on enlightenment ideas of just rights and constitutional government. The guillotines and savage mobs of the French Revolution have often been compared unfavourably with these calm advocates of freedom. There was no equivalent to Lenin and his Bolshevik plotters aiming to destroy 'bourgeois democracy' and instal their own class-based ideology, in the Russian Revolution.

This rather rosy picture ignores some other manifestations of committees. The French revolutionary excesses were directed by a Committee of Public Safety, run by well-educated, enlightened, middle-class people. The Congressional Un-American Activities Committee imposed damaging censures on those whose ideas and ideals were seen to be *un*-American in the Cold War. There was no guillotine, but ostracism, disgrace and isolation. This was not a world away from the committees of the Revolutionary era, enforcing economic sanctions, isolating loyalists and conniving at acts of violence. The congress of the McCarthy era was complicit in highly illiberal and prejudiced activities which opponents found difficult to stop because of the ability of the Red Scare leaders to mobilise public opinion. In the Cold War period, there was demonisation of opposition and susceptibility to rumours about communist plots and foreign invasion. This was not too far away from the colonial opposition to Britain in 1774. Committees and congresses are quite capable of repressive behaviour

There are some omissions in the commonly accepted story. First is the opposition to the committees and congress. Second is the nature of the congress itself and third is the increasing popular protest.

A common term used by historians to describe the elections of both committees and congress is 'extra-legal'. Presumably this is to draw a distinction between acts, which were actually illegal, such as the destruction of property, the tarring and feathering of individuals and, towards the end of 1774, the seizure of arms. Electing bodies with the specific intention of organising opposition to government policy was rather less obviously illegal, though the activities they encouraged, such as boycotting trade and pressuring individuals to join boycotts, were by eighteenth-century standards totally illegal. They were covered by unconvincing protestations of loyalty to the Crown.

The assumption that the committees and congress spoke for Americans is false. To begin with, not all of British America was involved. The historian Kevin Philips[1] makes the point that five colonies – Quebec, Nova Scotia, Prince Edward Island, East Florida and West Florida – did not send representatives to the congress. The vanguard of protest was Massachusetts, Virginia, Connecticut and South Carolina.

In addition, there were substantial reservations about the development of what we might see as a state within a state by the end of 1774, especially with the growth of another set of committees set up by Congress to oversee non-importation of British goods – the so-called Committees of Observation. It is clear that by the time actual fighting broke out in April 1775, an alternative state had been established, albeit with significant local variations. The establishment of local militias and the seizure of arms had given that shadow state the means for armed resistance.

This was a long way from the wishes of a substantial number of colonists for reconciliation and ongoing loyalty to the Crown, but it was increasingly difficult for their views to be heard. In Georgia, a minister of religion called Haddon Smith wrote that the key issue was not whether Parliament had a right to tax colonists but whether Americans had a right to destroy private property with impunity. His defence of the British right to alter colonial charters led to him having to flee Georgia in August 1774. The same situation occurred when another clergyman, John Bullmann of Charleston preached against the right *of every silly clown and illiterate mechanic to censure the conduct of his governor*, arguing that social cohesion would break down if ordinary people did not accept authority. When he was dismissed by the Church committee, over eighty Charleston residents signed a petition on his behalf. The situation was looking dangerous and to avoid trouble Bullman left in March 1775. A pastor in Hebron, Connecticut, also criticised opposition and found himself surrounded by a hostile crowd of 300. He sought safety in Boston, but hostile letters were intercepted and there were more threats which forced him to leave America in October 1774. Local committees often went beyond corresponding with like-minded people. When the ship the *Magna Charta* (*sic*) landed tea in Charleston, the local correspondence committee took charge of making him promise to destroy it. When the elderly captain did not, a mob boarded the ship intending to tar and feather him, with the tacit approval of the committee. Though the captain escaped the mob, his treatment was poorly thought of by many in the port.

By the end of the year, with new committees enforcing the boycott and unauthorised local assemblies, there were a considerable amount of loyalist pamphlets. Revolutionary pamphlets and orations are often quoted but writings like Thomas Bradbury Chadler's *What Think Ye of Congress now?*, accusing the Sons of Liberty of trying to intimidate writers, printers, readers, speakers and thinkers who opposed opposition, complained that his own pamphlets had been burnt. Another writer from New York, James Rivington, complained that the people who had claimed to demand liberty wanted to *establish a power more arbitrary and tyrannical than anything we have hitherto complained of*. This seemed to be justified by local committees prohibiting the sale of New York loyalist pamphlets. The Massachusetts provincial congress, which had been formed in the wake of the general congress, tried to get Rivington's pamphlets banned in all colonies. This provoked expressions of sympathy for those concerned about committees and congresses.

The historian Mary Beth Norton has documented these examples and the prevalence of concern about the growth of agitation.[2] It prepared the way for the American War of Independence being a civil war, and many of the contemporary writers who were worried about the growing guild between both Britain and the colonies and between radicals and moderate, so-called Whigs and Tories, used this term.

This concern about revolution derived in part from a disapproval of mob activity, which as shown in chapter one, was a feature of colonial life before 1763 and was to be a major factor in the making of the Constitution. It was also to do with the benefits of association with Britain economically and respect for the Crown.

This was quite abstract, as in the eighteenth-century monarchs did not pay state visits to the Empire and even in their own countries few people actually saw them, let alone talked to them. George III did not ask his loyal subjects over a cup of tea how far they had come to see him. However, respect for the Crown was considered important as a cornerstone of order and deference. A distinction was made between the Crown and policies adopted by government and passed by parliament. Part of being English and enjoying those privileges and liberties of freeborn Englishmen was to be loyal subjects. Even radicals were careful to express conventional respect. For those who wanted reconciliation with Britain, loyalty to the Crown was more important emotionally. It was tied up with respect for the natural order, property and law. It is notable that only after more than a year of fighting between colonists and British troops, did the Second Continental Congress come to declare independence from the Crown and sanction a document justifying this by criticisms of the king.

These attitudes have to be understood when considering the First Continental Congress. Initial support for this came as a result of the reluctance of the colonies to agree with requests from the Boston Committee of Correspondence for another ban on British trade. After the closing of Boston port following the Tea Party, there were expressions of sympathy from the colonial assemblies but a reluctance to act unilaterally without a meeting of representatives in a congress. Such assemblies had been held before but the earliest was perhaps encouraged by Benjamin Franklin's famous cartoon of a severed snake.

This cartoon, often seen to be an encouragement for a united, independent America was actually pro-British and urged cooperation to support the struggle against common enemies in the French and Indian War. Franklin took the lead in a campaign to put Pennsylvania under Crown authority rather than under the Penn family, heirs of the colony's founder. The Stamp Act Congress was very different but did not discuss fundamental issues of rights, just aiming to coordinate opposition to specific measures.

The First Intercontinental Congress had its origins then in quite conservative aims of appealing to the Crown for an end to conflict which involved meeting American demands and recognising colonial rights. It did not please the radicals, and John Adams deplored its caution, even in the light of the news of the measures taken to change the Massachusetts charter and government. In his view there was too much 'nibbling and quibbling'. The delegates were products of a well-developed education system for the propertied elite and a profound interest in the ideas of the enlightenment and political theory, which have led some historians to see those ideas at the heart of the American Revolution. As seen in Chapter one, delegates were bound to meet the needs of their constituents and most had a remit to restore 'union and harmony' and to avoid the 'rivers of blood' predicted by Sam Adams in the wake of the Coercion Acts.

The meeting of the congress in Carpenters Hall in Philadelphia has sometimes misleadingly been described as secret. Delegates were not in any way secret as they made their way to Pennsylvania, often being met by enthusiastic crowds, curious to see the representatives.

In keeping with the legalistic frame of mind, the attenders set about establishing a special committee to establish the key academic or philosophical issue of 'American rights', which would be a basis for redressing grievances and explaining to the British why opposition was justified. The committee began this deliberation on September 5 and its final report was made on 22 September, but not adopted until October at the end of the congress. No wonder the Adams family were so frustrated. There were practical issues – Boston was suffering from a blockade. Its people had to put up with military occupation with all its inherent stresses and strains. The changes to the way Massachusetts was government seemed arbitrary. Given obvious grievances, why spend so much time on theory? The committee was made up of two members from each state. so for smaller states most, if not all of their delegates were tied up. The debate, as far as it can be reconstructed because the congress sessions were behind closed doors and the debates only partially published, was about Natural Rights and 'Laws of Nature'. Perhaps this was inevitable given the knowledge of these sorts of discussion in seventeenth-century Britain and the interest in writings such as those of John Locke, who argued that subjects had natural rights which went beyond any rights granted or nor granted by monarchs.

Conservative writers in Britain had reacted with frustration in the previous century about talk of these 'natural rights' as it was not clear quite what they were based on. Who would decide when monarchs infringed these natural rights to such an extent that they should no longer be obeyed? It seemed like anarchy if people could decide for themselves when their natural rights had been infringed. If elected assemblies could decide on the basis of their having been voted in by the people, then again that was dangerous. However, supporters of natural rights argued that there had to be a higher authority than the monarch or the state to protect life and liberty. European philosophers, in particularly Jean-Jacques Rousseau, had argued that legitimate rule depended on an unspoken contract between government and those it governed. If a government became tyrannical, then that contract was broken and the subjects had a right to rebel.

The problem came in fixing a point where there was such a tyranny and in deciding who should decide. Also, there were problems about where these 'rights' derived from.

It might have been easier to argue that British actions were unconstitutional or simply that they were just unfavourable or unfair, without going into matters of fundamental rights, laws of nature and philosophical justifications for resistance. It seemed that those who wanted a reconciliation were in favour of a more down to earth and pragmatic justification, that would allow Britain to withdraw unpopular measures without accepting quite revolutionary ideas about the whole nature of sovereignty and contractual theories of government.

However, the committee went for the nuclear option and made the basis of opposition not only the measures themselves, and not only on the view that Britain had been 'unconstitutional' in interfering with an established charter, but crucially that 'the laws of nature' justified opposition.

This was too much for the more conservative elements who, while opposing policies, did not actually oppose British overall rule and wanted to return to a mutually beneficial *modus vivendi*. One such was Jospeh Galloway from Philadelphia, angry at '*untenable principles, rearing wild and chimerical superstructures*'. He was sure that the congress did not want reconciliation, but independence. It was a view shared by the Governor of Boston, General Gage, who saw '*a desperate veering between justifications based on the laws of God and nature and arguments about violations of the Constitution*' and rights in the original charter. The purpose of this searching around for justification was a break with Britain in his view.

This movement towards independence was confirmed by the congress accepting the radical Suffolk Resolves, which contained the view that the king ruled not by right of birth but by 'assent' and talked of a covenant or contract between the monarch and his subjects vitiated by unjust and tyrannous measures,

The move towards these more provocative views may have been provoked by inaccurate rumours that British troops had killed Bostonians trying to confiscate gunpowder and by rumours that the fleet had bombarded the city.

In the end, the congress adopted measures to wage economic warfare against Britain by reviving the non-importation policy and agreeing to committees to organise this boycott. Though the sanctions against those who did not comply would be to 'name and shame', in practice this could easily lead to more extreme intimidation.

Interestingly, the congress did show some concern about these committees. The committees of correspondence had been chosen by various Town Meetings and had included more radical elements. To prevent this, congress insisted that only those who elected the existing state assemblies should vote for the committees of observation. This may have reflected a concern that events were moving too fast.

However, this was somewhat inconsistent because the delegates to congress had not been elected uniformly by the electors who normally chose representatives to the various state assemblies. The way that they were chosen varied considerably. In some cases, it was possible to elect representatives to the assembly at the same time as to the congress, as in Virginia. In other states less regular elections took place and *ad hoc* groups had made the decisions. Though the congress was not legal and did not conform to the usual assembly elections, and fell outside the control of the governors or any legitimate authority, this variation in electorates reduced its legitimacy in many eyes.

But of course, not all. For some, like the 19-year-old Alexander Hamilton, a revolution had already occurred. Hamilton was the illegitimate son of a well-born Scot who had been brought up in the West Indies and had come to study in America in 1772. For him it was not possible to question this group of men who had '*devised and recommended the only effectual means to secure the freedom of America*'. He saw them replacing the British parliament as a source of authority and Americans should regard their decisions as binding. His pamphlet *A Full Vindication of the Measures of the Congress*, written in New York in December 1774 – though not set to music in the musical – nevertheless goes a long way to seeing the first congress as equivalent to independence.

Once one 'extra-legal' body had been seen as being given legitimacy by being elected, however haphazardly, it was easy for other elected committees and assemblies to appear. When Governor Gage dissolved the Massachusetts assembly in October, the members moved to Salem, and from there finally to Cambridge and declared themselves the Massachusetts Provincial Congress with the radical John Hancock as presiding officer. This body took it on itself to raise taxes and also to prepare armed forces to defend itself. A committee claimed the right to call on the colonia's militia. The militias were to elect their officers and start training in earnest.

The shadow state emerged strongly with the creation of the Committees of Observation and Inspection to enforce the so-called Continental Association to boycott trade. At city, town and country level, elections were by registered voters, but the election of this sort of new local authority was something new. Previously officials had been appointed. The remit of these committees was to *'observe the conduct of all persons touching this (Continental Association)'* and the brief went further than trade. Committees were to publicise the names of all *'foes to the rights of British Americans'* so that there should be no dealings with them. Not only were British goods not to be imported, but also not to be consumed. A whole way of life was involved, as extravagance and entertainments such as plays, dancing and horse racing were not to be encouraged. Direct action began quickly after 1 December when Virginians seized and destroyed a cargo of tea and made threats to its importer. Those who made comments critical of protest actions or in favour of Britain were made to do public penance and, in some areas, public confessions. Public humiliations in Communist China years later were a practice that later America found shocking, but were part of their own history.

Opponents were increasingly subject to mob actions as the 'Tories' of Marshfield in Massachusetts found out when threats that the 'damned Tories' hands would be cut off'. Quakers in Pennsylvania who refused to sign loyalty to the Continental Association because of their traditional beliefs against taking oaths, found themselves being accused of disloyalty and threatened.

The divisions that emerged are not the staple of general histories of the progress toward independence, and the influence of communal popular actions gets less attention than the activities of the Enlightenment figures of Congress. But inequalities and social divisions in the colonies had led to a considerable number of poorer people normally excluded from politics taking a much more active role in protests.

The 'extra-legal' state within a state, encouraging popular action and sometimes violence, has curiously more often than not been a subject of disapproval in the US, even though it was the development which propelled America to independence. Mao Zedong's extra-legal state in China, in the famous Soviet set up after the Long March, was not praised as following an American example.

Britain faced by the start of 1775 a considerable threat with a virtual loss of control, popular violence, and an opposition convinced by its ideology that they were fighting tyranny and had a natural right to resist. When its troops were unreasonable enough to try and prevent an illegal arms build-up close to the most important British base in the colonies, they unleased what one historian has called a 'military fury' which had been building up since the end of that crucial year, 1774.

It would be concerning and possibly unacceptable for many to see the movement towards armed conflict and independence in terms of 'frenzy' as opposed to a growing desire for freedom. A long-forgotten study of loyalism published in 1958 contained this judgement, *'Will not posterity be amazed by the overreaction a three-penny duty on tea gave rise to. Will they not see it was as disgraceful to America as the witch craze frenzy?'*[3] Posterity has not, over the sixty years since then, made much connection between the growing hysteria in 1775 against Britain by a minority of the colonial population (discounting enslaved people and Indians much less) and the much-discussed witch craze hysteria in Salem in the 1690s, which seems to belong to a different era, even though both were centred on Massachusetts. However, periodic bouts of frenzied activity were common in colonial America. Sometimes they took the form of assaults on indigenous people, sometimes class-based disorders, sometimes, as in the Great Awakening, they concerned religion.

It does not help understanding to see the past through modern eyes and the level of violence in 'normal' eighteenth-century life has to be taken into account. Brutal punishments, public execution, beating of apprentices, indentured labour, children, enslaved people, soldiers and the frontier warfare against Indians would not have been seen by contemporaries as abnormal, any more than it would in Georgian England. This did not exclude finer feelings, education, hard work, enterprise, compassion, ideals and a love of liberty and independence. However, there is a distinction between justified enthusiasm to be free and behaviour more redolent of uncontrolled frenzy. In 1775, that distinction was becoming blurred.

Already, as the research of historians like Mary Beth Norton have shown, there was a growing intolerance to those who maintained loyalty or who were indifferent and still wanted to make a living by normal trading and did not want revolutionary austerity. In 1774, a young and ambitious settler of Scottish descent called Thomas Brown arrived in Georgia, with seventy-four indentured labourers to establish a plantation. Some studies give the impression that indentured labour had given way to a freer workforce, but it is interesting how often references to this continued practice of semi-enslavement persisted. Brown did well and became a local magistrate, swearing loyalty to the Crown as was customary. When hostilities broke out he was pressured to join the local patriots. He declined, as was his right to do so in a free country. A mob attacked his home, knocked him unconscious, stripped him and tied him up. They poured hot tar onto his legs and set it alight, they pulled out his hair and cut strips of his scalp.

Somehow Brown survived and made his way, now penniless, to South Carolina where he later raised a force of loyalist troops and pursued a brutal campaign of revenge against supporters of the Revolution.

It is not safe to generalise from incidents like this, many of which had their roots in local resentments not political causes, but it makes disturbing reading.

In the wider context, this incident does not seem untypical. Large crowds had been gathering in Massachusetts since the summer of 1774 to shut down courts. These crowds were often supported by local militia. At Worcester in August, some 6000 armed men defied authority and prevented the court hearing cases in the town.

The danger of armed conflict was great enough for General Gage to fortify the entrance to the city of Boston. For their part, local committees of safety accumulated arms and confiscated cannon from forts. In February 1775 over 200 British troops were sent to Marblehead to seize stolen cannon. Facing armed militia and realising the cannon had been spirited away, the commander did not provoke conflict. The town of Worcester had become an unlawful arms depot and was too well defended for British forces to take the weapons without a major clash. Some sort of armed encounter seemed inevitable. The fighting began when some 700 British troops were sent to Concord with orders to take or destroy arms. Local militia were warned, famously, that the British were coming, tried to stop them and eight Americans were killed. The troops entered Concord and destroyed some stores and gunpowder. They were attacked by a large force of local militia on the way back.

There remains an idea that patriotic local farmers hastily armed themselves and spontaneously attacked the British troops before volunteers swarmed towards Boston and besieged the British garrison, eventually forcing their withdrawal.

However, this is to ignore the shadow state that had been forming and the extensive military preparations made by the committees of safety and local militia. There was a large militia force ready – perhaps 14,000 strong in the colony – and preparations for riders to announce any attack and allow coordinated actions to take place. Once the local militias had attacked on the way back to Boston, men from Connecticut, New Hampshire, Rhode Island and Massachusetts were surrounding Boston and British regular forces faced 20,000 armed men.

This was an extension of the sort of mass communal actions described in chapter one, and a result of the development of a state within a state during 1774. Cannon had been stolen and stored away. The smugglers who were numerous and skilled had brought in munitions. Militias had drilled and practised shooting. Just as the Boston Tea Party was, in fact, a coordinated action rather than a spontaneous outpouring, so the initial actions which led to war resulted from a well-planned conspiracy by skilful organisers and propagandists like Sam Adams and other radical leaders. Accounts in which the British were the aggressors and fired first and that local lovers of liberty had leapt to the defence of their liberties were circulated both in the colonies and in Europe.

What really happened? As this is such an important event, the differing accounts will be quoted below to show the problems in finding the truth.

A loyalist source offers what those close to the governor knew. Anne, the sister of Henry Hulton, the chief customs commissioner in Boston, wrote to her friend, Elizabeth Lightbody, a few days after the 'shots that range round the world'. She recorded that about 800 grenadiers and light infantry were ferried over to Cambridge at 11 pm and marched to Concord. She says that the congress had been 'lately assembled' there and that Gage had news of 'a magazine', i.e. a stache of arms.

> *The people in the country (who are all furnished with arms and have what they call minute companies in every town ready to march on any alarm), had a signal it's supposed by a light from one of the steeples in Town, upon the troops embarking.*
>
> *The alarm spread through the country, so that before daybreak the people in general were in arms and on their march to Concord.*
>
> *About daybreak a number of the people appeared before the troops near Lexington. They were called to, to disperse, when they fired on the troops and ran off, upon which the Light Infantry pursued them and brought down about fifteen of them. The troops went on to Concord and executed the business they were set on.*

The letter then describes how the British troops on their way back:

> *found two or three of their people Lying in the agonies of death, scalped and their noses and ears cut off and eyes bored out – which exasperated the soldiers exceedingly – a prodigious number of people now occupying the hills, woods, and stone walls along the road.*
>
> *Facing fire from an enemy using walls and trees and out of windows of houses rather than in 'open field' the troops were harassed. The soldiers entered the houses from which shots had been fired and 'put all the men to death'.*

The letter estimated 50 British dead and 100 wounded and that they were outnumbered ten times, with 1000 American casualties.

On 20 April a Boston merchant wrote to his brother-in-law in Philadelphia with what he saw as shocking news. He also related the nocturnal expedition, but his account is different in significant respects.

> *The first advice we had was about eight o'clock in the morning, when it was reported that the troops had fired upon and killed five men in Lexington—. About twelve*

o'clock it was gave [sic] out by the general's aide de camps that no person was killed, and that a single gun had not been fired, which report was variously believed – but between one and two, certain accounts came that eight were killed outright and fourteen wounded of the inhabitants of Lexington – who had about forty men drawn out early in the morning near the meetinghouse to exercise. The party of the light infantry and grenadiers, to the number of about eight hundred, came up to them and ordered them to disperse. The commander of them replied that they were only innocently amusing themselves with exercise, that they had not any ammunition with them, and therefore should not molest or disturb them. Which answer not satisfying, the troops fired upon and killed three or four, the others took to their heels and the troops continued to fire. A few took refuge in the meeting house, when the soldiers shoved up the windows and pointed their guns in and killed three there. Thus much is best account I can learn of the beginning of this fatal day.

You must naturally suppose that such a piece would rouse the country (allowed the report to be true). The troops continued their march to Concord, entered the town, and refreshed themselves in the meeting and town house. In the latter place they found some ammunition and stores belonging to the country, which they found they could not bring away by reason that the country people had occupied all the posts around them. They therefore set fire to the house, which the people extinguished. They set fire a second time, which brought on a general engagement at about eleven o'clock. The troops took two pieces of cannon from the peasants, but their numbers increasing, they soon regained them, and the troops were obliged to retreat towards town. About noon they were joined by the other brigade under Earl Percy, when another very warm engagement came on at Lexington. I stood upon the hills in town and saw the engagement very plain. It was very bloody for seven hours. It's conjectured that one half the soldiers at least are killed. When I reflect and consider that the fight was between those whose parents but a few generations ago were brothers, I shudder at the thought, and there's no knowing where our calamities will end.

This was not from a firebrand but a moderate who had everything to lose from fighting, but he reports aggressive action by the British, whereas the first letter blames the minutemen.

An early newssheet account, dated 25 April, called *The Essex Gazette* printed 'an early report' of the events of 19 April and made no attempt at objectivity, comparing the actions of the troops as *'no less brutal that what our venerable ancestors received from the vilest of savages'*. It agreed that the people were alarmed (i.e. the alarm was given) and began to assemble at:

Lexington, 6 Miles below Concord, a Company of Militia of about 100 men mustered near the Meeting House. The Troops came in Sight of them just before Sunrise, running within a few Rods of them, the Commanding Officer accosted the Militia in Words to this Effect: – 'Disperse you Rebels – Damn you, throw down your Arms and disperse'. Upon which the Troops huzza'd and immediately one or two Officers discharged their Pistols, which were instantaneously followed by the Firing of 4 or 5 of the Soldiers, and then there seemed to be a general Discharge from the whole Body. Eight of our men were killed, and nine wounded.

At Concord they destroyed several Carriages, Carriage Wheels, and about 20 Barrels of Flour, all belonging to the Province. Here about 150 Men going towards a Bridge, of which the Enemy were in Possession, the latter fired and killed 2 of our men, who then returned the Fire and obliged the Enemy to retreat.

A few of our Men attacked a Party of twelve of the Enemy (carrying Stores and Provisions to the Troops), killed one of them, wounded several, made the Rest Prisoners, and took Possession of all their Arms, Stores, Provisions, &c. without any Loss on our Side.

The report then described in vivid terms looting, arson and murder in Lexington.

But the savage barbarity exercised upon the Bodies of our unfortunate Brethren who fell is almost incredible. Not content with shooting down the unarmed, aged, and infirm, they disregarded the Cries of the Wounded, killing them without Mercy, and mangling their Bodies in the most shocking Manner. We have the Pleasure to say that, notwithstanding the highest Provocations given by the Enemy, not one Instance of Cruelty that we have heard of was committed by our victorious Militia; but, listening to the merciful Dictates of the Christian Religion, they 'breathed higher Sentiments of Humanity'.

Truth is indeed often the first casualty of war, and the disparity in these accounts reflects the problem of knowing quite what happened and the way that differing sympathies led to very different accounts. The Essex newspaper was often the one most believed and similar descriptions were assiduously spread.

By 1835, when the writer Ralph Waldo Emerson produced these famous words, the legends had already begun:

By the rude bridge that arched the flood
Their flags to April's breeze unfurled,
Here once the embattled farmers stood,
And fired the shot heard round the world.

Schoolchildren learnt about the ride of the Boston messenger, Paul Revere, shouting 'The British are Coming' to rouse the 'embattled farmers'.

This is apocryphal and the truth is probably of a well-established system of signals and riders; Revere did not ride alone and failed to reach Concord. There is no evidence that he said, 'the British are coming'. It was not so much embattled farmers that the British met but trained local militia. In the interest of poetry, Emerson slipped up and said the shots 'heard round the world' was that of the armed farmers, implying that they had started the action, rather than the British. Given the uncertainty in the sources of what happened, it is a little disconcerting to read on Lexington's official website:

The first battle of the American Revolution took place in Lexington on April 19, 1775, and the town has long been known as 'The Birthplace of American Liberty'.

Not in the eyes of either Anne Hulton or the Boston merchant. Anne thought it the starting point of a possible massacre of the people of Boston and the merchant a disastrous civil war.

The increasingly heavy casualties in the armed conflict round Boston obviously changed the situation by the time Congress reconvened in May, and there is a generally accepted narrative of the way that the situation moved from a struggle for rights or an armed protest against British policies to a complete break and assertion of independence. Briefly it could be described in this way.

Congress reconvened on 10 May 1775. Since it adjourned in October 1774 there had been a determined speech by the king condemning the actions of Massachusetts and the Congress's adoption of the Suffolk Resolves, a powerful statement of grievances drafted in Suffolk, Massachusetts in September 1774. There had been a considerable development of initiatives for virtual self-government and then the outbreak of hostilities and the siege of Boston by large numbers of colonial militia men.

The original intention of Congress was to resolve the hostility and in July it approved the Olive Branch Petition, hoping even at this stage for a settlement. This was not accepted and on 23 August a royal proclamation declared America to be in open rebellion. Meanwhile, Congress prepared for war, and the success of the Patriots at the Battle of Bunker Hill on 17 June 1775 made its members more confident. As with the discussions in 1774, the elite delegates thought it important to establish just cause for resistance and the appointment of Washington to command a Continental Army. *The Declaration of the Causes and Necessity for Taking Up Arms* fell to the influential John Dickinson and Thomas Jefferson to draft.

Congress faced the task of creating the regulations, conditions and service for its army and paying for it. On 22 June it approved a million dollars in paper currency and another million was printed in July.

Congress adjourned in August and reconvened in September to consider seeking foreign aid and also responding to a traditional British weapon of naval blockade by legitimising attacks on British vessels. There was already a virtual state within a state by the end of 1774, but the creation of an army, issuing money, and seeking foreign recognition were tantamount to independence. There was some reluctance to take the final jump into independence given that even with the fighting and the success of Washington in forcing the British to evacuate, as well as the 'flight of the Governors' as the Crown's representatives left their colonies, there was no unanimity about creating a new country. But for the scholarly and legalistic congress delegates a key issue was legitimacy. Assemblies and governments had been set up in the colonies but why should they be obeyed when the Crown was still, in theory, the ruler. Pressure, however, was building up from writings like John Adams's *Thoughts on Government* and from a widely read work by an English radical, Thomas Paine, called *Common Sense*.

Congress used its own authority to allow each colony to create its own government in May and the crucial debate about formal independence took place in June. The draft of a Declaration of Independence was entrusted to Thomas Jefferson. His first draft was amended but agreed on 2 July and formally announced on 4 July. What had been inherent in a lot of the discussions and actions since 1765 was now made manifest; all the supporters of independence had to do was to overcome the indifference of a third of Americans, the hostility of another third and defeat the strongest naval power on earth with a highly trained professional army.

With the Declaration of Independence, perceptions of the Revolution move onto a new plane of idealism. Two people come to the forefront. One is Thomas Paine who wrote *Common Sense*, advocating full independence; the other was Thomas Jefferson who drafted the Declaration. Both have the highest of reputations, and the Declaration has iconic status as a document of universal significance.

To take Paine first, his pamphlet *Common Sense* made a case for independence and made a claim which many still think true:

> *I have never met with a man, either in England or America, who hath not confessed his opinion, that a separation between the countries, would take place one time or other.*

Paine (or Pain as he was born) is a cultural hero and now cited in connection with a variety of progressive causes as a visionary and reformer. He was born in Norfolk, England in 1739 and apprenticed to his father's business of corset marking. His life before 1777 was a catalogue of failure and personal loss. His businesses failed and he lost his posts in government service in customs and excise. His first wife died, and he separated from his second. He became interested in radical ideas when he moved to the Sussex town of Lewes and a meeting with Benjamin Franklin, then in England, led to his move to Philadelphia in 1774.

Short of money, with limited education and lacking much achievement in his life, he was drawn to radical journalism and was seen as a useful propagandist by supporters of independence like Benjamin Franklin and Benjamin Rush who financed the 47-page pamphlet which was originally to be called *Plain Truths* but became *Common Sense*.

No similar piece of writing has had such claims made for it, and histories are fairly unanimous about its huge sales. Some go for 100,000, others for 120,000 and some even for 500,000 by the end of the War of Independence. It is also said to have influenced the Constitution of Pennsylvania, Washington's conversion to independence and Jefferson's Declaration of Independence, and converted Americans to a final break with England.

However, a certain amount of common sense needs to be applied to *Common Sense*.[4] First, there are no actual sales figures and the pamphlet was largely printed in Philadelphia. Sales figures are entirely dependent on claims made by Paine himself, which varied and had no supporting evidence, especially since he received no royalties and had broken from the original publisher. He claimed to have sold both 100,000 and 120,000 and to have changed the course of history. In 1779 he wrote to the outgoing president of Congress that independence had followed within six months of the work's publication and 'before it was published it was a dangerous doctrine to speak of independence'. In the letter he claimed that 150,000 copies had been sold. By 1892, when a biography was published (incidentally to defend Paine, whose reputation had sunk badly after the Revolution) the figure of 500,000 was introduced and is perpetuated by online sources.

That would mean that every White household had bought a copy. If so, it would have been a bestseller to end all bestsellers. But this is utterly unlikely given that so many Americans were loyalists, that there was also illiteracy, and that American printing and distribution did not have the capacity for book production on this scale. Even the lowest figure would suggest that one in five White households bought a copy. That Americans in the south and west avidly sought out this publication and were moved to revolution by it seems the stuff of myth, but in any case, there is nothing more than anecdotal evidence of what impact the work had, even if it was widely circulated and its contents conveyed by word of mouth as well as purchase.

The problem with 'common sense' as a concept is that it assumes that all Americans had common views, and also that once they had read the assertions about monarchy, the mother country, the need for a republic and the negative view that government was a necessary evil, that their traditional notions and beliefs would be transformed. Again, this seems unlikely, and as with most propaganda it seems more likely to have reinforced existing beliefs than to have changed the minds of those whom we have encountered so far in this book, who were fearful of mob rule and of going against tradition and taking on a great power. Analysis of the appeal of the book with its persuasive down to earth language is more common than analysis of its actual effects.

By January 1775, regardless of what could be seen as a short rant by a foreigner, the *de facto* movement towards independence was in full swing. All sorts of grievances were in play, particularly about restrictions on migration and the measures taken by Britain against Massachusetts. There had already been pamphleteering. Paine was not original in this appeal to 'common sense'; John Dickinson in *A Declaration by the Representatives of the United Congress of North America* in 1774 had adopted what was a sort of formula justifying opposition by reference to 'the Great Creator, principles of Humanity and the dictates of Common Sense'. Paine put all this more directly and more radically. He argued that respect for monarchy was just based on tradition and fear. But a view that acceptance of monarchy was based on a covenant which could be ended had already been stated in the Suffolk Resolves. George III took so much exception to this declaration that he declared that the colonies were seeking independence before that was actually stated directly by Congress.

For such a widely read and influential popular hero, Paine's subsequent career was surprisingly uneven. His critical views on religion were unpopular and by the end of the war, he had become penniless and his writings unpopular. In a somewhat morally dubious move, he accepted the grant by New York of a confiscated loyalist farm which he did not manage successfully. The people whose wisdom and power he so praised turned against him quite dramatically after 1783. He fell out with Washington and published a letter accusing him of 'treacherous and private friendship and hypocrisy' and puzzled over whether he was 'an apostate or an imposter'. This was not a wise move at a time when Washington was an unassailable national hero. Paine went to France as he was so excited by the Revolution and dined off the plates of the executed Louis XVI. But he himself was nearly guillotined and his reputation plummeted. After his return to America in 1802, he was so unpopular that a coachman refused to take him as a passenger, fearing that God would send a thunderbolt to destroy any carriage transporting a godless revolutionary. Paine was dogged by ill luck through his life, apart from the shining moment in 1789 with *Common Sense*, so perhaps it is rather harsh to question the myth of his importance.

Jefferson's Declaration of Independence appears much more unassailable. The huge memorial in Washington stands as tribute to him as Founding Father and later president. His reputation as a wordsmith earned him the task of drafting the seminal document in American history. He had honed his skills in preparing the new constitution for Virginia in June and as a pamphleteer extolling the role of

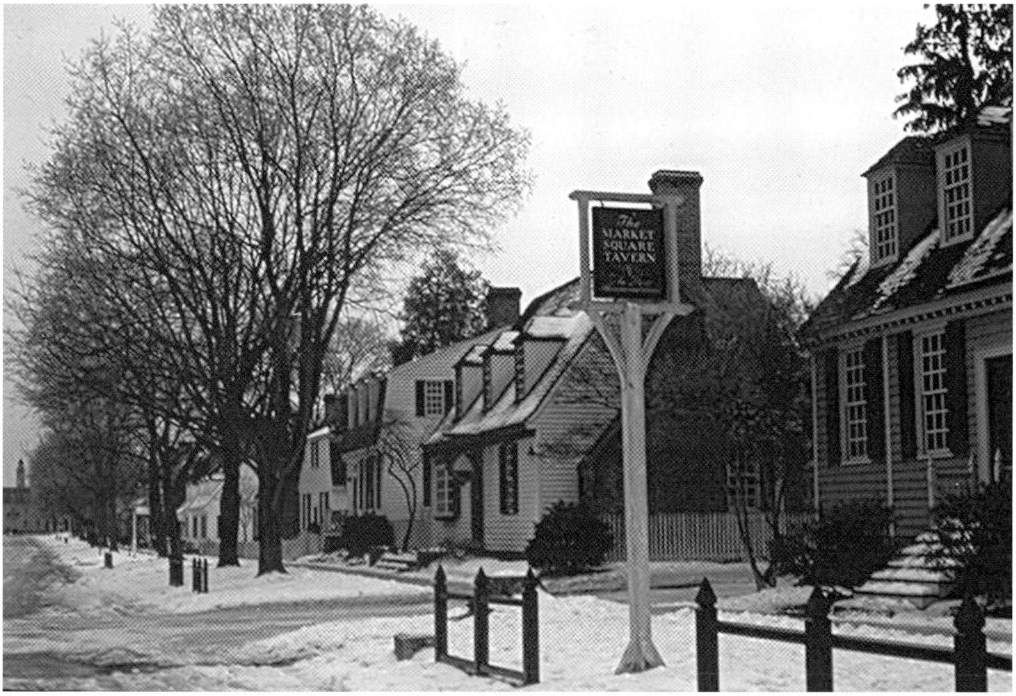

Colonial Williamsburg. A fine day out for generations of visitors but a selective portrayal of colonial life.

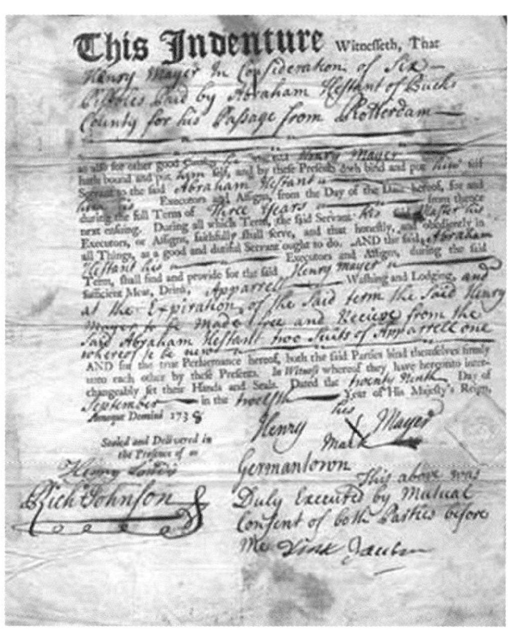

Benjamin Franklin was so famous that the great French sculptor, Houdon, made a bust of him during his stay in Paris. Detractors could buy a chamber pot with his face on.

Land of the unfree. In this agreement, Henry Mayes sells himself into servitude for three years in return for the price of the voyage to the new world.

A British print of the death of General Braddock at the hands of Iroquois warriors during the French and Indian Wars. His enemies do not seem to be portrayed.

The Stamp Act as seen in *The Pennsylvania Journal* in 1765. A modest duty on documents was seen as an existential threat.

This famous print of the attack on John Malcolm, published in Boston, is approving of the action.

This British print of the same time, October 1777, is not.

The Boston printer Paul Revere depicts the 'Boston Massacre' of 1777.

Revere's ride to warn the people of Concord, Massachusetts, of the approach of the British caught the imagination of later generations, as in this inaccurate picture of 1916. 'The torch bearer of the Revolution' was later court martialled by his own side.

William Howe depicted in 1777. This liberal-minded and intelligent commander was far from being an upper-class fool. Six feet tall, he was notorious for an affair in Boston with Elizabeth Loring, the wife of a loyalist.

The very stuff of legend, a later portrayal of Washington crossing the Delaware to attack the Hessians at Trenton.

A print of 1787 depicts Washington.

A portrait of 1840 shows a more familiar image.

The painting by David Trumball shows Burgoyne making a gentlemanly agreement to surrender at Saratoga.

A French print by comparison ridicules Burgoyne as a turkey. Saratoga was the tipping point for the French to enter the war formally.

A later print of the fictitious Molly Pitcher of the mid-nineteenth century.

A work of 1914 celebrating the contribution of African Americans to the war, seems not to show many Black soldiers.

The famous portrait of Joseph Brant by Romney. One of many portraits of this ambitious leader.

Banastre Tarleton, the swaggering British officer of the campaign in the South. Tarleton did not entirely deserve his reputation for brutality.

The end of the war saw a return to enslavement for many. This print of the 1780s depicts dancing, but the reality was harsher.

Signing the Constitution, a later depiction from 1856.

1. Washington, George, Va.
2. Franklin, Benjamin, Pa.
3. Madison, James, Va.
4. Hamilton, Alexander, N.Y.
5. Morris, Gouverneur, Pa.
6. Morris, Robert, Pa.
7. Wilson, James, Pa.
8. Pinckney, Chas. Cotesworth, S.C.
9. Pinckney, Chas., S.C.
10. Rutledge, John, S.C.
11. Butler, Pierce, S.C.
12. Sherman, Roger, Conn.
13. Johnson, William Samuel, Conn.
14. McHenry, James, Md.
15. Read, George, Del.
16. Bassett, Richard, Del.
17. Spaight, Richard Dobbs, N.C.
18. Blount, William, N.C.
19. Williamson, Hugh, N.C.
20. Jenifer, Daniel of St. Thomas, Md.
21. King, Rufus, Mass.
22. Gorham, Nathaniel, Mass.
23. Dayton, Jonathan, N.J.
24. Carroll, Daniel, Md.
25. Few, William, Ga.
26. Baldwin, Abraham, Ga.
27. Langdon, John, N.H.
28. Gilman, Nicholas, N.H.
29. Livingston, William, N.J.
30. Paterson, William, N.J.
31. Mifflin, Thomas, Pa.
32. Clymer, George, Pa.
33. FitzSimons, Thomas, Pa.
34. Ingersoll, Jared, Pa.
35. Bedford, Gunning, Jr., Del.
36. Brearley, David, N.J.
37. Dickinson, John, Del.
38. Blair, John, Va.
39. Broom, Jacob, Del.
40. Jackson, William, Secretary

A key was provided in 1940.

In 1863, survivors of the war were photographed by the Reverend Ellis Hilliard. Seeing these pictures brings home the period much more than prints. All this really happened.

Congress. As a plantation owner of the fine estate of Monticello with its tobacco and, of course, its enslaved workers, he was seen as part of an enlightened elite in the Republic of American Letters, as the growth of enlightened learning in the colonies has been termed. His was a life far away from the rootless, radical Paine, who may or may not have been a seminal influence on him.

The writer and historian Bill O'Reilly[5] describes Jefferson at work at Philadelphia. He had observed the debates and heard Richard Henry Lee's proposal that 'these united colonies ought to be free and independent states' and absolved from allegiance and any political connection with Great Britain, but it was far from certain that Congress would accept full independence. Only seven colonies were definitely for it. Jefferson was entrusted with this highly important draft as he had a strong reputation in Virginia as a scholar and writer. But he had personal worries about his wife, Martha, who was weak, pregnant and had already lost a child, Alone in a lodging house for two weeks in June 1776 he struggled to make a case for independence.

What was agreed was an edited version of Jefferson's original and it is interesting to see what Congress deleted:

He [King George] has waged cruel war against human nature itself, violating its most sacred rights of life and liberty in the persons of a distant people who never offended him, captivating & carrying them into slavery in another hemisphere or to incur miserable death in their transportation thither. This piratical warfare, the opprobrium of infidel powers, is the warfare of the Christian King of Great Britain. Determined to keep open a market where Men should be bought & sold, he has suppressed every legislative attempt to prohibit or restrain this execrable commerce. And that this assemblage of horrors might want no fact of distinguished die, he is now exciting those very people to rise in arms among us, and to purchase that liberty of which he has deprived them, by murdering the people on whom he has obtruded them: thus paying off former crimes committed again the Liberties of one people, with crimes which he urges them to commit against the lives of another.

South Carolina and Georgia were uneasy about a critical view of slavery, but it is also one of the more ridiculous parts of the Declaration. It argued that slavery was bad and blamed the king for it but also blamed him for offering freedom to enslaved people who joined the British. Jefferson's father-in-law had fathered a number of slaves and so Martha Jefferson was half-sister to a number of enslaved people at Monticello, so blaming the British for slavery may seem a little bizarre.

Jefferson provided, or rather reheated, the theoretical justifications but the motives for a declaration went beyond ideological concerns. Practical issues required that Congress and the individual colonial governments should have more legitimacy since they needed to get foreign aid, regulate trade, raise and pay armed forces and provide law and order, which protected property. They had to avoid charges of anarchy and sanctioning a general lawless rampage by the lower orders, whom they now needed in uniform and ready to die for the cause. They also needed to avoid being merely rebels and fight as citizens of a sovereign country. But this needed some theoretical underpinning. Jefferson, though in the middle of major concerns in his personal affairs, did the job, drawing on previous arguments both in Congress and in the flood of pamphlets justifying resistance. Not only did the Declaration express, in quite understandable terms, the complex ideas of natural law, it also offered a range of practical grievances in pros which was effective for its day and generally respected. However, Jefferson did not speak for all Americans and some of the ideas and evidence seemed quite flawed and, if analysed, continue to be problematic. Working alone and distracted by concerns for his wife, it is perhaps remarkable that his final Declaration was as coherent as it was. What is also striking is the lack of debate about it, compared to the anguished discussions about natural law justifications in the First Congress in September 1774; the delegates spend only days revising his draft – beginning a long American practice of appeasing the slaveholding states.

The famous opening preamble has achieved fame as a fundamental statement of democracy and liberty:

> *We hold these truths to be self-evident, that all men are created equal, that they are endowed by their Creator with certain unalienable rights, that among these are life, liberty, and the pursuit of happiness. That, to secure these rights, governments are instituted among men, deriving their just powers from the consent of the governed. That, whenever any form of government becomes destructive of these ends, it is the right of the people to alter or to abolish it, and to institute new government, laying its foundation on such principles, and organizing its powers in such form, as to them shall seem most likely to effect their safety and happiness.*

Perhaps all this really did seem self-evident by the time the resistance to Britain had reached the stage of war, but there are some problems. The idea of a self-evident truth is similar to Paine's *Common Sense* argument – it is so obvious that there can be no discussion. But the justification is not obvious. It relies on a huge assumption that there are 'inalienable rights' and that they are granted by God. However, God's word – the Bible – is more about duties and responsibility and obedience. When Moses brought back the Ten Commandments, the Israelites did not form a committee to discuss them. When Jesus said 'render under Caesar' what is due to him, he did not exclude taxes which people did not want to pay. The Declaration did not explain quite where in the Bible this granting of inalienable rights was made. The delegates did not see the contradiction of a statement that 'all men are created equal and endowed by their creator with certain inalienable rights' when so many of the population were in a state of enslavement. These noble words were written while Jefferson was being looked after by an enslaved person, Richard Hemmings. As for the rights to life, liberty and the pursuit of happiness being inalienable, this was agreed to in a time of war, which involved forcing men into a Continental Army in which death was a very real possibility, given that it was fighting a highly trained professional army, which unlike all the colonists, had enlisted voluntarily. The pursuit of happiness by living in their own lands and being protected from invasion by settlers and hunters was not accorded by the Virginians to the Indians on the border with the enlarged province of Quebec. Liberty of opinion was not accorded to loyalists any more than it had been accorded to royal officials, tea importers or men like Thomas Brown of Georgia (see above). But in dangerous times, there had to be a strong moral basis for opposition which went beyond a desire for land or freedom from taxes and customs dues. The unequal struggle against the might of Britain needed idealism, or if not that, at least a strong sense of grievance, and the Declaration also expounded the ills and oppressions imposed on Americans. Many of the complaints were far from being self-evident truths and few were substantiated. The impression is that George III had no reason to do any of the heinous things he was attacked for, a long list of which includes:

For imposing taxes on us without our consent;

For depriving us, in many cases, of the benefits of trial by jury;

For transporting us beyond seas to be tried for pretended offences;

For abolishing the free system of English laws in a neighbouring province, establishing therein an arbitrary government, and enlarging its boundaries, so as to render it at once an example and fit instrument for introducing the same absolute rule into these colonies;

For taking away our charters, abolishing our most valuable laws, and altering fundamentally the forms of our governments;

For suspending our own legislatures and declaring themselves invested with power to legislate for us in all cases whatsoever;

He has abdicated government here, by declaring us out of his protection, and waging war against us;

He has plundered our seas, ravaged our coasts, burnt our towns, and destroyed the lives of our people;

> *He is at this time transporting large armies of foreign mercenaries to complete the works of death, desolation, and tyranny, already begun with circumstances of cruelty and perfidy scarcely paralleled in the most barbarous ages, and totally unworthy of the head of a civilized nation;*
>
> *He has constrained our fellow citizens, taken captive on the high seas, to bear arms against their country, to become the executioners of their friends and brethren, or to fall themselves by their hand;*
>
> *He has excited domestic insurrections amongst us, and has endeavoured to bring on the inhabitants of our frontiers, the merciless Indian savages.*

Not all found these accusations plausible, but loyalist criticisms are generally not as widely publicised as this key revolutionary document.

Much less well known, for example, is the rebuttal written by Thomas Hutchinson, Governor of Virginia from 1771 to 1774. He questioned whether the colonists were in fact a whole people or distinct from Britain. He challenged the idea of taxation requiring consent and defended actions taken in response to rebellion. All this is of course debatable and is part of its time. The following, though, has quite a modern flavour:

> *Only I could wish to ask the Delegates of Maryland, Virginia, and the Carolinas how their Constituents justify the depriving of more than a hundred thousand Africans of their rights to liberty and the pursuit of happiness, and in some degree to their lives, if these rights are so absolutely unalienable.*

Hutchinson refuted in some detail many of the claims made, for example:

> *DECLARATION:*   *For taking away our Charters, abolishing our most valuable laws, altering fundamentally the forms of our Governments. For suspending our own legislatures and declaring themselves invested with power to legislate for us in all cases whatsoever.*
>
> *HUTCHINSON:*   *There has been no Colony Charter altered except that of Massachusetts Bay. The only instance of the suspension of any legislative power is that of the Province of New York for refusing to comply with an Act of Parliament for quartering the King's troops posted there.*

Overall, Hutchinson made some important points. He rightly observed that there had previously been little discussion of actual impendence as opposed to resistance. Implicit in this was the view that the colonists had not been properly consulted:

the professed reason for publishing the Declaration was a decent respect to the opinions of mankind, yet the real design was to reconcile the people of America to that Independence which always before they had been made to believe was not intended.

He also argued that discussion was limited by pressure on those who opposed, contradicting the idea of democracy and freedom:

Discerning men have concealed their sentiments, because under the present free government in America, no man may, by writing or speaking, contradict any part of this Declaration without being deemed an enemy to his country, and exposed to the rage and fury of the populace.

There are objections to most of the claims in the Declaration, some of which refer to proposals not actually carried out and to misconceptions, for example that the Hessian troops in the English forces were merely mercenaries. There was no exemplification of some of the claims. In Quebec, for instance, 'the free system of English laws' was not abolished as the province had been French.

However, the important point is not to engage in a discussion about the rights and wrongs of a Declaration and a Refutation but rather to make clear that whatever its later reputation, at the time there was not universal acceptance of the claims and assertions it contains. It is also important that the independence referred to a severing of ties with, and loyalties to Britain and its monarch, not to the creation of a united country. Hutchinson made this clear when he refuted the assumption that Americans were a whole and distinct people united behind a noble cause of liberty. The initial proposition put forward by Lee made it clear that independence referred to the individual colonies who attended the congress. The Declaration was not necessarily about the creation of a new United States – that came about because of the protracted war

Hutchinson's concern about enslavement was still being expressed over eighty years later by Abraham Lincoln, in a famous series of debates about whether enslavement should be allowed to spread to new territories. It is worth quoting and considering:

I should like to know if taking this old Declaration of Independence which declares that all men are equal upon principle, and making exceptions to it – where will it stop? If one man says it does not mean a Negro, why does not another say it does not mean some other man? If that Declaration is not true, let us tear it up [Cries of No! No!]. Let us stick to it, then, let us stand firmly by it, then.

The signers of the Declaration had it clearly in their minds that the 'men' who were equal were free White men, not enslaved men, not Indians, not women.

But the Declaration still had a great deal of emotional power when used in a very different context to justify a view that when it said men, it should mean just that and whole groups of humans should not be excluded.

By 1776 a minority of Americans had taken disputes about relatively limited matters of import duties and taxation to a new level. It was not the tea but the principle of representation. Finally, it was not just a matter of various grievances about coercive acts which did not apply to the colonies as a whole and increased military presence, but a matter of natural rights and independence. Dissenting voices like Hutchinson's and rational counter arguments did not stand much of a chanced to be considered in the turmoil of war. However, conservative views had been increasingly subjected to abuse and violence even before the fighting began. Whether or not independence could be sustained was now dependent on what happened on the battlefield.

What began as local militiamen taking on outnumbered British troops developed into a war with various protagonists. Loyalists also resorted to arms. Both sides attempted to gain support from parts of the American population that were most endangered and oppressed – enslaved people and African Americans and the Indigenous peoples. This amounted to what has rightly been called 'the First Civil War'. The normal title – 'The War of American Independence' – was perhaps more applicable to a wider struggle involving not just Britain and her colonists but also France, Spain and the Netherlands. The re-enactments rarely involve these various groups and generally the period of conflict between 1775 and 1783, as depicted in ceremonies and movies, is rather selectively edited. It is very unlikely that without the war developing into an international conflict the British would have lost America

The following chapters deal with the struggle, but this can only be understood in the light of a more divided people with more varied motivation for war than textbooks and general narratives often suggest.

Notes

1. Kevin Phillips, *1775 A Good Year for Revolution*, Penguin, 2012.
2. Mary Beth Norton, *1774 The Long Year of Revolution*, New York, 2020.
3. Claude Halsted Van Tyne, *The Loyalists in the American Revolution*, Mass, 1958.
4. The myth of Paine's sales has been convincingly debunked by the historian Ray Raphael in the *Journal of the American Revolution* (2013) but it still appears in textbooks.
5. Bill O'Reilly, *Killing England*, Henry Holt, 2017.

Chapter 5

The Armed Struggle 1775–1779

Military accounts often see more continuity between the heady days of early victory and the remainder of the war than actually existed. The attack on the troops at Lexington and the swarm of armed militia and volunteers that descended on Boston, driving the British to retreat to New York, were an isolated series of events. It probably has more in common with some of the 'mob' or, if seen more favourably, 'communally based protest', that were a feature of eighteenth-century America. Instead of just prisoners being released or officials terrorised, this was a larger scale and bloodier conflict which had more significant consequences. However, the triumphant Americans mainly were not keen to be engaged into a drawn-out struggle involving travel outside their region and the rigours of military life for an indefinite period. The new commander, George Washington, was no Fidel Castro and had no desire to lead a revolutionary crowd. His vision was of a regular army able to engage with the European military tactics of the British Army. He was not an egalitarian and maintained an English style of distance from troops whom he saw as his social inferior. His insistence on European forms of address – he was 'Your Excellency' – and military discipline and formality was a long way from the swarming hoard of the first encounters. Though many think that the war was a matter of ambushes and irregular fighters with local knowledge taking advantage of formal European military tactics followed by Britain, this was not the case. The most successful example of a smaller, irregular force using the terrain, surprise and fighting in small groups, often from hidden positions, had been in 1754 when the Iroquois Indians defeated a British forced led by General Braddock, who was accompanied by George Washington in an advance on the French Fort Duquesne (which is modern Pittsburgh), during the war with France and its Indian allies. This might have been the characteristic of the later War of Independence, but in fact this was not usually the case.

In the end, the war was lost by Britain because of the intervention by foreign forces, particularly France, and by increasing lack of political will to maintain a costly and uncertain conflict on a huge area which had brought foreign involvement. The war was not a heroic parade of square-jawed heroes and feeble, bewigged British in unsuitable red coats led by upper class fools. It involved a great deal of hardship, relatively heavy losses in proportion to the population, and a great deal of internal conflict among colonists and brutal violence. Victory brought heartache and exile to a large number of loyalists, and its final outcome was disappointing in some respects. Independence led to uncertainty about the future and some quite profound divisions about the nature of the new republic. A lot of conflicts followed the end of the war and there were losers as well as gainers among the American population.

The war began with a brutal and confused encounter between colonial militia and British troops. It was not the intention of the British commander, General Gage, to start a conflict and he had been avoiding confrontation for some time. The war that followed was not really in the best interests of either side, and it was difficult to see how it could be won easily or what the outcome would be.

From the American side, it must have been clear that the patriot cause did not have the overwhelming support of colonists, hence the gap between the start of fighting and the Declaration of Independence. Though local enthusiasm and weight of numbers might initially have secured the exhilarating experience of locals driving back the professional troops, the prospect of a war against the British Navy and Army was fraught with danger. The main communication between the colonies was by sea. A long, sparsely populated and defended coastline would be open to British attack, and British sea power would allow freedom of movement for Britain. The main ports of the colonists would be vulnerable by sea while British control of Canada and a possible base in New York, a city noted for its loyalism, would threaten the colonies. Also, the colonies were vulnerable from Indian attack. As Britain was the main defender of Indian rights, it was likely that the alliance of the Seven Years War would be revived and turned not against France, but against the colonists who were so eager to seize frontier lands. Also, it would be possible – and indeed this happened – for Britain to promise freedom to the enslaved peoples in return for support. A British blockade would be able to strangle American trade, and the lack of manufacturing made the colonists likely to lack the means to produce munitions. The colonists had the advantage of being on the defensive, as in the second civil war of the 1860s, the rebel side had only to hold out, get foreign aid and wait for the official government to feel that the war was becoming too unpopular and costly to pursue. However, that meant being able to sustain a defence with troops not as well disciplined and not likely to be able to withstand British military power in set piece battles as opposed to sieges and ambushes. On the plus side, there was a huge area for Britain to pacify and there were commanders who had military experience, like Washington, or who were talented amateurs. There was also the hope of foreign intervention. As soon as hostilities started, there were secret discussions between Congress and Britain's enemies, with some notable clandestine negotiations for arms sales with France and Spain, involving the famous playwright Beaumarchais of *The Marriage of Figaro* fame.

Britain had the money and the military resources to fight a successful war, in the sense of being able to inflict defeats on an army without the training, discipline and experience of its troops. It did not lack strong leaders. The indecisive General Gage was replaced by the much stronger William Howe. The idea that the British generals were dim-witted, upper-class fools is not borne out by the successes obtained and the very determined opposition offered. The British had a record of success, not only in foreign wars but also in suppressing domestic opposition, as in the crushing and brutal suppression of a Scottish Highland revolt led by Bonnie Prince Charlie some thirty years earlier at the Battle of Culloden in 1746. However, the problem lay with poor internal communications, unfamiliar terrain, long lines of communication and the sheer size of territory to be pacified.

British military training centred on the pitched battle that was the staple of European warfare in the eighteenth century. European armies employed similar weapons, and the staple of infantry warfare was the smooth bore musket. This weapon had a narrow range and was not very accurate. Its power lay in its use by massed infantry firing their single shots rapidly. The cumbersome process of charging the pan of the musket, of inserting a ball down the barrel and pressing it down with a ramrod, cocking, aiming and firing did not produce rapid fire. However, with effective drilling and firing in alternative ranks, it could lead to surprisingly quick repeated volleys. Without rifled barrels, however, individual accuracy was limited. Artillery, especially if deployed close enough for the deadly grapeshot to be used, offered more chances for death and destruction but a key element was the final bayonet charge. The muskets and bayonets were the equivalent of a long deadly spear and the violence of a bayonet charge could disconcert inexperienced enemy troops. Given the British Army's expertise in drilling, musketry and bayonetting, there is no doubt that they made a formidable enemy. However, as the first encounter showed, against rifle fire by concealed marksmen not deployed in close formations but acting in smaller independent groups, the military skills so well-honed for European warfare were less effective. Though not all battles would be fought in the unusual circumstances of the first encounters in Boston and its outskirts.

A bigger issue is that of possible outcomes. If there had been enough successful encounters to convince Britain to accept independence, then the congress would have been left with a series of divided independent colonies and a divided population. There was no guarantee that the economic damage caused by the interruption of trade with Britain, and particularly the British West Indies, would be repaired easily. There had already been disputes between colonies, for example between Virginia and Pennsylvania, about ownership of the lands on the western frontier. There were considerable differences between the southern states and their large, enslaved populations and those states with less dependence on slavery. Some areas like the Canadian provinces had not joined the struggle. There would be the danger of the independent colonies being in conflict with other European powers without having the protection of the British state. It was also likely that war with Britain would involve considerable loss of life, the sacrificing of individual rights and the creation and maintenance of a standing army which many particularly disliked.

For Britain, a victory would restore prestige and be a victory for order over rebellion and anarchy, but would have raised the issue of how to rule America. Loyalist opinion, though substantial, had not been enough to counter the much more vigorous patriot opposition. The British governors had not been able to stop the creation of a state within a state. It was very different raising a force to oppose a rebellion from having the resources to maintain a permanent occupation of hostile territory and keeping its population from the extended Quebec province. Making alliances with Indians and freeing slaves were not very palatable policies for the British, and a war risked European intervention and the loss of those parts of the Americas which really mattered, the ultra-profitable West Indies. A long war would also create problems at home where there was sympathy with fellow Englishmen, and even if this idealism was not common, loss of trade and high costs in pursuit of a far-off Empire would not have been popular. The type of Imperial enthusiasm which characterised later nineteenth-century and early twentieth-century Britain, with Empire Days and maps of the world with Britain's Empire in red in every school, was not present in the late eighteenth century.

The Early Campaigns Boston and Canada

The very doubtful prospects for both sides were cruelly revealed in the opening campaign, if that is the correct word, for the fighting round Boston and the dismal American invasion of Canada. After being forced back to Boston, the British troops faced a siege, as armed men, militia and volunteers poured in to surround the city. Remarkably, Congress managed to appoint a commander – George Washington – and to form the units into a cohesive enough force to erect fences and defensive works round the city. A striking example of military enterprise by an amateur colonial commander, Henry Knox, succeeded in seizing cannon from Fort Ticonderoga and adding them to the artillery already seized from British forts. Gage had been joined by more aggressive leaders, notably General Howe. In an attempt to break the siege by regaining Breed's Hill, Howe had a clear plan, with a preliminary artillery barrage, but he underestimated his enemy. Though the hill was taken, the British suffered a high number of casualties, particularly among officers. The idea that officers simply stood at the rear and ordered forward the expendable cannon fodder is not supported by the loss of so many senior commanders. Howe himself took an active part in the battle and led from the front in a way that eighteenth-century leaders, according to many military histories, did not do until Napoleon showed them how. The relatively inexperienced British troops. faced with some devastating fire from defensive positions, hesitated before pressing home the dreaded bayonet charge and lost momentum, though in the end the Americans were driven off the hill.

The Battle of Bunker Hill, as this battle is inaccurately known, increased American confidence and shook British ideas that they were merely attacking 'rabble'. In fact, they had faced well drilled militia units that had been preparing for conflict for some time and whose commanders had purged pro-British elements. The relatively heavy losses prevented any further British attacks, and both sides settled in for a siege. Congress authorised the raising of the Continental Army under the command of George Washington.

There is sometimes a confusion, as the Continental Army was not the same as the militiamen who had fought on Breed's Hill. These farmer fighters had no long-term commitment and went back to their local areas. The drive to recruit a new regular Continental Army was a remarkable task. Ten companies of riflemen were raised – from Virginia, Pennsylvania and Maryland – and the besieging militiamen were commissioned as regular soldiers, though the enlistment was limited.

Washington was disappointed with the numbers who joined – only 10,000 of the 20,000 hoped for. As opposed to membership of the militia, there was less status attached to the new army, which often attracted those who had not shared in the pre-war prosperity of the colonies. Men without property or prospects and often not well rooted in their local communities were attracted by cash bounties and promises, some even by uniforms. Washington's new army, gathered by July 1775, did not have a common uniform and the colonial authorities did not have a common way of recruitment. Washington faced a high level of desertion. The population base for recruitment was limited. There may have been out of 2.5 million, an able-bodied White male population of 425,000 who were able to be recruited. During the course of the war over 200,000 were recruited – a very high figure given loyalists and those who objected to war; women and free Blacks, initially recruited and then banned by Washington from service, had to be discounted.

Washington was frustrated enough by late November 1775 by his bored and malingering recruits to write:

A dirty, mercenary spirit pervades the whole army that I should not be at all surprised at any disaster that may happen.

A volunteer called Joseph Hodgkins wrote home to his wife in Ipswich, '*Our men enlist very slow*' and hoped that the soldiers would have 'the virtue' to stay all winter and not desert for fear 'we may be made slaves forever'.

The desertion rate was high, partly because many of the new army were much younger than they are depicted in movies. Some of the new soldiers left memoirs written later in life – Jeremiah Greenman, the son of a sailor from Rhode Island was 17, Joseph Martin and Ebenezer Fox were even younger at 15 and 12. It was common for employers to send their apprentices off to war. Eighteenth-century America was a much younger society. Younger people could be spared more than adult workers and poorer people more than those with farms and businesses to run.

The Continental Army did not reflect the range of people in America but was generally made up of younger and poorer males. A writer in a Connecticut newspaper in 1777, quoted in the revealing book by Ray Raphael, refers to local people 'recruiting the children and servants of their neighbours'. As property requirements excluded the younger and poorer from voting, it is quite disturbing that these were so heavily represented in the fight for 'no taxation without representation'. Equally disturbing to the heroic image of the Revolution is the practice of local constables arresting poor men for vagrancy, then selling them as substitutes so that richer citizens could avoid being compelled to fight. To modern readers, this has something of President Putin's filling of Russian ranks in his war in Ukraine with criminals from Russian jails, rather than the idealism of the Declaration of Independence.

A more traditional image of burly heroism was seen when a band of nearly a hundred backwoods Virginian riflemen arrived outside Boston in July, led by a dashing commander called Daniel Morgan, wearing hunting shirts, carrying scalping knives and ready to back the Liberty or Death inscriptions on their shirts. However, when Morgan and 1100 volunteers went to attack Canada in September, the results were not encouraging. An American force took Montreal, but an attack on Quebec proved, as with Breed's Hill, that frontal assaults were likely to be costly, and the colonial volunteers were forced to retreat, with one of their most daring commanders, Benedict Arnold (later to earn fame as America's most notorious traitor), suffering a serious leg injury and Morgan and his riflemen were captured. Rather than being massacred or maltreated, they were freed on parole on the understanding that they would not resume fighting until British prisoners had been similarly freed.

Morgan was a seasoned and determined fighter and it would be ridiculous to categorise the whole American fighting force as poor or deserters or malingerers. However, it must be said that they were more likely to die from the chronic spread of disease than in heroic armed conflict. The reality of eighteenth-century warfare was that with poor medical care and uneven hygiene, disease was more likely to put soldiers out of action than the next biggest threat – artillery. It was harder for the soldiers to kill each other with bayonets likely to miss the vital areas of the body not protected by bone or with musket balls which were not especially accurate killers.

There was an element of bad luck for Britain, but in the parallel campaign undertaken by what was known as the Continental Army, an invasion of Canada, the dangers of the war became all too apparent. Despite being bolstered by this being seen by some as an anti-Catholic crusade, the attack failed miserably. It was not a given that patriotic fervour would triumph over corrupt old world British forces.

During the long siege of Boston, Howe was faced with disease and shortages and the heavy losses and unexpectedly high level of colonial opposition. Washington put considerable effort into mounting artillery on the surrounding hills. A raid on Fort Ticonderoga gave him valuable amounts of guns and ammunition, though it was never used in a grand assault on the city, widely blocked by Congress. It was not possible to bombard the city so a waiting game ensued. Eventually this led to the decision to evacuate Boston. The 11,000 British forces, together with over a thousand loyalists, not by any means all rich merchants and officials, but ordinary farmers and artisans as well, were evacuated by sea to Halifax, Nova Scotia in March 1776. Faced with 20,000 armed opponents and with the loss of so many officers, there was not much alternative. Howe was eager to get to New York which was far more loyal – Boston was very heavily associated with opposition – and with such a lot of resistance in the surrounding countryside it was too hard to defend. An attempt to capture Charleston had been repulsed by the Americans, so much hope was placed on the Middle Colonies.

Some accounts make these events decisive – a sort of equivalent to the failure of the Schlieffen plan in 1914 or Gettysburg in 1863 in the second civil war. It has been claimed that after the evacuation of Boston, there was little hope of a British victory. But this is to look at history in the light of what eventually happened. The failure in Canada, the number of loyalists who decided to give up everything to leave and the poor discipline and quality of many of the colonial forces should also be noted. There was no obligation for many for long service, and most of the besiegers of Boston went home and had to be replaced by the army that Washington eventually took to New York. There he faced an overwhelming British response as reinforcements were sent on a large scale to resolve the American issue once and for all.

In a way, the fighting up to this point was more an extension of the protests against British rule since 1765 than a war. Independence was not an aim until July 1776. Britain did not deploy her full power until well into 1776. A substantial colonial army operating outside its local area was not evident until 1776. The balance of probabilities that Britain would be able to restore some sort of authority was more tilted to the British side with the arrival of reinforcements.

New York

Washington was eager to defend New York as both sides saw it a strategic key. The British plan was to divide the New England colonies by taking New York and driving up the Hudson valley. Washington prioritised building up defences and hoped for a repeat of Bunker Hill in which British frontal assaults would be met by a determined defence and heavy casualties.

What was the surprise element was the sheer scale of British reinforcement, with 32,000 men and 130 ships. It has been described as the largest British expeditionary force before the two world wars. British military expertise and Howe's experience as a leader would outweigh the hastily assembled colonial forces and Washington's inexperience of directing large forces. New York was a very hard place to defend against an enemy with strong sea power as was made very obvious when, in September, Howe's forces landed on Long Island after a frightening barrage delivered by British warships.

The complexities of the campaign can be reduced to a simple outline. Washington hoped to draw British forces onto defence lines, but the strategy failed. Key forts failed to hold out despite their natural defences. His forces were in grave danger of being encircled and cut off and he was forced to withdraw into New Jersey, in what was more of a scramble than an orderly evacuation. There was a real possibility that Howe might win an outright victory and destroy the Continental Army, but delays and limited knowledge of the battlefield area prevented that.

Given the very large-scale British force, it was probably inevitable that Washington's hastily assembled and trained forces would not sustain their defence. However, there were some disturbing elements to this campaign which counter some of the more favourable views of Washington as conducting a Dunkirk-like evacuation.

The first is the proposal from Charles Lee, whom Washington sent to organise the defence of New York when Howe evacuated Boston, that loyalists be rounded up and taken off to Connecticut to avoid a sort of 'fifth column' in a city which was very divided about the whole idea of rebellion. Loyalism was not an unreasonable position or treason, and this seems like an extension of the violence and intimidation that had become commonplace by at least some elements within the Patriot ranks. Congress blocked the proposal, but it is a worrying incident for those who see the struggle in terms of 'good' and 'evil'. It contrasts with the reluctance of Howe to sanction a slaughter of the defenders of one of the main forts defended by the Continental Army. Indeed, William Howe and his brother, Admiral Richard Howe, who commanded the naval fleet, were both liberal-minded Whigs who had opposed the policies towards America and hoped for reconciliation.

The second incident was perhaps more serious as Washington wanted to abandon any attempt to defend New York City and move into Manhattan. Conscious of loyalist sentiment, and knowing that most of the city's property was owned by 'Tories', he wanted to burn it down. Congress refused but nevertheless arsonists destroyed large amounts of the city and at least one historian has argued that Washington subordinates knew his wishes and unofficially implemented them. Arsonists were lynched by angry mobs and the decisions between loyalists and patriots or 'Tories and Whigs' were increased. The war was taking on the characteristics of a civil war. There had already been fighting between the two groups in South Carolina, so it was not just a case of Patriots against Redcoats.

Nor was it a case of flexible and 'democratic' Americans against stiff, inflexible British commanded by unimaginative aristocrats. Howe's plans worked well and he avoided wasteful frontal assaults. By using the navy, he landed men in effective amphibious operations, unusual for the time. His movements stood a good chance of cutting Washington's armies off and only a plea by his generals induced Washington to make a last-minute decision to withdraw, which saved total defeat.

The contrast between the well-provisioned British and the neglected and dispirited Continental forces was very apparent. It was not the remote and uncaring aristocratic British who neglected their men but the Americans. Letters home reveal men sleeping out in the rain without tents or shelter, desperately trying to keep their weapons dry, suffering the cold from being in the summer clothes they were wearing when they marched from Boston, and with low morale. Two major fortifications were surrendered without significant resistance.

Washington is usually presented as a determined and heroic figure for keeping his force together when it was suffering from great hardship. Part of the respect Americans have for those who fought in this war is based on men enduring hardship in the case of liberty. However, fewer ask quite why it was that the leadership permitted this hardship, not just at the start of the war in New York, but right through and especially when the army went into winter quarters at Brandywine 1776–7 and more famously at Valley Forge in 1777–8.

While it was true that eighteenth-century armies did invariably suffer hardship, this was often when they were fighting away from their own country. But the Continental 'Winter Soldiers' were not fighting overseas and there was a wanton neglect. It was shown early on when Washington appealed to the government of Connecticut for clothing and supplies and was told that the local militia needed these. Washington was in a state of considerable frustration in what was a learning curve for him as leader. He had limited empathy for raw troops faced with formidable British fire power. When his men panicked at the British bombardment at Kips Landing – one of Howe's most successful tactical moves – Washington rode into their midst shouting abuse and waving his sword until he was nearly surrounded by a troop of Hessian soldiers in British service. Only a quick-thinking aide grabbed the bridle and took him back to safety. Commanding a large force is very different from commanding a Virginian militia unit, and the General's greatness was not much in evidence. Washington rallied his forces before the imminent arrival of the British reinforcements by a proclamation:

> *The time is now at hand which must probably determine whether Americans are to be Freemen or slaves; whether they are to have any property they can call their own, whether their Houses and Farms are to be pillaged and destroyed. The fate of unborn millions will now depend, under God, on the courage and conduct of this army – our cruel and unrelenting enemy leaves us no choice but a brave resistance or the most abject submission. This is all we can expect – We have therefore to resolve to conquer or die.*

Like many of the public statements it seems problematic. There was no evidence of any intention of British forces to do all this, and indeed Howe was prepared for negotiations. The patriot treatment of loyalists could well come under the 'cruel and unrelenting' description. Just as Congress was starting to debate the Declaration of Independence, Washington deprived one of his lifeguards, Thomas Hickey, of his life by hanging him for a supposed loyalist plot to assassinate the General, ordering large numbers of the Continental Army to watch Hickey's death throes. The destruction of property in the burning of New York exceeded anything done by Britain.

Washington rallied his forces before the imminent arrival of the British reinforcements by a proclamation. Washington's reputation, however, rests heavily on his leadership at the conclusion of the extended retreat and the famous image has been the main way that Washington's generalship has been remembered.

Washington's army had been retreating through 1776 and had lost New Jersey and was in Philadelphia by the end of the year. Though his men were in a poor state, some lacking adequate clothing and supplies, Washington made a bold move. The British were established in Princeton but had unwisely divided their forces so a relatively small force of Hessian troops faced the bulk of Washington's defeated and despondent army over the Delaware River at Trenton. Washington had been reinforced by local militias, and he planned an attack on Trenton for 26 December 1776. He divided his forces to cross both north and south of Trenton. However, the sudden onset of bad weather – rain, sleet and snow – led to ice floes in the river and prevented the southern crossing. Washington took his ill-clad and freezing troops in flat boats and ferries. The famous painting does not show them huddled against the weather and the bright sky is dramatic but inaccurate. Safely over the river, his men encountered a force of Virginians who had decided independently on an attack and are not often mentioned. The myth was that the Hessian soldiers had not recovered from heavily drinking on Christmas night, but in fact they had posted patrols, but they had been stood down. There was no expectation of an American attack, as most of the time the Continental Army had been on the defensive. Washington divided his troops and achieved surprise and was able to use light artillery. The Hessian commander was killed and there were heavy casualties, but 500 Hessians escaped as Washington was not able to cut off the escape route from the village. Military plans hardly ever work exactly but this was one of the war's most noteworthy achievements. But it was not entirely clear what to do next. Washington fell back on his most characteristic strategy and dug in at Trenton. Luckily for him, the British, under Lord Cornwallis, who outnumbered Washington decided on an attack after a tiring and difficult march from the base in Princeton. A re-run of Bunker Hill resulted in heavy British losses. However, Washington faced a daunting prospect and responded imaginatively by marching unexpectedly on Princeton and taking the British base. Again there were heavy British losses, and the counter attacks succeeded in regaining New Jersey and denting British prestige.

The disappointing thing for Washington after these feats was that his army, whose soldiers were not committed by contracts to perpetual service, melted away. When he went into winter quarters at Morristown, he had barely 2000 men. Congress was forced into longer term recruitment but this often-caused difficulties. Bounties were offered but some recruits lacked patriotic enthusiasm and disappeared with the money. Those who did not return after an amnesty faced ferocious punishments, not often described in accounts which celebrate the endurance and patriotism of the Continental Army. Its survival had a lot to do with Washington's leadership but also with miscalculation by that of Britain, especially dispersing troops in New Jersey, and assuming that the American forces no longer proved a threat. There were then also tactical errors in assaulting the American defences without sufficient preparation and not anticipating a flanking march and not posting forces on the roads leading out of Trenton.

All war to an extent depends on a mixture of planning, heroism, leadership and mistakes. At the back of the fighting of 1776 was a key hope for the Americans and a key fear for Britain – French intervention. Already there had been informal help from France and Spain but hesitation about directly intervening in a rebellion by the monarchs of those countries. But it made obvious sense to take advantage of British weakness and so the victories at Trenton and Princeton were significant. Just as in the Second World War when Britain, before 1941, waited in hope for America to come to its rescue, so the Americans waited for French and Spanish intervention to allow their survival. Despite some obvious Continental weaknesses, the British had failed to secure the expected fatal blow by destroying Washington's army and taking advantage of colonial divisions in 1776; disease, death and disablement in battle had also reduced Howe's forces.

Washington's army still faced severe structural issues – the short-term recruitment, the problems of supply and the poor provision of clothing and food. For all its successes, the army lacked the discipline and infrastructure of a European force and was reliant on enemy miscalculations.

Saratoga

These miscalculations were to have important consequences in 1777 with a grand strategic plan for an invasion from Canada to advance towards New York and cut New England off from the other colonies. This ended in disaster at Saratoga in October 1777.

The Saratoga campaign was commanded by General John Burgoyne, unusual in military history in being a playwright and being played in a movie by Laurence Olivier. In Shaw's play *The Devil's Disciple*, he appears as a suave, humane and enlightened figure. In reality, he was vain, overambitious, careless of casualties and willing to make highly inhumane threats.

The British forces in Canada had been planning an invasion under Sir Guy Carleton but because of political intrigue 'Gentleman Johnny', replaced him. The plan, conceived in London in the winter of 1776, was to advance from Canada with a main force under Burgoyne of British regulars, German troops, Canadian militia, loyalists and pro-British Indians with a large artillery train. The main force would take Fort Ticonderoga. The advance would proceed by using water transports over Lake Champlain. As a diversion, a smaller force under Colonel St Leger would advance down the Mohawk Valley and attack the final objective, the town of Albany, in conjunction with Burgoyne's main army.

There is some misunderstanding that Burgoyne expected to join Howe's force at Albany but somehow the orders were not posted by the Secretary for War, Lord George Germaine. Burgoyne hoped that after taking Albany, Howe would be ordered to join him and the large concentration of force would have divided New England from the other colonies and somehow force an end to the war, though quite how was not entirely clear, as is common with many grand strategic plans in military history. In fact, Howe was intent on the more obvious objective of taking Philadelphia and forcing Washington's army into a full-scale battle. He told Burgoyne that he would not be coming to Albany before the expedition set off in June 1776. In no sense did Burgoyne expect Howe to be waiting for him.

The type of expedition which was planned would have been difficult for a modern army, with full communications, drones, observations, tanks and planes. For an eighteenth-century army which depended on horses and wagons, telescopes, scouts and spies, it was hazardous. Burgoyne did not know what enemy numbers he faced and the further south he went he became more dependent on long lines of communications. Also, like most eighteenth-century armies, it was a sort of bizarre cavalcade of camp followers, wives, mistresses, and casual female labour. These women who are often invisible in accounts of military campaigns acted as cooks, washerwomen and company. Children, too, accompanied the army. Burgoyne's creature comforts were taken in six wagons in a procession of horse drawn vehicles. In addition, some 138 artillery pieces were hauled along. Secrecy and surprise were not part of the plan. Burgoyne differed from a modern British expedition is his deliberate policy of threats and terror. He had a force of Indians ready and threatened to unleash them on those who persisted in the 'phantastic' act of rebellion and also threatened a scorched earth policy of destruction of farms. All this gave the Patriots unlimited propaganda opportunities.

The idea of a parade-ground-type advance of Redcoats with fifes and drums advancing blindly into fire by buckskinned Americans is not really accurate. The advancing force had Canadian volunteers and loyalists consistent with the idea of a civil war. Burgoyne was also sure that once in Albany he would be joined by large numbers of loyalists. That this was a part of his plan shows the degree of division among the colonists.

Perhaps the most unrealistic part of the plan was the diversionary attack by St Leger as the two forces could not communicate effectively. Also, if there were problems it would be difficult to coordinate a rescue by the British forces in New York under General Clinton.

Burgoyne was lucky that American forces had not been assembled at the first objective, Fort Ticonderoga, which would be a base for the 55-mile advance on Albany. The fort was abandoned without the costly assault that British forces would have found necessary. There was a fierce clash between colonists and

British, but the colonial forces withdrew. Despite losses in this fighting and from the usual sickness and exhaustion, the way seemed clear for the plan to succeed.

The first problem after the surprise success was the difficulty of taking a cumbersome force through roads blocked by the Americans by felled trees, barricades and destroyed bridges. The second problem was that little thought had been given to how to get across the Hudson River to take the defended town of Albany. River crossings were always difficult, especially under fire. Quite why Burgoyne had not thought of this before is a mystery, except that eighteenth-century military training and practice was much more fixed on formal battlefield encounters than on this sort of expedition, which is more like the activity undertaken by modern armies with much more developed weaponry and communications infrastructure. Anyway, he decided not on a direct march on Albany, but on a longer route to a place called Fort Miller some forty miles north of Albany. However, the roads were poor and the forests denser so he would have to break with the long chain of supplies. One solution would be to take supplies from a known rebel supply dump at Bennington and rely on foraging and 'living off the land'. At this point the plan unravelled. Assuming that Bennington was lightly defended, Burgoyne sent a force of about 750 troops under a German commander named Baum. In fact, there had been a rallying of support from local militia and advance warning of the British move and in sort of rerun of Lexington, the British found heavy defences and suffered a large number of casualties which depleted Burgoyne's force.

Short now of men and supplies, the great man decided to plough on. What he did not know was that a similar popular swarm of volunteers and New England militia to the attack on Boston in 1775 now rallied to the defence of Albany. Here was a repeat of one of those great communal acts of defiance that had characterised colonial life and reached its peak in the siege of Boston. The uninspiring American leader, General Horatio Gates, was moved to some unusual decisive action, and he used a Polish-born engineer to construct a fortification to defend Albany on what was known as the Bevis Heights.

Meanwhile, another part of the plan disintegrated as the diversionary force found more resistance than expected, fought a gruesome hand to hand battle and then retreated to Canada. The Indian allies proved unreliable, and St Leger had not expected the sheer numbers of militiamen to oppose him.

With inadequate military intelligence, diminished numbers, limited supplies and now without hopes of reinforcement from St Leger, Burgoyne hoped a final push and then support from New York might still win the day. A flanking attack over the meadows of a loyalist farm called Freeman's Farm once again showed the advantages of defence over attack. The British attack stalled. By 5 October, Burgoyne's commanders were urging an ordered retreat. But like his distant successors in the First World War, 'Gentlemen Johnny' staked all on a final push. The Battle of Bevis Heights however ended much like the attack at Freeman's Farm.

The British withdrew to a makeshift camp which was hellish. Bombarded by American artillery, short of food, with men suffering from hideous wounds and no sign of any help from the British commander in New York, in incessant rain and outnumbered, there were two choices. There could be a free for all, every man for himself retreat through the forests back to Ticonderoga or a negotiated surrender.

Burgoyne was no shrinking violet and unlike many of his successors he had been in the thick of battle. He had a horse shot from under him and his coat pierced by musket balls. But reality stared him in the face and Gates accepted generous terms. Regulars would be allowed to sail back to Britain and the Canadians and loyalists would be given safe conducts to return home. Given the indignation about Burgoyne's use of Indians and the furore when news spread of the murder of an American woman, Jane McCrae, by Indians in the service of Britain as well as various rumours of the massacre of children, this was quite lucky.

The surrender was not accompanied by jeering but was seen in a sort of awed silence, but it was to have huge consequences. The American conduct of the campaign had not been very brilliant in itself. Large numbers of the colonial troops had been unfit for battle because of the problems of organisation and as usual there had been desertion at harvest time. The leaders had been at odds with Gates intriguing against his fellow commander, Philip Schuyler. One of the most dashing American commanders, Benedict Arnold, had been ordered from the battlefield. The defence of Ticonderoga had been neglected. Though resistance had been brave and determined at the key battles of Bennington and the two final conflicts, there had been numerical advantage, and the Americans were fighting their usual defensive campaigns. Also, they were fortunate that Burgoyne had been slow to advance on Albany before it could be reinforced and had decided not to save his army by a withdrawal but to insist on a final attack, which was opposed by his own commanders and unlikely to succeed. But that is war. What was important was that, for whatever reason, a British army had surrendered and the chances of regaining control of the colonies had lessened to such an extent that the vital foreign aid could now be given.

In the short term, the progress of the war itself was not as affected by this victory as greatly as might have been expected. The comparison with 1775 is instructive. There a similar mass movement brought a British defeat at Boston, but the American forces proved no match for professional British troops in manoeuvring on Manhattan and in New Jersey. In 1777 there was another important victory, but Washington's army could not defeat Howe in open warfare at two encounters at Brandywine and Germantown, or prevent Britain occupying the very significant city of Philadelphia. Like Gettysburg in 1863, the Saratoga battles in retrospect were a turning point, but the war continued, and the outcome was still not certain. Nowhere is this clearer than in the winter quarters to which Washington withdrew in December 1777.

There is a well-known picture painted by John Trumbull in 1822 (the so-called 'painter of the Revolution'). Burgoyne is shown with Gates, though the proffering of the sword is probably made up. In reality, Gates was shorter and less imposing. The dominant figure in white is Daniel Morgan, the celebrated Virginian hero. No women, children, rain, mud or casualties are shown, and the baroness's account suggests a more private discussion. Afterwards the officers dined together which seems to link to the kindness shown to her.

The memoirs of the wife of Baron von Riederser give a flavour of the horrors and humanity of Saratoga.

Before the surrender a terrible cannonade began, and the fire was principally directed against the house, where we had hoped to find a refuge, (where there were women and crippled soldiers). A poor soldier, who was about to have a leg amputated, lost the other by one of these balls.

The want of water continuing to distress us, we could not but be extremely glad to find a soldier's wife so spirited as to fetch some from the river, an occupation from which the boldest might have shrunk, as the Americans shot every one who approached it. They told us afterwards that they spared her on account of her sex....

On the 17th of October, the capitulation was carried into effect. The generals waited upon the American General Gates, and the troops surrendered themselves prisoners of war and laid down their arms. The time had now come for the good woman who had risked her life to supply us with water, to receive the reward of her services. Each of us threw a handful of money into her apron; and she thus received more than twenty guineas. At such a moment at least, if at no other, the heart easily overflows with gratitude.

At last, my husband's groom brought me a message to join him with the children. I once more seated myself in my dear calash, and, while riding through the American camp, was gratified to observe that no body looked at us with disrespect, but, on the contrary, greeted us, and seemed touched at the sight of a captive mother with three children.

Valley Forge

After the failures of 1777, Washington took his army into winter quarters in an unsuitable and barren site at Valley Forge. The severe winter conditions and shortages of basic needs took their toll. By March 1778, despite having recruited more than the initial 800 soldiers, the army was not in a good shape. At that point the story takes a strange turn with the arrival of a self-styled, fraudulent, homosexual German captain

Friedrich Steuben was a Prussian officer who had fought in the Seven Years War as a captain in the army of Frederick the Great. After 1763 he moved to the small state of Hohenzollern-Hechingen in the Black Forest, where he became a leading minister. He gained the title of Baron by the good offices of a neighbouring princess, Frederica of Baden-Baden, but gained little money and was discharged in 1777, drifting to Paris. There he met US envoys Benjamin Franklin and Silas Deane, who concocted a backstory that he had been a leading general under Frederick the Great but had mislaid proof of his appointments and passed him off as a military expert. By 1778, the Continental Army had had enough foreign volunteers and when he arrived at Valley Forge, Washington barely noticed him. Steuben changed the story when he realised there were German officers there and claimed to be a general in the small German state of Baden.

Steuben must have been convincing because Washington gave him the post of acting inspector general as a self-styled military expert. He had little English, but his fluent French allowed him to communicate with officers like Hamilton. His later memoirs reveal the poor state of the army. Regiments were not of a standard size, some being less than thirty men. There was no clear way of knowing how many were actually present. Lack of regular pay had led to absenteeism, and many were working as servants or earning money as bankers or blacksmiths. Steuben found that weapons were poorly looked after, and the dress standards were poor. Some troops were literally naked, and officers were seen in blankets, Marching was done in single file, not in compact formation, and sentry posts were random. Hygiene arrangements were also poor.

Granted, Steuben was a liar, but there is enough corroborating evidence to suggest that the training, discipline, provisioning and housing of troops were poor even after the army had been in existence for over two years.

Steuben addressed himself to the task of writing military manuals, laboriously copied in longhand and issued. He drilled troops in person, then thought to be below the dignity of officers. He formed a model company to show the rest of the army how to march, stand in a military manner, and carry out Prussian-type movements such as the oblique order. All this would have delighted modern drill sergeants, but more useful was musket training, rapid firing techniques and bayonet drill.

But what effect did this have on actual fighting?

When the British evacuated Philadelphia, Washington's troops pursued them into New Jersey and there was an encounter at Monmouth Courthouse on 28 June, which was not very decisive, though it was actually the largest scale battle in the war. The British General Clinton gave an account of it in which he says that '*Mr W began his attack upon my rearguard. It was necessary to meet him to give my baggage train time to get to safety*'. Clinton also saw that the American forward troops had been separated from the main force and hoped to encircle them, but 'nothing but the intolerable heat prevented this'. A heat of 94° (Fahrenheit) in the shade tired his troops but they still were strong enough to hold the American attack until the baggage train was safe. Clinton did not mention any particular vigour or novelty in deployment of his enemy and his comment was 'we left Washington very sore'. After the battle, Washington had General Lee court martialled for withdrawing. Ironically, it was during this battle that the legend of Molly Pitcher began – Mary Ludwig Hays was said to have loaded a cannon and started a myth of an Amazonian female combatant called Molly Pitcher. Women in battle was hardly the Prussianised military machine that Steuben was said to have created

The strange thing about Valley Forge and the supposed retraining of the army into a great fighting instrument is that Washington is so often seen as someone outside the situation, enduring hardship stoically, not someone who was actually responsible for the organisation of the army. Though admirable to employ this military expert, even though a fraud, the question arises as to why it was so necessary. It was obviously sensible to change obvious things like the position of latrines and absenteeism, but had it not occurred to the American leaders? Washington had far too much on his shoulders because of the whole nature of the Continental Army and did not have a reliable chief of staff, such as Napoleon's brilliant quartermaster Berthier. Washington aimed to defeat the British in European style military operations but previously had not ensured that his men had the skills that Steuben so valiantly taught. Perhaps this was sensible as American successes up to December 1777 did not depend on them. However, the evidence from existing letters of soldiers confirms a fairly constant failure of the American leadership to supply basic needs, especially during the winter.

In an article in the *Pennsylvania Magazine of History and Biography* a writer made the argument that Washington allowed thousands of his men to starve and freeze to death because he was unwilling to override Congress and the State Governors. In the writer's view this was admirable. Instead of wintering in an established town with adequate accommodation and supplies, Washington accepted Congress' wish to station himself between British occupied Philadelphia and York, where Congress had fled to in order to protect them. He remained dependent on reluctant provision of supplies from Pennsylvania without using military authority to requisition. The barns of Pennsylvania farmers remained full, and they were happy to sell produce to the British for gold, but food was not seized when they refused to sell for Continental paper money. The *reductio ad absurdum* came when a supply of substandard shoes arrived at Valley Forge which were not wearable and Washington advised they be boiled for food.

Washington gained great credit both then and subsequently for sharing his men's hardships, living in a cold hut for instance (though some did not even have that). The article claimed that by abiding by the decisions of Congress and accepting the poor support of local governors and farmers, Washington was putting law before power and setting an example for the future United States. That a United States was not a concept in 1778 was not considered. That he was put in this position somewhat undermines the nature of the struggle for liberty at local levels. That he accepted this, argues misplaced priorities and perhaps an excessive concern that Congress might replace him by the more successful General Gates who had forced the surrender of Burgoyne. Considering the massive disregard for strict legality in starting the Revolution and the lack of concern for the property of loyalists, Washington's scruples seem rather selective and hard on the lower orders who made up the bulk of the army. The hated tyrannical British took greater care of their troops, which is not, in eighteenth-century terms, saying much.

The Later War

After Saratoga, the nature of the war changed. Washington, after his admiration for Prussian drill and his concern to be seen as a civilised military leader of Roman-type stoicism, wanted formal campaigns. However, the attacks on Indian Territory following Saratoga displayed a much greater level of brutality. The shift of focus of war to the South after 1780 also revealed much more of a brutal civil war, and the frustrations of some elements of the British forces saw more atrocity and what might be seen as more of a 'total war' than previously which involved civilians, though Burgoyne's warnings to the local population presaged this.

The other change which was perhaps more obvious was the internationalisation of the conflict by the entry of foreign powers, particularly France. Though it is now so generally accepted by historians that it has ceased to be contentious, the outcome of the war depended heavily not on Americans but on foreigners. This is still not the accepted popular view of the war which is seen much more in terms of a series of heroic tableaux. First Paul Revere's ride to Concord to warn the minute men. He did not ride alone and never reached Concord and there is no record of him shouting 'The British are Coming'. Fewer people know that he was actually court martialled by his fellow patriots later in the war than of his role in 1775. Then there is Bunker Hill, by which people mean Breed's

Hill and the furious patriotic farmers with their rifles defeating the Redcoats. In fact they were militia and in fact not all had rifles, which were relatively rare. They did not defeat the British, though the high casualty levels made the Redcoats' victory somewhat pyrrhic. Then The Crossing of the Delaware – the heroic comeback rather than the ignominious retreat that led to it. The escape of over 500 Hessians is not too much mentioned, nor is the fact that this encounter did not stop the British taking Philadelphia the next year.

Then Saratoga, even if this victory depended more on British problems and miscalculations and a lot of the American troops had deserted, leaving in one memoir's words 'a lot of youngsters and feeble boys'. The next tableau is Valley Forge, showing that mismanagement can still be seen as heroic. The destructive and often sordid struggle in the Carolinas in the years 1780 and 1781 is not usually part of the patriotic tableaux except right at the end with the surrender at Yorktown. The tableaux rarely include loyalists, women, Indians or Black people or depict failures and strongly suggest the war was won by a mixture of dedicated leadership and patriotic enthusiasm and self-sacrifice. The narrative thrust of many accounts are an elaboration of these snapshots and have tended to establish a narrative and a pattern on the events. The later stages of the war, however, were dominated by elements which the popular storyboard tends to play down – foreigners and loyalists.

The support from France, Spain and the United Provinces was not marginal but absolutely crucial in terms of resources, and eventually men and particularly naval power.

When France signed a formal alliance in 1778, the nature of the war changed. By the end of the Battle of Monmouth in June 1779 the outcome of the war was still uncertain. Eighteenth-century warfare in Europe did not often produce decisive results, despite the efforts of military leaders to manoeuvre even more efficiently. Frederick the Great of Prussia devoted his reign to warfare but never unseated his rivals or achieved gains commensurate with the costs and loss of life involved. This was largely because the warring countries never developed war-winning technology. They fought each other in much the same way, with much the same weapons. The war in America was fought in different circumstances with fewer formal battles, but it depended a lot on a weaker Continental Army falling back on defences.

Both sides faced formidable challenges in bringing the war to a decisive conclusion. The British had lost their chance of an early decisive victory but could rely on their forces not to desert and were not dependent on local governors to supply their troops. Sea power have them the opportunity for more flexible strategies and enabled them to defend New York as a major base. However, a decisive battle eluded them. Also, the war's initial popularity at home was fading.

Bold offensive strokes such as Burgoyne's invasion fell foul of logistical problems beyond the capacity of eighteenth-century forces and the difficulty of assaulting defended positions. However, despite the supposedly important reforms in eighteenth-century military drilling, the ability of Washington to win a decisive field victory or to wage the sort of total war where all resources are commandeered to back military success was quite limited. The French revolutionaries twenty years later were able to wield iron control over supplies and the civilian war effort, but this was beyond the American leadership because it was wedded to defending the privileges and liberties of the individual independent states. It was a similar organisational failure that led the Confederate States to lose the second civil war in 1865 and the North's willingness to control resources that led to victory. However, unlike the continental side after 1777, the southern rebels did not have the vital support of foreign powers. The Continental forces had not shown a willingness or ability to wage total war. Also, if some elements in Britain were opposed to war, then this was equally true of America. There was a substantial body of loyalist opinion that would have supported a negotiated settlement.

An interesting 'what if..?' scenario might be considered. What if there had not been foreign intervention? What if France and then Spain and the Netherlands had not diverted British forces and led to a vital loss of control of the seas? What if highly professional French forces had not at a crucial time strengthened Washington's men? Would Britain have ever been able to control America again even if there had been military victories? Had the moment passed for a decisive last stand encounter? How much longer would a war have been possible to sustain? On the American side, how much longer could Washington sustain armies in winter quarters without taking much greater powers of requisitioning and control and establishing just the sort of 'tyranny' that the war was being waged to end. Might stalemate and exhaustion have led to some sort of settlement, perhaps with individual states staying with Britain and some having independence? Or with all former colonies continuing to have economic ties with Britain and having decisions made by Britain having to be agreed by colonial assemblies and having elected governors?

The problem is that, given the violent conflict and the passions and propaganda, none of this seems likely, but again outright military victory also does not seem likely either.

In the end, the treaties with the European countries gave the Continentals the hope of final victory and dictated key British actions. Philadelphia was evacuated to ensure that the vital British stronghold of New York could be defended. This shifted the British strategy southwards to make optimum use of sea power and loyalism. The war moved into another phase.

Chapter 6

The Wider War and the Issue of Loyalism

By 1779 there were signs of a change in the war. This was very clearly seen in Washington's decision to launch a major campaign against the Iroquois Confederation in upper New York. The scale of this and the resources allocated to it by Congress – some $800,000 and 3000 men with artillery divided into four commands – seem surprising. Though there had been some raiding on the New York and Pennsylvania frontier in 1778, a campaign against Indians, even if they were pro-British and cooperated with loyalist rangers, was not a war winner.

There had been an attack by a mixture of British troops, Tories and Seneca Indians and the destruction of a settlement in Wyoming Valley which was widely reported as a massacre. This had led to a vicious reprisal by militiamen, not regular troops, involving the impaling of children on bayonets and the destruction of an Indian settlement. So emotions were running high, but the decision for the expedition was taken at a high level with the leading commanders Gates, Schuyler and Washington involved, and with the support of Congress who allocated valuable resources to it.

Whatever the motive – and this is disputed with some arguing that it was an attempt to clear away the Iroquois to make way for a post-war settlement and some seeing it as pure genocide – the actual orders of Washington show a different way of waging war to the formal drills of Baron Steuben and eighteenth-century military conventions.

He instructed the overall leader, General John Sullivan:

to chastise and intimidate the hostile nations, to countenance and encourage the friendly ones, and to relieve our frontiers from the depredations to which they would otherwise be exposed. To effect these purposes it is proposed to carry the war into the heart of the country of the Six Nations, to cut off their settlements, destroy their next year's crops, and to do them every other mischief which time and circumstances will permit.

In case Sullivan should not be clear, he wrote again in March 1779 of:

the necessity of pushing the Indians to the greatest practicable distance from their own settlements and our frontiers [and] …making the destruction of their settlements so final and complete as to put it out of their power to derive the smallest succor from them.

For the army it was a matter of either the Indians accepting civilization or death – rather a far cry from the famous 'liberty or death' and meaningless as the Iroquois were not primitive nomads, but had established farms, homesteads, villages and towns. They had a developed political society and were adept at diplomatic negotiations to establish a confederation of peoples. One young Continental officer noted in his journal that an Indian town along the Susquehanna was:

built on each side of the River with good Log houses with Stone Chimneys and glass windows it likewise had a Church & burying grounds.

The campaign lasted from March to September 1779 and though there was a day long battle at Newport, the main elements were destruction of settlements, crops and as much killing as possible. It is significant that the atrocities were not committed by local militia with a long history of hostility to the Indians and rivalry with loyalists, but by regular troops supposedly drilled to a high level of perfection by the mendacious Baron. What comes to mind reading accounts of this prolonged destructive episode is not so much the colonial charm of Williamsburg or the elegant surrender at Saratoga but the much later experience of Vietnam, with its disdain for enemies of a different race, the destruction of crops and brutal ill treatment of captives, and the infamous massacre of civilians. Incensed by the fate of a Continental patrol, in which two of the dead soldiers were left with their heads on poles and their bodies showing mutilation, the colonial troops resorted to terror. There were scalpings and one gruesome recorded incident of an Indian having his legs skinned to provide leggings for a Continental officer. A future American secretary of war observed an Indian woman and child burned to death in a hut. Incidents like this may or may not be typical, but the official records of death and destruction seem to suggest a brutal prosecution of war on a scale not seen in the struggle hitherto. There is agreement that 160,000 bushels of corn were destroyed, three major settlements and 40 villages were destroyed. The death toll overall has been estimated at 4500 with 5000 seeking refuge at the British Fort Niagara. There was a sizeable death toll of these – perhaps one in five given the limited food supplies available.

What is striking is that like more modern conflicts with conventional forces ranged against guerrilla units in difficult terrain, scorched earth tactics can only go so far. The Iroquois managed to rally 2000 fighters and pursue 'shadow war' that forced the invaders out. By 1780 quite substantial raiding had begun again on the frontiers. The precedent for later wars had been set but like so many campaigns in this war, no decisive result, though the death and destruction had permanently weakened the six nations.

In the context of the failure of the reformed army to bring the British to a decisive defeat and the stalemate in New York, with Britain still able to defend its major base by sea, did the Continental leadership want to exert its power over what it perceived to be relatively helpless civilians and take out its frustrations? There are plenty of occasions in history when this happened – the attacks by the Ottoman leaders on the Armenians in 1915, for example. However understandable, the direction of travel of the war was not in line with some of the high ideals of the Declaration. Not that it was one sided. The British too, by recruiting loyalists, irregulars and Indian allies and in some cases dressing up as Indians in the frontier region to attack patriots, were guilty of dragging down the morality of warfare.

For his part in the struggle against Britain in 1778 and his reluctance to wage total war, Washington was high-minded. He rejected a proposal to devastate the area between Philadelphia and Valley Forge to prevent farmers producing food to sell to the British. The conventions of taking prisoners, having prisoner exchanges, and respecting flags of truce were respected in a way that they were certainly not in Sullivan's campaign. If the men of the American Enlightenment who fought for their freedom saw all men as equal, then this was not evident in the way war was fought against enemies of different races.

The Sullivan campaign had more of an element of civil war than the more formal warfare in Pennsylvania in the previous year or at Monmouth. In the later stages of the war this became even more pronounced as the focus shifted southward. The savage nature of conflict, too, continued

What is striking is the hopes that Britain had during the war of engaging loyalist support. The opponents of Revolution still get short shrift but they figured heavily in British calculations. That was the rationale for the decision to shift the war southwards.

After 1778, the war took on more of the character of a civil war with the British decision for a southern strategy to exploit the divisions in South Carolina between 'Whigs and Tories' and to wage economic warfare. The wealth of the colonies was dependent on the southern plantations of tobacco, indigo and rice. Here, too, was the largest slave population. Getting loyalist support, threatening to destroy farmland and inducing the slaves to join Britain in return for freedom might have a more crippling effect on the Revolution than the previous European style manoeuvrings or the failed grand strategy of the Saratoga campaign.

The battle at Saratoga did have serious consequences for the final outcome of the war, though in itself it was not decisive. Owing to the nature of warfare in the eighteenth century, decisive encounters were rare. As with European land warfare, neither side had a technological advantage. Weapons did not change much in the eighteenth century and both sides faced similar problems with logistics and large-scale movement. Also, both sides faced a similar scourge – that of disease which killed and incapacitated more troops than actual fighting.

Though small-scale manoeuvres like the famous attack at Trenton would be strikingly successful, larger plans were more problematic. One constant in the British effort was to divide the northern from the southern colonies, but that had not proved successful. Washington aimed to bring his army into a formal battle but there was no great decisive clash. By 1779 both sides were finding it hard to maintain the strength of their forces and were facing stalemate. Washington's forces mutinied because of lack of pay and poor conditions and Congress never managed to create a well-resourced nation in arms along the lines of the armies of revolutionary France and Napoleon. Total war was not on the agenda.

What Saratoga changed was the explicit support given by Britain's continental enemies, France and Spain. Without this, an American victory would have been in doubt despite the humiliating British reversal at Saratoga. Britain had to ensure the possession of the immensely valuable West Indies and if possible, to take some more French islands. There was the danger of well trained and armed French forces backing Washington and also the danger of losing the vital control of the seas.

From 1778, British policy changed to a southern-based strategy and an attempt to mobilise loyalist allies. Though this failed, it was not entirely unrealistic. As this short study has shown, there was considerable opposition to the way that protests against British policies had developed and no consensus about the outbreak of armed resistance and the Declaration of Independence.

Historians acknowledge this and often state the view of John Adams, that a third were committed patriots, a third were loyal to the crown and a third were unenthused by both sides. However, there is no evidence to support this, and Adams was not even talking directly about the American Revolution. It has passed into history as a fact when in reality there is no way of knowing the extent of loyalism or patriot commitment. This is partly because it was not unusual for people to change sides, or to express support for one side or the other when they were in control of a local area to avoid violence and recrimination. It is a phenomenon familiar in many colonial conflicts, as locals feared inciting attacks from psyched up soldiers or guerrillas. The situation in the Carolinas after 1780 is not unlike the situation in South Vietnam during the Vietnam

War in that respect. Individual studies clearly show that not all who took part in the fighting were committed to either 'the glorious cause' or to the monarchy of George III. Local rivalries and social tensions often determined which side people supported and whether that support continued when the going got tough.

A good example is Ethan Allen and his famous Green Mountain Boys, so much a part of the heroic legend of Revolution. Allen was less concerned about liberty from Britain as liberty to do what he liked in Vermont and considered allying with Britain before committing to the Revolutionary cause. The most famous case of side switching was of course Benedict Arnold, the gung-ho patriot leader who joined Britain and earned lasting shame. It is as though all the resentment about 'betrayal' of the American cause was channelled towards this one man. In fact, there were a great many instances on both sides, but the impression is given of rather more fixed allegiances among White Americans. The fluctuations among erstwhile Indian allies was seen as justification for ill treatment after the war ended.

From the start, Britain assumed a great deal of loyalist opinion. This is sometimes seen as delusional and evidence of lack of understanding of the colonial mind set and character. However, it did seem quite rational. The benefits of trade, the high standards of living among colonists, the cultural influence of Britain and the relatively trivial amounts of money involved in taxation disputes might well have encouraged a view that Britain faced opposition from irrational and ill-disposed radicals rather than from a whole people. It was difficult to see that there was tyranny when the colonists had a degree of self-government, with ordinary people having far greater opportunities for political involvement than in Britain itself.

It was not a question of only a privileged view supporting traditional allegiances. There was no specific 'loyalist profile' and local circumstances often dictated how men and women thought. Nor was it a question of unthinking and old-fashioned royalism against modern enlightenment thinking.

An interesting example of enlightened loyalism was that of a Massachusetts lawyer, Jonathan Sewell, who published a series of essays between 1763 and 1775. Sewell thought very highly of the American spirit and predicted that eventually the energy and enterprise of the colonists would result in the new world dominating the western hemisphere. His plan was for a federal system of self-government within the Empire which anticipated the dominions of the Empire. This progress he saw being undermined by unrealistic and undisciplined protests by the lower orders and by those who had worked themselves into a frenzy quite unjustified by actual grievances.

Some risk plunging their wives and children into certain poverty. Others act like pilgrims but know not where they are bound; others are plundering and destroying, rushing into the arms of slavery. And all in honour of the Goddess Liberty.

These views were unpopular with his neighbours, and he was banished and his property confiscated in 1778. Like many loyalists he ended up in Canada where his son took part in a movement for greater constitutional self-government in New Brunswick. He offered a different path for a distinct American identity which foresaw future international influence.

It became increasingly dangerous to express opposition to the patriot cause because of the prevalence of crowd actions and because of the increasing bitterness caused by losses and hardships of war. The British were slow to harness loyalist fears and resentments by offering good terms to those who joined their forces and also by protecting them against attacks.

Not surprisingly, the assumption was that a massive show of force would rally loyalists and result in the defeat of the rebels quickly. The main role of the loyalists would not be in the fighting but in the reconstruction of British rule following the victory of Howe and his professional soldiers.

Nevertheless, loyalist soldiers were recruited and in surprisingly large numbers, given the lack of equal status and benefits compared with the recruitment of German troops and the standard conditions of service for the British volunteers.

The so called 'Provincial Service' or loyalist regiments do not feature strongly in textbook accounts or depictions in films. The historian Paul H. Smith[1] calculated that 15,000 colonists served at one time or another in these units and another 10,000 served in part-time loyalist militia formations called Associations. This was less than expected – clothing and supplies were sent over from Britain for 7000 expected volunteers in August 1777 for example, when the total did not exceed 3000. By 1778 loyalists under arms were 7400.

After Saratoga, Britain made a more determined attempt to recruit troops in America by increasing the recruitment bounty to a generous 3 guineas and offering more in the way of hospital expenses and facilities. By 1780 there were 10,000 loyalists in British service.

Given the total population was around two million and the relatively small numbers involved in actual fighting on both sides, this was quite a significant figure. It does not include Indian allies or Black men and women who assisted the British troops. Recruitment was overseen by enthusiastic British officers like Major Fergusson, killed at King's Mountain in South Carolina in October 1780. Certain groups were particularly keen to serve, notably Scottish Highlanders from Nova Scotia, but volunteers came from New York, Pennsylvania and the Carolinas.

Though Britain was disappointed by actual enlistment, loyalism became central to British plans and hence to the war from 1778. The predominant military activity was in the South because of the belief that British forces operating there would gather overwhelming loyal support and would also be supported by Indian allies and by freed Black slaves. So loyalism was not just an embarrassing footnote to the main story of independence but absolutely central, as it dominated British policy.

It was that policy pursued from late 1779 that initially seemed to indicate that despite the failure to bring Washington to a decisive defeat or to divide the colonies, Britain still might win. It was also the policy that brought about defeat when initial victories could not be consolidated and hopes for a general loyalist uprising did not materialise.

The story of the southern campaign can be quickly told and indeed usually is. For most students, the war was effectively over after Saratoga. But that is to look at the war with the benefit of hindsight. Similar judgements are made about the war in Vietnam which often ends in popular understanding with the Tet Offensive of 1968, actually a US victory, but more often remembered as a defeat. Similarly, the civil war is often seen as virtually over with the southern defeat at Gettysburg in 1863, even though the most intensive fighting was to take place in 1864 and 1865. Visitors flock to Gettysburg, and films feature it because of its drama, while the brutal slogging matches round Richmond which ground down the southern forces do not feature nearly so much in public interest or imagination.

The Southern Campaign of the War of Independence is significant not only because it demonstrated that British power was still considerable. It is also where the true nature of the war as 'the first civil war' is the most vividly seen. The flocking of the Minute Men to attack Boston in 1775, the heroic crossing of the frozen Delaware in 1777 and the staunch fighting of the militia to overcome 'Gentleman' John Burgoyne at Saratoga are the staple elements of the birth of a nation. The often sordid violence of the later campaigning, with obscure and often brutal battles leading to a final victory, which owed a lot to French help and a temporary loss of British control of the sea, is less appealing. Final victory depended a lot on British errors, foreign assistance and costly assault on defensive positions. It was also the result of a lack of British will to carry on with a war whose returns were uncertain. The war ended without the Continental Army being able to regain New York and with Canada firmly under British control.

But back to 1779. Far from being on the point of surrender, British hopes were surprisingly high and there was another grand plan. New York was firmly under control and the British commander, Sir Henry Clinton, was confident in naval supremacy, despite the often irritating activities of colonial privateers who raided British shipping, and under the enterprising John Paul Jones even raided shipping in the River Thames. However, this was not typical and strong British naval power allowed an expedition to take Savannah and control Georgia. Britain had another strong base in Florida. Control of the southern end of the colonies and New York in the north offered Britain a strategic advantage. If a strong expedition could take Charleston in South Carolina and encourage loyalists to affirm their support of Britain, then Washington would be forced to abandon the South. Limiting the scope of the revolt. It was believed that North Carolina had a substantial loyalist element which would leave Virginia vulnerable.

The initial plan worked well. Charleston fell to the British in May 1780. This was probably the worst setback to the Continental forces of the entire war. The port was besieged, and relief forces were prevented from defending the city by the rapid actions of a force under an officer who can be seen either as dashing or psychopathic according to one's point of view – Banastre Tarleton.

There now emerges another one of history's might-have-beens. What if Sir Henry Clinton had set up a form of government in South Carolina that gave stability under the British Crown and had managed to attract loyalists alienated by patriots? What if more substantial loyalist regiments had been formed and had acted in a disciplined way? What if Britain had made optimum use of alliances with the Indians? What if the slave holding plantation elites which had generally supported the Revolution had been weakened by freeing the slaves? What if Britain had managed to coordinate the different groups who were unhappy about the effects of the Revolution and established stable rule in Georgia and North Carolina as well? The British controlled Canada, New York, and Florida. If the lower South were added, then even if there was no decisive military victory in the other states, there might have been more incentive for a negotiated settlement. The consequences would have been huge. Slavery was legally ended in the British Empire in 1833 and it would have been substantially weakened where it was most entrenched. A United States would have been smaller and might have maintained more links with Britain, where its economic advantage lay. Concern about possible attempts of Spain and France to regain land might have recreated the military links with Britain forged in the Seven Years War. The deep divisions that eventually led to the second civil war might have been avoided. The whole history of the rise of the US as a superpower in its own right might have been different.

Well, perhaps. But like most 'what if' scenarios, it is probably not worth pursuing as in the real world of the years 1780 and 1781, real human beings took flawed decisions based on flawed information and flawed assumptions. Clinton did not prioritise establishing a renewed civil society, possibly because he did not consider it worth his while to do so after his military success and possibly because he overestimated loyalism. Or perhaps it was simply beyond him. His second in command, Lord Cornwallis, neglected what seems obvious and was in fact following Clinton's instruction – to focus on holding on to South Carolina. Instead, he took his forces into North Carolina and then, for reasons which seem incomprehensible, into Virginia where he allowed his men to be besieged and defeated at Yorktown. The idea that the British Navy would also have enough control of the sea to support troops near the coast was a given, but for a crucial period in 1781 the French Navy achieved a control of American waters that had normally eluded them. The assumption that loyalist feeling would translate into military strength was simply false. Recruitment was insufficient, and fear of patriot reprisals, together with a lack of determined effort of the British to protect their allies and win them over, resulted in failure. However, to expect otherwise from eighteenth-century military and civil leaders would be unrealistic in the context of the time. Hanging militiamen who had joined the British and then deserted was not likely to win support, but Lord Cornwallis was a soldier of his time who expected obedience from the lower orders. Faced with irregular patriot resistance, the loyalists were allowed to wage war in their own way and aided and abetted by officers like the infamous Tarleton. The conflict degenerated into a brutal civil war which caused so much disruption that the better solution for many was a patriot victory.

There are mistakes here that other commanders and leaders made in different periods and perhaps are a natural consequence of prolonged periods of warfare and assumptions about superiority. The British could not be flexible enough to build up support and in the Southern Campaign, the patriots or Whigs found strong leadership and fought in a highly effective and determined way. This meant that the whole nature of the war changed but the determining feature lay in the way that it had become an international conflict.

In the end, the civil war was determined not by what Britain did or did not do, or how gallantly or brutally Americans battled with each other, but by foreign intervention at a crucial time and the distraction of Britain to defend its most valuable possessions,

We have left the British celebrating the capture of Charleston. However, even this came at a cost. Troops had to be taken from Georgia, leading to a weakening of British control there. Britain did not have the very large numbers of men that Howe had employed in his defeat of the Continental Army in 1776. General Cornwallis was lucky when a force of Continental regulars and Virginia and North Carolina militia launched an attack on the British base at Camden. The American General Gates had a belief in the fighting ability of the militia after their success in defensive warfare at Saratoga. However, his troops lacked cavalry, and British mounted attacks were decisive. Camden has been seen as the most successful formal battle fought by the British in the war.

In retrospect, all the British commander Cornwallis had to do was to consolidate control of South Carolina. However, the fates were not with him. Firstly, the patriots relied more and more on partisan tactics, forming independent companies under skilled commanders such as Francis Marion and Andrew Pickens. This made it difficult to maintain British control. Then Cornwallis decided to move into North Carolina. The arrival of a force of some 800 loyalists from North Carolina led Cornwallis to think that he had to protect loyalists there and his arrival would lead to a general movement towards Britain. The third development was the decision to split his forces and to allow a loyalist force under Major Ferguson to operate independently of the main British Army.

The war was assuming the character of a civil war more and more and an irregular force of patriots defeated and killed Ferguson by storming a defensive position he had set up at King's Mountain.

Cornwallis now permitted extensive irregular warfare rather than engaging in formal battle, something conducted with some relish by his subordinate Banastre Tarleton. However, the expected mass loyalist support did not materialise, and he had failed to maintain control over the Carolinas. There was no strategic objective to aim at and the momentum of the British campaign stalled. Under the leadership of one of the Continental Army's most energetic military leaders, Nathaniel Greene, the patriots regained the initiative. Their aims were much clearer – to harass and defeat the British forces and to revive support for the cause. In January 1781, an important if quite small victory over Tarleton and his Tory militia at Cowpens gave the Patriots confidence. In March 1781, there was a more extended formal battle at Guilford Courthouse. The British were technically the victors but suffered quite heavy losses. There was now little incentive for people to join the British forces and the main assumption of British strategy of mobilising loyalist support had been proved to be over optimistic.

On top of all the problems, Britain now suffered from divided command. Clinton hankered after an attack on Philadelphia from New York and wanted Cornwallis to hold his position and send men for a version of a 'big push' against the rebel capital. Instead, Cornwallis decided that it was not possible to hold the Carolinas and instead moved into Virginia.

The last clash between Cornwallis and Greene in South Carolina at Eutaw Springs in September 1781 was a pretty desperate affair. The Continental soldiers were so badly equipped they were reduced to wrapping moss round their bodies to keep warm, and were virtually starving. Fighting was bitter hand to hand scrapping. Greene's losses amounted to a quarter of his forces, and he once again was forced to withdraw, but British losses were proportionately higher.

By now it was difficult to see what Britain could do. The French had committed troops to support Washington. The main concern for Britain was the West Indies, and the French fleet had managed to gain naval supremacy off the coast of Virginia. Cornwallis dug in behind lines of fortifications at the Yorktown Peninsula but could not get reinforcements or defeat a larger Continental attack by Washington.

Though 6000 men surrendered at Yorktown, Britain still had 22,000 troops in America, but one of the crucial failures had been to turn loyalist sympathies into actual military success. The battles in the South had not been great victories for the Patriots – but they had been costly for the British.

Arguably, the crucial element was the failure of Britain to get the loyalist support they had hoped for and had built their entire strategy on. Thus loyalism, far from being a sort of footnote, was crucial. It was strong enough for Britain to build its hopes on, though in the end not strong enough for it to bring about an end to the Revolution. It certainly meant that the war was in a very considerable measure a civil war. It has been said that the conflict had many different elements: a war of national liberation, a guerrilla war, a war of class conflict, a global war and domestic rebellion. This made gaining outright victory problematic.

The losing side not only suffered at the time, but in terms of their historical reputation. The historical attention given to them is far less than to the winners, and in popular imagination they often seem like a treacherous minority, on a par with the collaborators in the Nazi empire of the Second World War. The consequences of being on the losing side for various groups were considerable in terms of material loss, discrimination, exile or ongoing enslavement.

But who were the loyalists? They were certainly not all wealthy merchants or landowners who had grown rich by trading with Britain. A study of New York in 1776 showed that the revolutionaries acted against all sorts of enemies – innkeepers, labourers, apprentices, blacksmiths, leatherworkers. In addition, there were farmers of varying degrees of wealth. On one estate in the Hudson Valley the poorer tenant farmers were loyal to the king because an unpopular landowner had declared for the Revolution. However, of the major landowners of the area, most were loyal. There seemed no economic divide between Whigs and Tories. The disputes had a long history and were part of the social unrest and crowd discontent noted earlier

Crowd violence was often a feature of why there was so much resentment against the Patriots. There was also reaction against conscription and taxes imposed by the Revolutionary authorities,. In 1780, hundreds in Sussex County, Delaware, formed an Association to protest against taxation. These Associations were common but not much about them appears in standard histories. The Patriots often looked down on those who were unwilling to contribute to the

Revolution. One Patriot in Maryland saw local loyalists as living in '*a poor wretched hut crowded with children, naked and hungry*' and was angered that such lower-class people wanted '*to knock down independence*'. The Scottish Highland immigrants of the Mohawk Valley were largely Catholics brought over by a loyalist family called Johnson. Faced with a large force of mostly Protestant rebels the highlanders escaped to Canada, where they allied with pro-British Indians and raided the border areas.

Families could be divided as in most civil wars. The most spectacular example is the Franklin family. Benjamin made the transition from being a supporter of British rule to being a revolutionary. His son William, a royal governor, maintained his allegiance to the Crown. When he was imprisoned in particularly harsh conditions, his father Benjamin continued to disown him and did not try to gain either his release or better conditions. Such family divisions have been commonly written about in the second civil war and are the subject of many western films, but they are much less discussed in the first civil war.

The pressure on people to conform and join the cause of freedom is also not much part of the overall awareness of the Revolution. In the films, *Revolution* and especially *The Patriot*, there is no enforced oath taking and the protagonists join the cause without compulsion. There is little sign of community pressure. In Morristown, New Jersey over a hundred who refused to join the Rebellion were sentenced to death and reprieved only if they took an oath. Forced affirmation because of local pressure is a theme of Arthur Miller's play *The Crucible*, set during the witch craze in Salem in the 1690s. The hero, a symbol of freedom, refuses to sign a false confession of witchcraft to save his life. Written as a parable of the McCarthy era, when public hysteria identified and vilified those who were un-American and forced recantations, his liberal stance was clear. The play has become a classic of American schools and colleges. But what if he had set in in the Revolutionary era and the theme was not about something obviously ridiculous to a modern audience like belief in witchcraft, but rather the right not to go against one's conscience and join a revolution which one did not believe in? That might have gone against too many accepted values – liberty, the right to be independent, the birth of democracy and so on. But, what if the cause of liberty becomes so oppressive that it destroys what it is intended to protect? The gallows at Morristown is something of a warning and the repression of the Revolutionary committees goes some way to explaining why there was opposition to the cause of independence. There is a world of difference between the tyranny of tea duty and the tyranny of banishment, imprisonment and death for not accepting political views or a national cause.

Another manifestation of repression was legal discrimination against political enemies. Washington considered internment of opponents, New York removed legal protection for loyalists who had been assaulted and made it impossible for them to use courts to recover debts. The term 'lynching' did not derive from post-Civil War southern violence against former slaves but from the violent activities of a Colonel Lynch in Virginia against loyalists. The authorities made no effort to stop assaults and hangings from the tree in Lynch's Garden. The anti-communist hysteria of the late 1940s had plenty of precedents in the rantings of the Patriot press against 'the damned Tories'. The tarring and feathering of the 1760s progressed to harsher punishments, as when loyalist protestors in Delaware in 1780 were sentenced to be hanged, drawn and quartered followed by beheading.

Given this level of bitterness, the divisions between Whigs and Tories may well have become less a matter of political principle or social resentments and more a matter of cumulative desire for revenge. Also, fear of retribution by the dominant force may well have led to people judging it prudent to join whoever was in control, only to suffer punishment when areas changed hands, thus building up more of a cycle of violence and resentment.

There are too many accounts of violent incidents for these to be dismissed as propaganda by the different sides, and they were notably part of the later stages of the war which degenerated rapidly. The complexities of loyalism can be best illustrated by reference to North Carolina. As with South Carolina, there was a distinction in wealth and status between the richer colonists of the tidewater areas and those of the back country and the frontier. This had caused tensions before the war. The Governor's Council and the Assembly were dominated by the more prosperous families. The taxes imposed on the poorer people caused resentment as did legal dues. There had been various incidents of attacks on officials and protests with rioters being jailed and freed by crowds from 1759 to 1771. In that year, however, protest took the form of an armed clash between a thousand official militiamen and about 1500 protesters. The opponents of what were seen as unjust taxes and fees were known as Regulators. The fighting was seen as treason by the militia commanders who hanged one Regulator on the scene of the battle. An oath of allegiance was forced on 6000 dissidents and six more hanged. There was a threat of ongoing reprisals that was so severe that the British government and the royal governor, Martin, urged an amnesty. The Assembly and the Council were all for social discipline and more trials.

This social upheaval led North Carolina to support independence but it also led to divisions and increased bitterness. Sporadic uprisings and repression occurred between 1776–1780 but it was the British Southern Campaign that escalated conflict to a full civil war. Violent incident followed violent incident.

After the killings of six Patriots, two officers, Wade and Culp, decided on vengeance. Capturing a group of Tories, they ordered that their heads should be split by sabres. The party went on to a house of a Tory called Daniel Macmillan who was shot multiple times and then finished off. Another inhabitant called Allan McSweenie had his hands tied, was hit and then his head was split open by a sabre in sight of his wife and child. Two young women were stripped and robbed.

A party of Tories fell on a Whig neighbour called John Cornelison and hit and shot him so that he fell into his own fire. A friend followed one of the assailants into Tennessee where he shot him through the cracks of a log cabin. The victorious Whigs pursued their enemies through court proceedings and trials and there were considerable confiscations of land and property.

Not all of the civil war was haphazard atrocity. David Fanning conducted a campaign of some thirty-six skirmishes, leading varying numbers of loyalist troops ranging from a hundred to a thousand from 1776 to 1782, before fleeing to Florida and then to Nova Scotia.

The civil war in the South followed this pattern. Local committees tried to enforce uniformity, triggering resistance based on existing grievances and rivalries. Reprisals led to further reprisals. Alongside the campaigns waged by the formal armies, irregular groups formed on both sides, out of control by the commanders of both armies. When violence became habitual, it was sometimes a matter of circumstance that led to the choosing of sides. In 1780, a Patriot militia captain called William Green was captured during the British capture of Charleston by a Tory patrol. Though he escaped, he decided to actually join the Tories. Captured again, this time by Patriots, he was condemned to be hanged but escaped. However, he decided for reasons unknown to fight for the Patriots.

The relish for violence seems to have grown. One of the leaders of the partisan group led by the Patriot Francis Marion, a certain Hugh Ervin, deserted in frustration that his leader would not sanction the indiscriminate murder of Tories. Another murderous Whig called Maurice Murphy beat his aged uncle to death when he denounced him for overstepping the mark in his violent behaviour. Bloody Bill Cuningham began as a Whig partisan but joined the Tories. He killed a Whig called Richie, who had killed Cunningham's younger brother. This former Patriot formed a band of 300 men who terrorised the region round the South Carolina settlement of Ninety Six and won notoriety for sabring to death thirty-five captured Whigs in Laurens County. He later escaped to England where he was given a pension. Violent action was not the prerogative of male Whigs and Tories. In 1781, Nancy Hunt's house was occupied by six Tory militia. As they relaxed their guard she shot two of them and held off the others until her husband arrived and hanged them.

The decline in 'civilised' warfare, if such a thing exists, has been seen in the activities of a British officer vividly portrayed in the film *The Patriot* by Jason

Isaacs, whose thinly disguised British officer orders reprisals and pursues personal vendetta. Little of this is accurate. The film shows little of the inter-communal violence that was more a feature of the Southern Campaign and civil war.

Tarleton was a young lieutenant colonel, not from an aristocratic but from a mercantile family in Liverpool, put in charge of the British Legion of regular troops and Tory militia. Formed in New York in 1778, this was a unit of fast-moving cavalrymen who had local knowledge and were used to combat the Patriot militia bands in South Carolina. Together with another loyalist unit, Ferguson's Queen's Rangers, Tarleton's men took a major role in preventing the relief of Charleston in 1780 by a daring night attack on reinforcements. On 29 May, Tarleton and his men attacked a retreating Continental force, under a commander called Buford, at Waxhaw Creek on the border of South and North Carolina. In the furious charge Tarleton's horse was shot from under him. His men were eager to avenge him and some killed surrendering enemy soldiers. This gave Tarleton a reputation as a 'butcher', and killing prisoners became known as Tarleton's quarter. It was practised by Patriot forces at the later battle of King's Mountain, in which the body of Ferguson was mutilated and his men slaughtered – Tarleton had, in fact, offered Buford surrender terms before the charge and did not, once recovered from his fall, pursue his retreating army to the point of wholesale slaughter. His evil reputation was more a matter of propaganda and legend. Tarleton's forces were defeated at Cowpens, but he fought in a very determined way for the rest of the war, at one time nearly capturing Jefferson in a raid into Virginia. Tarleton was not merely a commander of an irregular anti-partisan force but a professional officer who led a regular formation in some skilful and daring raids.

Regular loyalist troops were demonised by legends such as the Waxhaw Massacre. Militia units suffered from brutal reprisals and were themselves guilty of atrocities in an uncontrolled struggle that seemed to be very divorced from the ideals of 1775.

Note

1. Paul H Smith, *Loyalists and Redcoats*, University of North Carolina, 1964.

Chapter 7

Women and the American Revolution

The Revolution and the war for liberty did not transform the women of the eighteenth century into the women of the twenty-first century. Colonial life was predominantly rural and depended on the contribution of women to the household. It was based on their subordination to their fathers and then their husbands. The war intensified the importance of women in the home because their responsibilities grew when men went to war. They were also deeply affected when the war brought the fighting to individual households. The level of sexual and physical violence or exploitation almost certainly went up, though this has not been a major source of study. Women's contribution to the war was linked to following husbands into camps and sometimes battles and to providing household-type services to fighting men – washing, cleaning, cooking, and emotional and physical comfort. A major development was not towards modern independence or political and social equality but in boosting their role in the family as Republican mothers. The focus on a few individuals who seemed to indicate a more modern progress has been to distort the reality for most White women. Highly publicised, the fighting role of 'Molly Pitcher' in the battle of Monmouth was a myth. No such woman existed. A few women did take part in the fighting but made minimal difference to its outcome. The casting of Abigail Adams, the wife of the future president John Adams, as a prototype feminist and pioneers of women's rights has been wishful thinking. The brutal truth is that the minority elite of White men who led the resistance to Britain needed support from other groups. This included women, the unpropertied White population, freed Black slaves and, where possible, Indian allies. There was no longer-term intention to reward this support by social, political or economic change. Women stayed predominantly in the home after the war and had no meaningful political rights until the twentieth century. Slavery was entrenched. Indian rights were eroded. When it seemed that individual states might become too democratic, the elite ensured its own supremacy through a new constitution and the suppression of social unrest. This chapter focuses on White women. The position of women in other ethnic groups was different and will be considered in the next chapter.

The political opportunities for women in colonial America were limited, but they contributed to political life in a wider sense than voting or being active in assemblies. They took part in non-consumption activities; they supported protests and boycotts; they expressed views in writing. They held and made clear their views, both in support of actions against Britain and in defence of loyalism. There is evidence of their interest and involvement in the debates and divisions which led to war.

During the fighting, very few actually took part, through there are examples of some disguising themselves as men and they may have taken part in actual conflict. However, in other ways they contributed to the war as camp followers of the Continental Army, acting as support for the soldiers, nursing, cooking, cleaning and sometimes spying. On the all-important home front they ran farms and business in the absence of husbands, brothers and fathers, shouldering extra responsibilities. Both as patriots and loyalists they often dealt with military occupation and, to varying degrees, offered resistance.

After the war they were influential in a movement called Revolutionary Motherhood and maintained an interest in political life, though only for a while did they actually vote – and then only single property-owners were eligible.

The Study of Individuals

It is difficult to assess their role in bringing about the Revolution. Until the emergence of organisations to promote women's rights in the 1840s, accounts of the Revolution offered little about their role or roles. There was a revival of interest in the mid-century when collections of deeds of women were made. Elizabeth F. Ellet produced two volumes in 1850 of biographical descriptions based on interviews entitled *The Women of the American Revolution*. She was intent on showing how individual women could have personal influence by their actions.

However, though extensive, the often vivid description of revolutionary acts and words was quite random and included examples of varying degrees of significance.

Ellet describes the life of the English-born Esther Reed, wife of the Governor of Philadelphia, who had fled from Howe's forces in 1776, lost her children to smallpox and, despite ill health, led a campaign to raise money from the women of Philadelphia in 1779.

Notwithstanding the feeble state of her health, Mrs Reed entered upon her duties with great animation. The work was congenial to her feelings. It was charity in its genuine form and from its purest source – the voluntary outpouring from the heart,

It was not stimulated by the excitements of the day – neither fancy fairs nor bazaars, but the American women met, and seeing the necessity that asked interposition, relieved it. They solicited money and other contributions directly, and for a precise and avowed object. They labored with their needles and sacrificed their trinkets and jewels. The result was very remarkable. The aggregate amount of contributions in the city and county of Philadelphia was not less than 7,500 dollars, specie; much of it, too, paid in hard money at a time of the greatest appreciation.

Catharine Greene, the wife of the famous General Nathaniel Greene, made her contribution by being a loyal companion and running a household in the South for the general. The approval of the conventional role of a wife in Elizabeth Ellet's writing is worth quoting at length to show expectations which were likely to be held in the Revolutionary era:

Mrs. Greene joined her husband in the South after the close of the active campaign of 1781 and remained with him till the end of the war, residing on the islands during the heats of summer, and the rest of the time at head-quarters. In the spring of 1783, she returned to the North where she remained till the General had completed his arrangements for removing to the South. They then established themselves at Mulberry Grove, on a plantation which had been presented to Greene by the State of Georgia.

Mrs. Greene's first impressions of southern life and manners are painted in lively colors in her letters to northern friends. The following passage is from one to Miss Flagg:

'If you expect to be an inhabitant of this country, you must not think to sit down with your netting pins; but on the contrary, employ half your time at the toilet, one quarter to paying and receiving visits; the other quarter to scolding servants, with a hard thump every now and then over the head; or singing, dancing, reading, writing, or saying your prayers. The latter is here quite a phenomenon; but you need not tell how you employ your time.'

The letters of General Greene to his wife breathe the most entire confidence and affection. His respect for her judgment and good sense is shown in the freedom with which he expresses his thoughts and unfolds his hopes and plans. He evidently looked to her for support and sympathy in all his cares and troubles.

Other biographies offer a more vigorous type of marital support than in Mrs Greene's ladylike activities.

Mary Draper of Massachusetts fed a hundred militiamen after the Battle of Lexington. Hannah Israel, 19 and pregnant in 1777, had seen her husband captured as a member of a local Committee of Safety of Wilmington, Delaware. When a body of soldiers came to kill his cattle, Hannah drove the animals off, despite being ordered to stop and actually fired on. Mary Anne Gibbs, a

13-year-old daughter of a plantation owner at Charleston saved a young boy who had been left behind in the mansion when British troops occupied it in 1779. Though the house was under fire from American troops, this girl ran back and took the boy to safety. Her aunt ordered the rescue of a badly wounded nephew from a field of battle and nursed him back to health.

In the civil war in North Carolina in 1781, Martha Bratton, the wife of a Whig commander, was questioned by loyalist militia about her husband:

Animated by the spirit of deadly animosity towards the Whigs which then raged; one of the militia seized a reaping hook that hung in the courtyard and brought it to her throat with the intention to kill her.. Still she refused to give information that would endanger her husband's safety.

The wealth of information gleaned from interviews and memoirs is overwhelming and accompanied by pictures of the women. Saved from obscurity by a remarkable chronicle, the examples range from perfectly banal activities, such as providing Burgoyne with a good meal after Saratoga, to show the moral superiority of the American victors, to much more violent episodes.

Sometimes an encounter with eminent personalities is revealing. Dorcas Richardson of South Carolina aided her husband, who was a leading partisan, to hide out from the Tarleton legion. She smuggled food to his hiding place and endured some harsh treatment from Tarleton's men, who pretended they had found and killed her husband, wiping blood from their sabres. Tarleton is said to have been sympathetic but acquiesced in attempts to force her to reveal her husband's whereabouts. He is also said to have burnt the plantation and hanged a young rebel in full view of Mrs Richardson. The given source of all this is, however, not from a published memoir but from the reminiscences of Dr Joseph Johnson of Charleston. Had Tarleton become so much of a 'demon' that he appeared in various reminiscences even though he had not actually been present? There are similar narratives of his misdeeds which were written or given in evidence sometime after the war. The two volumes do not include loyalist women.

However, though it shows the wide variety of the ways that women reacted to the circumstances of war, it is difficult to draw overall conclusions from what should be a highly valuable source book, though something of a grab bag of memories. In it can be found women as spies, passing on information; women as resisters; women as supporters and comforters to their men folk; women withstanding hardships; and women as fundraisers. The examples were chosen to show moral strength and womanly virtues – loyalty, defenders of the home, hardship and so on. Sometimes an entirely unwomanly spirit is also seen. Dicey

Langstone was given a gun to look after by her brother and there was a password agreed before she handed it over to his fellow patriot militiamen. When a group came to take possession, they refused to give this password and laughingly said they had it anyway. Dicey cocked the weapon and thrust it into the man's face telling him that 'if the gun is in your possession, take charge of her!' The man gave the password. Is this revealing about attitudes in general or was Dicey Livingstone just a high-spirited young woman, used to weapons and influenced by the way that civil war in South Carolina had overturned social norms?

Elizabeth Ellet did not give a potted biography of some of the figures that have most intrigued more modern chroniclers of individuals, but the same problems occur when trying to assess their importance. It might be helpful to consider a number of individuals: Molly Pitcher, Margaret Corbin, Deborah Samson, Molly Briant, Betsy Ross and Abigail Adams.

There is now a great deal of writing about women both as active supporters of political causes and about the impact of war on women. As the war had many characteristics of a civil war and as it affected so many families and households in a way that the French and American wars had not, it follows that women were profoundly affected. However, the extent to which women actually affected the outbreak and outcome of the Revolution and whether it brought about significant change for them remains difficult to assess.

Writing has tended to focus more on individuals than on larger groups. Also, the overall picture has been distorted by focusing on individual examples of women's participation in the Revolution, regardless of how typical it was or what it actually achieved. For all that, many traditional accounts simply neglect women's contributions or relegate them to dutiful paragraphs in a White male narrative. It has been observed that in a standard and substantial narrative history of the war there is one mention of a woman.

Abigail Adams emerged as a pioneer of women's rights. Born in Massachusetts in 1744, her father was a slave owning Congregationalist minister. Abigail married a lawyer, John Adams, who was to be a leading figure in the opposition to Britain. Their marriage was relatively unusual in that Abigail freely expressed views on current topics and they engaged in vigorous debates. When John Adams was away as a delegate to the Continental Congress, she wrote to him on 31 March 1776 and one particular letter has become a classic of women's rights:

I long to hear that you have declared an independency. And, by the way, in the new code of laws which I suppose it will be necessary for you to make, I desire you would remember the ladies and be more generous and favorable to them than your ancestors. Do not put such unlimited power into the hands of the husbands. Remember, all men would be tyrants if they could. If particular care and attention is not paid to the ladies, we are determined to foment a rebellion and will not hold ourselves bound by any laws in which we have no voice or representation.

That your sex are naturally tyrannical is a truth so thoroughly established as to admit of no dispute; but such of you as wish to be happy willingly give up – the harsh tide of master for the more tender and endearing one of friend. Why, then, not put it out of the power of the vicious and the lawless to use us with cruelty and indignity with impunity? Men of sense in all ages abhor those customs which treat us only as the servants of your sex; regard us then as being placed by Providence under your protection, and in imitation of the Supreme Being make use of that power only for our happiness.

A lot of weight has been put on this seemingly feminist stance. However, Abigail, despite being the husband of one president and the mother of another, did not see a political role for women outside normal domestic responsibilities. Her concern was for property rights and the unequal laws governing a woman's right to her own property. Read in this light and in the light of a tendency for the couple to enjoy intellectual sparring, the letter is less of a general call to arms for equality and political rights. Adams' reply is less quoted, but it should not be taken as an angry response:

As to your extraordinary code of laws, I cannot but laugh. We have been told that our struggle has loosened the bonds of government everywhere; that children and apprentices were disobedient; that schools and colleges were grown turbulent; that Indians slighted their guardians, and negroes grew insolent to their masters. But your letter was the first intimation that another tribe, more numerous and powerful than all the rest, were grown discontented. This is rather too coarse a compliment, but you are so saucy, I won't blot it out.

Depend upon it, we know better than to repeal our masculine systems. Although they are in full force, you know they are little more than theory. We dare not exert our power in its full latitude. We are obliged to go fair and softly, and, in practice, you know we are the subjects. We have only the name of masters, and rather than give up this, which would completely subject us to the despotism of the petticoat, I hope General Washington and all our brave heroes would fight.

Adams, like many of the advocates of liberty in the 1770s, did not believe in democracy and opposed a proposal to allow unpropertied men to vote for the new Massachusetts Assembly on the grounds that they were not independent and worked for masters. He thought women had as good judgment and as independent minds as those men who are wholly destitute of property: It was not any inherent lack of understanding but rather a lack of independence that meant that women should not be active citizens.

… there will be no end of it. New claims will arise. Women will demand a vote. Lads from 12 to 21 will think their rights not enough attended to, and every man, who has not a farthing, will demand an equal voice with any other in all acts of state. It tends to confound and destroy all distinctions, and prostrate all ranks, to one common level

In essence this was a position that his wife accepted, though she did come back at her husband in what was probably quite a playful tone rather than that of an embittered outburst.

I cannot say that I think you are very generous to the ladies; for, whilst you are proclaiming peace and goodwill to men, emancipating all nations, you insist upon retaining an absolute power over wives. But you must remember that arbitrary power is like most other things which are very hard, very liable to be broken; and, notwithstanding all your wise laws and maxims, we have it in our power, not only to free ourselves, but to subdue our masters, and without violence, throw both your natural and legal authority at our feet

What was being argued here was not a Suffragette position or an anticipation of the later feminism, but an instance of age-old influence of women in the domestic and marital sphere. The French Revolution did throw up some radical ideas of equal voting and political rights for women, but this is not the thrust of this marital sparring and very little political progress emerged from the sacrifices and hard work that women contributed to the Revolution. John Adams was a well-read liberal figure, but his views about women were rooted in the past.

Women were not passive victims of male warfare nor helpless or so engrossed in domestic life that they did not have opinions and passions about the conflicts of the Revolutionary period. However, there is limited evidence that whatever individuals did in the war, or the activities of groups in promoting the struggle for freedom, that women did not share the prevailing attitudes to their proper role in society. That role, as Abigail Adams made clear, was not necessarily to be subordinate in the domestic sphere or to be absent from the public sphere.

In the aftermath of the Revolution, the tendency was for the role of women as a whole to be downplayed while, paradoxically, legends were created about individuals who had represented women's heroism or commitment. The most lasting was that of Betsy Ross, the supposed creator of the American flag. Initially the Revolutionaries had used all sorts of flags, often versions of the British Union Jack, with additions to show dissent. In 1777, Congress specified a national flag with stars and stripes. Betsy Ross or Elizabeth Griscom Ross was the wife of a sea captain who had a flourishing embroidery, dressmaking and upholstery business in Philadelphia. There is some evidence she did make flags but in 1870 her grandson gave an account of her key role in the creation of the Stars and Stripes:

> *Sitting sewing in her shop one day with her girls around her, several gentlemen entered. She recognized one of these as the uncle of her deceased husband, Col. George Ross, a delegate from Pennsylvania to Congress. She also knew the handsome form and features of the dignified, yet graceful and polite Commander in Chief, who, while he was yet Colonel Washington had visited her shop both professionally and socially many times, (a friendship caused by her connection with the Ross family) they announced themselves as a committee of congress, and stated that they had been appointed to prepare a flag, and asked her if she thought she could make one, to which she replied, with her usual modesty and self reliance, that 'she did not know but she could try; she had never made one but if the pattern were shown to her she had not doubt of her ability to do it'.*

This gave rise to a whole Betsy Ross legend. There is a museum in her house in Philadelphia, a silent movie in 1917 and a stamp in 1952. In the musical *Hello Dolly!* there is a song, 'When the Parade Passes By', in which the heroine sings 'Betsy Ross's Flag is Passing'. As late as 2017 a book was published with the title *Betsy Ross and the Making of America,* which suggests there might be some connection between the Revolution and the embroideress. Engagingly, the author admits to a lack of evidence from any personal letters or diaries and a reliance on adverts, probate documents, tools of the trade, accounts and so on. The sad fact is that there is no evidence at all for the visit of Washington or that the flag of 1777 was in any way linked to Mrs Ross.

The same is true of another manufactured heroine, 'Molly Pitcher', who has a much of a real existence as 'G.I. Joe' The image of Mollie Pitcher was widely depicted as an example of female heroism and patriotism. However, it is not quite clear whether this was to indicate the typicality of a woman joining in a battle and firing a cannon alongside men or the exceptionality of this – something so out of the ordinary that it was worth recording as a wonderful individual act. Given the lack of depiction of women in the military paintings of the period, the latter is probably true.

The names of individual women who did participate are much less well known than the symbolic and fictitious Mollie. Modern research has rescued them from obscurity. Mary Ludwig Hayes accompanied her husband to war in 1778, two years after he joined an artillery regiment. In the Battle of Monmouth, she was bringing water to the artillerymen when her husband was incapacitated, and she took over firing his cannon. The memoirs of a soldier called Plumb Martin mention this, so this a rare example of verification of military action undertaken by a woman. There is less verification for stories about her – a tough character who smoked and chewed tobacco and was unfazed by a musket ball passing between her legs. As she was one of the few women who was awarded a pension, it seems likely that she saw action. Another possible model for 'Mollie' was Margaret Corbin who served in the same regiment and took her husband's place when he was killed at the Battle of Fort Washington. Unlike Mary Hayes she wore uniform – something done by only relatively few women. Wounded, captured and then paroled, she was employed as a guard at West Point and was buried there in 1800. Deborah Samson has been the subject of a lot of interest as a rare example of a women who disguised herself as a man to serve in a Massachusetts regiment. There are more examples of this in the civil war of the 1860s and though it seems unlikely, the limited unclothed bathing and removing of clothing in barracks of the period made such impersonation possible. She had the nickname 'Mollie' because of her smooth skin and indeed was not a tall or manly person. She later appeared in quite a feminine way, though in male uniform, on stage singing patriotic songs celebrating her exploits. Quite what they were is unclear, but she did succeed in getting a pension from Congress after the war.

The problem of focusing on individuals like this is that it tends to obscure the scale of female participation in the Revolution and the war. It also distorts reality. The perception of eighteenth-century campaigning is that it was like the campaigns of the twentieth century. Women were not in the trenches of the First World War but in the rear, ready to receive casualties as nurses or act as support staff. Hitler's Blitzkrieg was an all-male affair. D-Day landings were made by men only.

However, though largely invisible in accounts and pictures, eighteenth-century armies had large numbers of women. One historian has estimated that when Burgoyne moved down from Canada in his ill-fated campaign which culminated in defeat at Saratoga, he had 1000 women with him and 8000 men – an astonishing ratio. An observer of his army in Boston after the defeat recorded 'great numbers of women' carting children, pots and even furniture. The Continental Army would not have been different, but the problems of supply and shelter reduced the numbers, Washington wanted no more than one woman to every thirteen men – still remarkable by most modern standards, as they were not soldiers.

Taken as a given in the period, the presence of so many women and children was not often recorded in military accounts, giving a picture of warfare which has an important element missing.

Historians who have looked at account books and pension applications as well as casual references in memoirs have suggested a possible participation of 20,000 American women in the campaigns. Women sometimes had no choice except to follow their husbands and not all were householders who bravely carried on farming work. If recruits or volunteers were without property then the only thing preventing utter destitution was army pay and work in the camps as laundresses, cooks, or in some cases, prostitutes. As this support work was necessary, many women were on a sort of semi-official basis. Some were in uniform, but only a minority, and in camp subject to military discipline. There are instances of women being court martialled. In the heat of battle, it was a small step from providing food and water to the men at the front to actually stepping in. Sarah Osborne was with her husband as a camp follower when the Continental Army was besieging the British at Yorktown and brought coffee, water and food to the men in the trenches. She also washed and mended clothes. During her time with the army, which she accompanied from 1780, she had two children who were brought up in the camps and battlefields. The distinction between home, family life and the military world was not always clear.

It is the sheer scale of this participation which is masked by limited biographical narratives. But how committed were women to the political cause and how were the majority who did not follow the armies affected by war?

The general view is that the Revolution politicised women. This took various forms. The widespread discussion about the measures imposed by Britain in American households involved women in debates. The decision to resist was often a male one, but wives and daughters could not be unaffected. In May 1770, John Adams warned Abigail, his wife, that by opposing British measures he had likely brought ruin to himself, to her and to their children. He recorded that she replied 'I am willing in this cause to run all risks with you'. The historian Carol Berkin[1] has perceptively seen the Revolution as stretching the notion of help-mate and taking women into the public sphere.

Colonial America put great store on the family unit and the supportive role of the wife. Women were expected to be faithful, to keep the home and to obey. Married women lost independence, property rights and did not have equality in matters of inheritance, but family life depended a lot on their energy, domestic skills and versatility. Their economic role was of considerable importance. The 1760s saw the domestic sphere merge into the public sphere. The key element was the boycott of British goods and the development of American alternatives. Suddenly, what had been thought of as routine and unimportant domestic activity took on political significance, with women as producers of alternative goods and changing their habits as consumers to support politically motivated boycotts.

Women in a predominantly rural society had supported men in all sorts of agricultural work, planting, harvesting, husbandry, accounts, using firearms and knives to defend frontier settlements. If widowed, the whole responsibility of running farms and businesses had fallen to them. When the Revolution started these skills were extended.

The crowd actions of the 1760s involved women as well as men and there are examples of fiercely held political opinions. In June 1768, a young Boston woman called Charity Clark wrote a letter to an English friend which has become well known:

'If you English folks won't give us the liberty we ask, I will try to gather a number of ladies with spinning wheels, we will learn to weave and will found a new Arcadia.

As will be seen, the new Arcadia was elusive, but spinning became a political act, albeit one associated with traditional, domestic activity. The most famous example of this sort of female support for economic rebellion is the Edenton Compact of October 1774, when fifty-one women in Edenton, North Carolina, met at the home of Mrs King and agreed to boycott British made products. Spinning groups, sewing bees, and boycotts of tea were protests entirely in accordance with colonial ideas of women's role. Wholesome, domestic, patriotic, supportive. Women, too, could support the male cause by instructing the young. There survives an Alphabet for Little Masters and Mistresses published in 1775 for mothers:

A, stands for Americans, who scorn to be slaves;
B, for Boston, where fortitude their freedom saves;
C, stands for Congress, which, though loyal, will be free;
D, stands for defence, 'gainst force and tyranny!

A supposed jolly and larkish poem in 1769, published in Boston, gives women some advice on how to show their political sympathies. The patronising tone and the focus on clothes and tea drinking (bohea was a form of strong, British imported tea) shows a depressingly sexist and dismissive tone by modern standards.

Young ladies in town, and those that live 'round
Wear none but your own country linen;
Of economy boast, let your pride be the most
To show clothes of your own make and spinnin'.
What if homespun, they say, be not quite as gay
As brocades. Be not in a passion
For once it is known 'tis much worn in town
One and all will cry out 'tis the fashion!

And as one all agree, that you'll not married be,
To such as will wear London factory;
But at first sight refuse, tell 'em you will choose,
As encourage our own manufactory.
No more ribbons wear, nor in rich silks appear,
Love your country much better than fine things,
Begin without passion, 'twill soon be the fashion,
To grace your smooth locks with a twine string.
Throw away your bohea, and your green hyson tea,
And all things of a new fashioned duty;
Get in a good store of the choice Labrador,
There'll soon he enough here to suit ye.
These do without fear and to all you'll appear,
Fair charming, true, lovely and clever,
Though the times remain darkish,
Young men will be sparkish,
And love you much stronger than ever.

For thirty-two months, starting in March 1768, more than sixty spinning meetings were held from Harpswell, Maine, to Huntington, Long Island.

However, another side was shown in the participation of women in the crowd actions, such as during protests about the Stamp Act. The Daughters of Liberty emerged as groups of women in Massachusetts acting as a female equivalent to the Sons of Liberty but mostly confining themselves to boycott, spinning and fundraising. The heroine of these groups was a women called Sarah Bardlee (or Bradley) Fulton who lived in Medford. She was born in 1740, so like many of the enthusiasts for liberty she was quite young when she helped to organise some of the female activities. However, from 1773 myth overtakes reality and she was credited with a leading role in the Boston Tea Party, suggesting that the protestors disguise themselves as Mohawk Indians. She is widely remembered as 'the mother of the Boston Tea Party'. This claim is repeated in many historical articles but her connection to this pivotal event in American history is recounted through anecdotes from two historical sources: a letter by Eliza M. Gill, published in the *Boston Evening Traveler* in 1873 and an article by Helen T. Wild for the inauguration of the Daughters of the American Revolution's Sarah Bradley Fulton Chapter in 1897. A story that she resisted the seizure of cattle by a British raiding party during the war and was a spy for Washington is based only on family legends and anecdotes. However, the city of Medford has a special day named after her. In October 2024 there were celebrations, the appearance of George Washington on a horse and an exhibition of her dress. All this seems redolent to more sceptical observers of the Jedidiah Springfield celebrations in 'The Simpsons' in which the town honours the mythical achievements of its founder and is outraged when Lisa reveals them to have been untrue. The reborn Daughters of the American Revolution in the late nineteenth century exaggerated the degree of organisation of their forerunners.

They did boost enthusiasm for the opposition to Britain and once the war started, they did help with fundraising and support the Continental Army.

In 1780, Esther Reed organised a fundraising campaign in Philadelphia with military precision. A strong admirer of Joan of Arc and a believer in women's duty to support the cause, she sent her women supporters to every street in June 1780. She had appealed to patriotic women to abandon buying 'vain ornaments', expensive clothes and having elaborate hairdos. The money saved should be given to support Washington's men. In the end, and even with a lot of Quaker disapproval, she raised $300,000 from 1600 donors. There is no 'Esther Reed' day, perhaps because she came from a city not a small town.

Charity-style fundraising, the proper education of children, sewing and spinning, parading, renouncing frivolity and even encouraging some dressing up were all things that could be celebrated and remembered in the aftermath of the Revolution. They could also be embellished by later generations and family legends could be turned into supposedly definitive historical accounts. The bravery and enterprise of a few hardy women who actually fought were a sort of 'cherry' on a very wholesome cake.

Some of the darker realities were not so welcome. Riots and group violence were not what post-Revolutionary America wanted its women to have been involved in. Sexual molestation and violence during a civil war were not part of the Betsy Ross style legends and female loyalism was not part of a post-independence Republican Motherhood movement.

It is a theme of this short study that popular crowd action and violence was a feature of colonial life and the Revolutionary period. This was evident in the large number of food riots that occurred and involved large numbers of women. These were not women like Betsy Ross or the Edmonton ladies. These were more like the camp followers, female participants who were airbrushed out of popular mental pictures of the Revolution.

The heroic deeds of women celebrated after the Revolution made little mention of their participation in a significant number of food and price riots which took place in the North in the years 1776 to 1779. There were over thirty instances of crowd actions against merchants and retailers accused of hoarding and overcharging, ignoring the attempts of the revolutionary committees to control prices. What provoked public anger were inflated prices for tea, sugar and molasses. The riots were not only in farming regions but also in cities such as New York, Boston and Philadelphia. What was significant was the extensive participation of women and the political nature of the protests.

Women had been involved in popular urban protests before the Revolution but the events of 1776–1779 saw a surprising increase in actions which supported male protests and also were independent of them.

In 1778, Abigail Adams recorded in her journal an incident in Massachusetts involving a wealthy merchant accused of hoarding coffee to sell later at inflated prices:

A number of females, say a hundred, assembled with a cart. One seized him by his neck and tossed him in the cart. He delivered the keys when they tipped up the cart. The women took away the coffee, assaulted some servants while 'a large concourse of men stood amazed'. There were rumours that the women had beaten the merchant on his behind, but Abigail Adams discounted these. The coffee was handed over to the local committee of safety for sale at the going rate, so this was not a food riot as much as a desire to ensure that prices were fair.

This was not an isolated incident, but no legendary, heroic individual leader emerged to be celebrated in later years. No equivalent to the spurious 'Mother of the Boston Tea Party' was thrown up. It had a communal nature and was similar to the later activities of women in Paris during the French Revolution when there were concerns about prices.

Women were involved in a riot in July 1776 in Longmeadow, Massachusetts, when the merchants Jonathan and Ezekial Hale were forced by a crowd to reduce rum and molasses prices. As with the Boston Tea Party, there was a blackening of faces and some dressed as Indians in an improvised fashion. A more forceful demonstration resulted in the seizure of goods from another merchant.

Women also took independent action in August 1776 at Fishkill, New York against a tea merchant called Josephus Lefferts accused of hoarding tea. This was so unpopular that even members of his own family joined in, and a committee of women organised the confiscation of the tea, which was sold at the regulated price and the profit given to the local Committee of Safety to support the patriot cause.

There was a clear political justification in these disturbances that inflated prices were a barrier to the success of the revolutionary cause. It has been argued that women were a vital element in these and subsequent disturbances because of their economic role. Women were consumers and also providers – they managed household budgets and had a concept of what was fair. They also often ran ships and taverns. Thus, in disputes and actions about fair prices their private experience was central and so merged into public activity. It was thought natural that they should have an input.

They also became more assertive. In 1776, there was an incident at Kingston, New York, in which they surrounded the chamber of the local safety committee and demanded tea which was in short supply and highly priced. They threatened that they would see that their husbands would not fight in the Continental Army unless their demands were met.

In the spring and summer of 1777 there was considerable unrest in Boston. A 500-strong crowd had threatened to hang five 'Tory' merchants who were monopolists and accused of price inflation. The men were carried out of town in a cart and threats were made against other traders. Perhaps the cart had seized popular imagination because it also featured in an attack on Thomas Boyston in late July, this time exclusively by women, which Abigail Adams described:

In Poughkeepsie, NY a crowd of women attacked the shopkeeper Peter Messier to seize tea and there was some vandalism. It did seem that women were participating more and more in these patriotic disturbances. In August 1777 at East Hartford Connecticut a group met at a local tavern and marched a mile to the store of a man called Pitkin and seized 218 pounds of sugar. They drove off a man on horseback, possibly Mr. Pitkin. The attack was censured however by the local Whigs as the sugar had been for the army.

What is interesting is the degree of organisation involved in these sporadic outbursts of unrest and the parallels with Revolutionary France – the organised march, for instance, a pre-echo of a much more famous march of the women in October 1789.

Taken together with the more peaceful activities of the boycotts and fundraising, these more radical acts do indicate a movement of women from the private sphere of homes, farms, and small businesses to the more politicised activities of economic pressure. The problem is to assess the impact.

By 1779 there were concerns about radical actions. Popular support had been vital for opponents of British rule before the outbreak of armed conflict. When the war began, the underprivileged elements of colonial society were needed – the unpropertied, the women, the Indians and to some extent the Black population. However, as the war went on there was increasing concern in Congress and among the Revolutionary leaders. The Continental Army was developed into more of a standard European force with elite officers. The easing of price controls and the lack of support by established revolutionary authorities brought the popular disturbances to an end. As will be shown, the end of the war did not bring much recognition of the political and military support of women.

Naturally, most historians in the US writing about women focus on the active participation in revolution and war, and are reluctant to focus on women as victims. However, the effects of years of dislocation and uncertainty had as considerable effect on women, especially perhaps those who were not sympathetic to the revolutionary cause. These were far from being a small, unreasonable minority and their experience should not be forgotten.

The exposure to violence was inevitable as the war spread. Some victims became famous. Jane McCrea was killed by Indians in a famous and well-publicised incident during the Saratoga campaign, but, generally, indigenous peoples did not indulge in sexual violence. A widely quoted comment gave rise to the view that sexual assault was common in the war.

In a 1776 letter written by Francis, Lord Rawdon, of the Sixty-Third Regiment of Foot, Lord Rawdon, Adjutant to General Clinton, describes to his uncle, the Earl of Huntingdon, sexual abuse actions throughout New Jersey in flippant terms:

> *The fair nymphs of this isle are in wonderful tribulation, as the fresh meat our men have got here has made them a riotous as satyrs. A girl cannot step into the bushes to pluck a rose without running the most imminent risk of being ravished, and they are so little accustomed to these vigorous methods that they don't bear them with the proper resignation, and of consequence we have most entertaining courts martial every day.*

In fact, only a small number of court martials dealt with rape accusations, though that may be seen in different ways. Either troops did not assault women as a matter of course, or assault was not seen as a serious matter, perhaps mirroring contemporary attitudes to rape common in both England and America that did not give complaints from women about assaults very high priority.

American propaganda made a lot of sexual assaults by British troops, using it as a metaphor that the colonies were being violated by Britain. American men could be rallied to the cause of liberty by the need to protect their womenfolk. Nevertheless, there are documented accounts of sexual abuse by British and Hessian troops and some evidence of assaults on loyalists. Rape was seen as an attack on male property in colonial America, so assaults on those not so valued were probably not recorded. Assaults on camp followers, for instance, as opposed to the wives and daughters of property owners were less likely to be recorded. Also no Black woman, either slave or free, could bring a charge of assault and there would be no record of assaults on Indian women.

Most evidence concerns the campaigns in New Jersey in 1776, when civilian lives and property were under attack from Howe's army. Depositions were collected in a collection of papers and affidavits 'concerning the plunderings, burnings and revenges' committed by the British in New Jersey by Congress.

One notable example was the evidence from Hunterdon County, New Jersey, of three young women called Sarah and Elizabeth Cain and Abigail Palmer. According to their testimony, Abigail, then 13, was threatened by five British soldiers who threatened to knock her eyes out. She was subjected to three days of sexual abuse and 15-year-old Elizabeth Cain was also abused. The soldiers threatened to shoot the girls unless they accompanied them to the camp. Sarah explained in testimony given in March 1777:

> *... [soldiers said she] should go with them, to their Camp about three quarter of a mile from the place, or swore they would poison her or Blow her Brains out ... then charged his Bayonet against her Breast, and swore he would Run her thro the Heart if she Refused to go, when she this Deponent Beged and Intreated to be Excused, & told them she could not leave her Parents, but they Damn'd her Parents & said what was her Parents to them & then two of them seiz'd hold of her & dragd her into a Back Room against all her cries...*

There was no suggestion that rape was a deliberate policy and two soldiers called John Dunn and John Lusty were tried and executed for the rape of a woman, Elizabeth Johnstone, in New York in 1776. Some women were reluctant to undergo the shame in complaining as in the case of a farmer's wife assaulted by Hessian troops in Princeton in 1777.

The scale of abuse is difficult to judge, particularly when the war intensified and became more overtly a war of terror as in the Southern Campaigns. American propaganda stressed the sexual violence, as in this example from 1778 by Jonathan Austin of Boston:

> *does not the ear tingle when it hears the shrieks of helpless virgins, dreadful victims to lust & barbarity, while the grey hairs & expressive groans of an aged parent, witness to his daughter's shame, plead in vain... These monsters exceed even the most barbarous nation... Lead your sons, ye fathers, not to the altar of Paganism, and under the tutelage of some unknown deity, but to the saved altar of freedom, & while the guardian God of America is witness to the solemn obligation, MAKE THEM SWEAR that they will never be friends to a power, who are thus sacrificing their dearest privileges.*

Images were often sexual in nature, possibly to provoke the 'tingle' mentioned above. After the Revolution this was even more so, as in a much-viewed depiction of the assault on Jane McCrae from 1808 and widely accepted as factual even though there were no witnesses.

Obviously, women were vulnerable, but not all violence was sexual and not all attacks were accepted without retaliation. In 1779, Elizabeth Bozarth's farm came under attack from Indian attackers. In the struggle she split open the head of one of the enemy with an axe, and killed another. During the Saratoga campaign a farmer, Catherine Schuyler, burnt whole fields of wheat rather than let Burgoyne's troops harvest it. More arson was attributed to a woman in the burning of New York in 1776, '*her visage besmeared with every mark of rage, despair, resolution and exalted heroism*'. In 1777, a band of loyalists attacked Poughkeepsie dressed as Indians. Captured and imprisoned, five were found to be women and three a mother and two daughters. Of course, women were also on the receiving end of violence. Women and children were reported to have been burnt alive in an Indian and Tory attack in 1778. Those who sheltered troops could be punished by both sides, even though they might have had little choice in the matter. Some women suffered theft and threats from both sides. After her belongings had been plundered by British troops, a woman called Elizabeth Wilkinson recorded her feelings in a way that accords with the impact of crime on modern victims and brings home the emotional impact of the dislocations of war:

> *The whole world appeared to me as a theatre in which nothing was acted but cruelty, bloodshed and oppression; where neither age nor sex escaped the horrors of injustice and violence.*
>
> *We could neither eat, drink nor sleep in peace. The least noise alarmed us. Our nights were wearisome and painful; our days spent in anxiety and melancholy.*

Frontier life could be hard, and death was closer and more frequent in everyday life than for most modern Americans, but the emotional trauma of loss was considerable. One account of women watching fighting in 1778 in Wyoming Valley brings home the impact of war. A farmer, Hector de Crevecoeur, recorded:

> *Each wife, each father, each mother could easily distinguish each husband and son as they fell. Hundreds of women and children, now widows and orphans, with pale and dejected countenances, sitting on the few bundles they had brought with them, keeping their little unconscious children as close to them as possible.*

The extension of the war to the South was hard on many women. The depredations of both sides in destroying homes and taking revenge for irregular military forces marauding eroded distinctions between regular warfare and brutal civil war. Women were both victims and protagonists. Sarah Jones's family were prominent Patriots in Georgia. Her husband was imprisoned when the British took Savannah. Her son and two brothers died in the fighting and she was forced to flee with her younger children. The Governor of South Carolina reported to Congress in 1780 that the British raids had '*hanged many people, burnt house and turned women and children naked into the woods*'. On the other hand, women were reported burning down Tory houses in South Carolina and also taking part in a Tory ambush in North Carolina. Given that it is possible that 20 per cent of the White population of the Carolinas were loyalists and 100,000 acres of land changed hands during the retribution enacted by Patriots during and after the war, the impact on women must have been considerable. 200 people fled to England in 1776 alone and there was a mass exodus after the war to Nova Scotia, Jamaica and East Florida. The dangers of war were followed by homesickness and the challenges of making a new life.

Women faced the agony of losing family members, the dangers from the presence of armies and their allies, the dislocation of war with shortages, higher prices, additional responsibilities and for some the humiliation of defeat. Loyalists faced disapproval and ostracism, the loss of property and for many thousands, exile. On the other hand, there was the sense of participating in great events away from the confines of home, farm, family, and neighbourhood. For a small number there was literary recognition. For more there was the sense of worth in participating in patriotic activities. For a small number there was the thrill of the battlefield and breaking out of traditional gender roles. For more there was the experience of war with its comradeship and excitement as well as its hardship and hard work. The whole experience of protest and revolution took more women into the public sphere. For some historians, the words of a Connecticut woman, Mary Fish, about the experience of revolution summed up a significant change:

> '*I have in some measure acted the heroine as well as my dear husband the hero.*'

Women are often said to have gained confidence to think and act on matters traditionally reserved for men. There were prominent women who advocated greater rights and who anticipated the feminist pioneers of the nineteenth and twentieth centuries – Mary Otis Warren and Judith Sargent Murray. However, the war did not produce substantial changes. The state of New Jersey did allow women to vote, but this was ended in 1807 and was a result of a curious omission in the colonial constitution drawn up in 1766, which allowed property owners to vote without specifying gender or race. In the post-war period, laws relating to voting used the term 'he or she', referring to voters. In the election of 1797, the votes of seventy-five women nearly have victory to a candidate from the Federalist Party over his Republican opponent. This individual was determined to gain his revenge, and in 1807 succeeded in getting the New Jersey assembly to pass a law specifically excluding women and Black citizens from the franchise.

So, from 1807 to 1920 no woman enjoyed the right to vote, and therefore half the population continued to be excluded from political rights. 'No Taxation without Representation' was a cause many women had sacrificed a great deal for, but it was not to apply to them.

One of the most feted female writers was Mercy Otis Warren, the wife of a Massachusetts political activist, who hosted dinner parties for those opposed to British policies and who wrote extensive verses, plays and essays which were published in 1790. She had no formal education, and her fame lies in her being one of the few women of the time to have her work published.

This example may well be enough to show the quality of her outpourings:

To the Hon. J. Winthrop, Esq.
Who, on the American Determination in 1774, to suspend all Commerce with
Britain, (except for the real necessaries of life) requested a poetical Life of the Articles
the Ladies might comprise under that Head.

Freedom may weep, and tyranny prevail,
And stubborn patriots either frown, or rail;
Let them of grave economy talk loud,
Prate prudent measures to the lift'ning crowd;
With all the rhetoric of ancient schools,
Despite the mode, and fashion's modish fools;
Or the fair liberty, who us'd to smile,
The guardian goddess of Britannia's isle,
In fable weeds, anticipate the blow,
Aim'd at Columbia by her royal foe;
And mark the period when inglorious kings,
Deal round the curses what a Churchill sings.

But what's the anguish of whole towns in tears,
Or trembling cities groaning out their fears?
The state may totter on proud ruin's brink,
The Sword be brandish'd, or the bark may sink;

More remarkable was the literary output of Phyllis Wheatley, a former slave who compared her own experience with that of the colonies as a whole. This was published in London in 1773:

Should you, my lord, while you peruse my song,
Wonder from whence my love of Freedom sprung,
Whence flow these wishes for the common good,
By feeling hearts alone best understood,

I, young in life, by seeming cruel fate,
Was snatch'd from Afric's fancy'd happy seat:
What pangs excruciating must molest,
What sorrows labour in my parent's breast?
Steel'd was that soul and by no misery mov'd,
That from a father seiz'd his babe belov'd:
Such, such my case. And can I then but pray
Others may never feel tyrannic sway?

The almost tragic element is that people who were members of a society which denied freedom to all except elite White men should write so expressively about ideals of freedom. Phyllis Wheatley admired Washington, even though he had slaves who, like herself, had suffered the 'cruel fate' of her poem.

What was the most influential result of the Revolution for women was a movement called Republican Motherhood. After all that had been endured by women far away from the sheltered world of Mercy Otis Warrern's strained and tedious odes, the 'message' was for women to have, as their purpose in life, the raising of children in a pure Republican and virtuous way. Sweaty and dirty heroism on the battlefield or defending your home by cleaving an attacker's skull with axes was not what was admired after victory, but instead true feminine virtue in the context of the all-important family. Years later it was much the same story. Rosie the Riveter, the propaganda heroine of the Second World War, had to go home and be a Stepford Wife in a new suburban home and, immaculately coiffured and in lovely dresses and high heels, bring up her 2.5 children to be God-fearing young Americans. As will be shown, it was much the same for all the allies of the Patriots – the impoverished, the Indians, the Black population, the French and the Spanish. Gratitude was in somewhat short supply as 'the Empire of Liberty' pursued its destiny.

The Republican Motherhood movement did continue the activity of groups of women in the public sphere, in the manner of the groups who opposed the immorality and frivolity of tea drinking and consuming luxury goods that was a strong element of the protests of the 1760s. What had to emerge from the fighting and the sacrifice was a better world; and women had a vital role in creating it that was very different from the role of men in government and politics.

On 10 July 1799 the local newspaper in Norwich, Connecticut published a speech by a local woman made at a celebratory picnic during the previous week's Fourth of July celebrations:

Let us then appreciate justly the rank of our sex, not indeed by an affection of political
science, nor like the voluptuous ladies of France, who insinuating themselves into the

cabinet have blended gallantry and state affairs, until the motley code has inscribed ruin upon the Empire. Nor do the hackneyed paths of Fashion and Frippery afford a just field to display female excellence.

In the narrow but liberal walks of domestic life our sphere lies. To act nobly in this be our aim. As mothers, wives, sisters, and daughters, we may all be important, teach our little boys, the inestimable value of Freedom, how to blend and harmonize the natural and social rights of man, and as early impressions are indelible, this assist our dear country, to be as glorious in maintaining, as it was great in gaining her immortal independence.

In many ways the speech represents some of the positive changes that the Revolution brought about. Colonial views about women were very restrictive. In terms of legal rights, political participation and social expectations – a system known as Coverture – women suffered from considerable restrictions by modern standards. By 1799 there had been obvious changes. The Revolution brought women into the public sphere as a matter of necessity. The widespread discussion of political rights and policy politicised the colonial world and women could not be excluded when their support was needed. The creation of a Republic brought about a focus on the classical world – the only real precedent for this type of government. As in the later French Revolution, there was quite widespread consideration of 'virtue'. The Republic had to be less corrupt that the old Europe and like the best examples of Rome, should encourage a major change in morals, purity, and higher values. How widespread these notions were can be seen in the speech. For this Norwich woman, the Republican woman should not attempt to meddle in politics by 'insinuating themselves' into political life by political salons or using their influence as wives and mistresses of politicians. Nor should they reject their public responsibilities by just focusing on 'fashion and frippery'. Their domestic role was seen as vital and even 'glorious' by teaching boys the key Enlightenment values of love of freedom and an understanding of 'the natural and social rights of man'. Without this, as in the Roman Republic, freedom might not be maintained. This showed an implicit understanding that the fate of Republics was far from certain. The Roman Republic had given way to dictatorship and Empire. They key to the survival of this new political ideal was education. Here women were central – not just mothers but 'wives, sisters and daughters'.

From a modern perspective, the total subordination of women to nurturing men and supporting a male-dominated world makes uneasy reading. Many women embraced Republican virtue with intensity. A letter to President Adams from a woman in 1798 is interesting in showing the influence of religion and knowledge of ancient history.

On 11 August 1798, Abigail Cunningham, of Lunenburg, Massachusetts wrote that she would be proud if her sons '*were Called to Action, in defence of their Country, to Count not their Lives Dear in Defiance of Foreign influence, and Defence of their Country's Cause*'. And if they were killed in action she would be like mothers in Ancient Sparta, '*who suspended their Lamentations for the Loss of their sons, or Husbands till they examined their clothing, to see whether the shot went in Behind or Before*'. She said she would be like Abraham in the Bible, '*who Led his Beloved son to the Alter [sic]*'.

The spelling might indicate a lack of formal education but the commitment to the public sphere at the expense of the private world of the family shows the effects of years of discussion of idealism and a certain militarisation of the colonial community.

Historians have established some changes as a result of the Revolution. Social attitudes encouraged women to choose their marriage partners on the basis of love, not just money or family pressure. Divorce was made easier. Education changed for those able to access it as more girls were taught the same subjects as boys – grammar, history, geography and arithmetic. Boston even stipulated this equality in a School Act of 1789. Women also took a bigger part in education, with many more female teachers and the emergence of large numbers of an American phenomenon, the 'school ma'am'. Optimists might see the basis for later change, the greater valuing of women and the emergence of some feminist pioneers. However, pessimists have analysed these advances in a more negative way. Like historian Kim Lorton, they have seen that these changes were regarded as necessary to support the creation of virtuous men to run a man's world. Men would need to demonstrate this virtue by winning love and not just offering wealth. Women would need to control men's desires – the early Republic took a more censorious view of pre-marital sex and out of wedlock pregnancy. White attitudes saw female sexual passion as more characteristic of other races. Easier divorce was to inculcate better male behaviour and to avoid domestic tyranny when British tyranny had been defeated. Education was needed for women to fulfil their responsibilities for educating their boys and young men. The fervour with which Republican motherhood was embraced shows the success of ideas which essentially put women back into the domestic sphere after a dangerous foray into male prerogatives of politics and war.

The complexity of change is shown in another letter to the President in April 1799, from a war widow called Margaret Smith from Kentucky. She protested against Adams's idea of creating a standing army and wanted her children not to be Republican heroes but to live virtuous lives, eat and drink and enjoy the fruit of their own labour. She put to Adams that a standing army went against ideas of liberty. She threatened to publish her letter in a local newspaper, though *The Kentucky Gazette* did not accept it.

Would an ordinary and not very well-educated woman have written such a letter before the Revolution, expressing essentially political views about a public issue? At the same time, she rejected the idea of her having, as a mother, the public responsibility of raising children to be committed republican citizens.

The last word goes to Sarah Hodgkins, a 24-year-old farmer's wife whose husband, Joseph, enlisted in 1775. Worried by their separation, she tried to carry on. Joseph did return but for many, husbands, lovers, brothers and fathers just disappeared. The bodies of one third of those killed were never returned and families had no idea where they were buried. Hundreds of women never knew what became of their men. They had to carry on, supporting where they could by sending clothes or food and falling back on their religious beliefs about God's will. High levels of anxiety must have resulted, intensified if women were in war zones or in areas which changed hands.

I have been here very busy all day to day a making you a Shirte… I have got it done and washed and Sister Perkins is now a ironing of it. I want to see you so very much. Sometimes I am almost impatient but considering it is Providence that has parted us I desire to Submite & be as contented as I can.

Notes

1. Carol Berkin, *Revolutionary Mothers*, Vintage, 2006.
2. Kimberley Lorton, *Historia*, East Illinois University, 2013.

Chapter 8

African Americans and the American Revolution

The colonists who took up arms for liberty in 1775 were in many ways prisoners of their own history and inherited a number of characteristics which rendered their ideals hypocritical. The earlier British migrants had faced a situation where land was plentiful and offered huge opportunities, which seventeenth-century Britain did not. However, labour was scarce and the White colonial population small. To meet the shortfall of labour there was a considerable dependence on indentured labour. Thousands of White migrants sold their liberty for the price of the passage to America and were, to all intents and purposes, slaves in a largely agrarian society. Where possible, the richer colonists also made use of Native American forced labour, but this was problematic, and they often preferred not to have the insecurity of workers being in possible contact with their tribes. However indentured labour was effective until the 1680s as settlement of new land spread. This type of contractual forced labour was usual in the home country and from Stuart England also came a reliance on violence to enforce discipline and authority. In the supposed land of liberty, the whips and stocks of the home country used to enforce the authority of both state and nobles were used freely. As in England, masters beat servants; husbands beat wives; parents beat children. Local authorities punished the poor and there were harsh penalties of branding and mutilation. Social inequality was taken as a given from the homeland and sexual inequality was an inherited norm. From the English oppression and colonisation of Ireland to the dispossession and repression of the native population of America was a short step. Where there were racial and cultural differences, it was easier to maintain slavery. By 1700, South Carolina had 1400 Native American slaves out of a total population of 12,580, and all colonies enslaved them. The ground had been well prepared for African slaves. A major study of American slavery by Peter Kolchin has outlined the developments which led to what later became known as 'the peculiar institution' of enforced labour which played such an important part in the making of America.

A Dutch sea captain brought the first African forced labour to the English colonies in 1619. However, there were only twenty and numbers remained small until the 1680s. It was expensive to import Africans from the Dutch and Portuguese traders, and given language difficulties it was difficult to train them. It made more sense to rely largely on European indentured labour with some Native Americans. Africans made up only a small part of the colonial population by the late 1670s. However, between 1680 and 1750 there was a very marked acceleration in the import of African slaves. As more White labour fulfilled the term in the indenture, so population grew and there was more demand for forced cheap labour. Virginia, for example, saw a doubling of population in the second half of the seventeenth century. The flow of White indentured labour slowed.

In the reign of Charles II, growing British naval power and enterprise saw the rise of the Royal Africa Company and the growth of slave trading. Slaves became more plentiful and cheaper. They also were more advantageous as they worked their whole lives and not just for a contracted period. They also bred slave children. Both White servants and slaves fled their captivity, but African slaves were easier to identify and recapture.

Initially Black and White forced labourers worked together, and it was possible for Black slaves to become free and even own land. However, there was a gradual separation between the races as increasing numbers of Africans were imported. To ensure control there were specific laws governing African slaves, which became harsher after initial attempts by various colonial legislatures to set down regulations. Increasingly there was a belief in 'breaking in'; in harsh punishments and specified legal inequalities.

The slave influx was part of a wider movement which saw perhaps 10 million Africans brought across the Atlantic from the sixteenth to the nineteenth century. The English colonies took between 600,000 and 650,000, far fewer than Brazil; and slaves were a smaller percentage of the population than in the West Indies colonies of the European powers.

The more unscrupulous exploitation of slave labour in the West Indies and Brazil involved a more continuous supply of labour. Better treatment in the English colonies in America allowed for more population growth, with the total African population reaching a million by the early nineteenth century. This meant that slaves born in America rather than Africa (so-called Creoles) outnumbered those born in Africa well before the 1780s. In one of the most remarkable developments in American history, the colonists, purely for economic motives, altered the whole nature of society by creating slave states and creating sizable communities of people of a very different racial and cultural background. The consequences were considerable and still being felt. The growing differences between North and South were to lead Americans into a prolonged and costly civil war in 1861 and racial issues have rarely been off the agenda since.

The rapid importation of Africans changed the colonies quite drastically. In 1670 there had been 597 Black people. On the verge of the Revolution in the 1770s, there were 460,000. Many were recent arrivals as the figure in 1750 had been 237,000 and in 1730, 90,000. The sharp rise was also seen in other areas – for example the French West Indian colonies and British Jamaica. However, these were more agrarian factories with the main aim of producing sugar. The American colonies consisted of different types of settlement. Where there was the need for labour for the cash crops of tobacco and rice, the number of Africans was considerably greater. North Carolina had 70,000 and South Carolina had 58,000 while Virginia had 188,000 and Maryland had 64,000. Further north there were far fewer slaves and free Black men and women. Maine had only 500, New Hampshire 650. But the idea that the North had only handfuls of slaves is wrong. Massachusetts had nearly 5000 and New York 20,000. Quakerly Pennsylvania still had 6000. Georgia's Black population doubled to 20,000 between 1770 and 1780.

All these figures are meaningless without seeing the proportion of the population. The total population of White and Black was about 2,200,000 in 1770 and 2,800,000 in 1780. Out of a population of about 450,000 in 1770, 188,000 were Black. South Carolina had 125,000 White people and 75,000 Black people. North Carolina had 180,000 White people and 70,000 Black people. Massachusetts, on the other hand, had 236,000 White people and 4800 Black people – a much smaller proportion typical of the northern colonies. Vermont had 10,000 White people and only 25 Black people.

What did all this mean? The colonists had transformed their populations in a relatively short time. Not only did the White population grow to 2.2 million in the thirty years before 1780, from about 1.2 million in 1750, but there was a big change in the racial composition of the colonies, a large rise in the Black population and major changes, particularly in the South, in the proportion of White to Black.

In history, population is one of the greatest agents of change in human history. It helped to propel the White colonists into conflict as population pressure created a desire for more land and more colonisation, which was blocked by control from the homeland. It also transformed the colonists into reliance on slave labour and accentuated differences between South and North.

However, in contrast with America's second civil war in the 1860s, it was not a cause of the conflict for independence directly. Both sides – that is the English government and its foreign troops and loyalist support among many colonists on one hand and the supporters of independence and their foreign allies and troops – believed in White racial superiority and in slavery as a form of property. If slaves were freed as a result of war, this did not reflect on either side any ideology opposed to slavery as such. Britain and France needed slave labour in its wealthy Caribbean islands. The economies of much of colonial agriculture depended on cheap slave labour. In any case, the Black population had grown so large relatively that it would be difficult to deal with if slavery were abolished. There had also emerged strong feelings of racial superiority that saw that Black labour was inherently inferior. The racialism that the early colonists had demonstrated towards the Native Inhabitants had established itself so firmly that it was transferred to people of a different race brought to the colonies from a land that few White colonists knew or understood.

The outcome of the war in military terms did not depend on the large numbers of Black Americans who supported the armies of both sides, but whose action in actual fighting was quite limited. However, it would have been impossible for such a large proportion of the colonial population not to have been involved in the Revolution and affected by it. The Revolution raised issues which affected the way that slavery was viewed and led to debates about the role of the African Americans. These issues are often subordinated in general accounts to the narrative of disputes and the nature and outcome of the fighting, marginalising very large numbers of people involved – Black men and women, Native Americans and women.

In the growing awareness of rights and liberties in the years before the outbreak of war, the clashes between Britain's government and 'patriots' and radicals among the colonists, there was limited involvement possible either among the slaves or among free Black citizens. In one respect, though, they did represent the spirit of an age in which traditions and authority were questioned by those who spoke for liberty. The liberty from taxation and barriers to westward expansion was of a very different kind than liberty from perpetual personal enslavement, but there were attempts to gain freedom by some enslaved people.

The surprising judgements reflect concerns among the colonial elite about slavery as an institution while not being prepared to take measures to end it or to relinquish their own slaves. This bizarre hypocrisy is strikingly seen in Jefferson's draft of the Declaration of Independence in 1776. Drawing up a list of the iniquities of George III which would justify independence, he includes slavery. The paragraph was removed after concerns raised by Virginia, but it is one of the strangest instances of delusion in US history. It was the desire for profit and land that brought about the huge influx of slaves, not George III or his ministers. Had the colonists wanted, the trade could have been ended and the use of slaves stopped. But abolitionism was very limited, and the opponents of slavery a minority. The great and good did have reservations. Benjamin Franklin stopped using slaves, for instance. However, Jefferson himself continued to use slaves at his estate in Monticello and even took one, Sally Hemmings, as his mistress while expressing worries about the immorality of slavery.

The protests against England did seem to focus on issues of little real relevance to the growing Black population. However, not all Black Americans were slaves, and some free Black citizens were affected by taxation and did share a general concern for liberty. Famously it was a Black American who was accused of starting the disturbance in Boston which led to the 'Massacre' of 1770.

Black Americans seem to suddenly emerge from a history dominated by the actions of the White elites and it is worth looking more closely at the one well-known figure in the protests against British rule leading to the Revolution. Crispus Attucks may not feature strongly in historical accounts, but he took a leading part in the so-called Boston massacre of 1770. He was born in Framingham, Massachusetts, around 1723. His father was of African descent, but his mother, Nancy, was a Native American and he took her name. He escaped slavery and ran away to sea in 1750. A brawny and tall individual, he was a well-known character on the docks of Boston. Witnesses put him at the head of a crowd, taunting and threatening British soldiers on 5 March 1770 in Boston armed with a club. When the soldiers fired, Attucks was struck in the chest and killed, along with four others. Patriots took his body, and it was given a place of honour and he became a martyr. A memorial was erected in his honour in the 1880s with a special poem honouring 'the first to defy and the first to die'.

A less favourable contemporary view was offered at the trial of the commander of the British troops by John Adams, who acted as defence council for the British – '*a motley rabble of saucy boys, Negroes, and mulattos, Irish teagues and outlandish jack* tars'. Adams was appealing to prejudice but it is interesting that he refers to 'negroes'. In a contemporary account of earlier disturbances over the Stamp Act, a Boston observer, John Williams, writes of the night of August 1765 when 'boys and negroes began to build bonfires in King Street and blew the whistles and horns that brought the Boston mob out of taverns, houses and garrets'. Before the Massacre soldiers clashed with a group of rope makers and a Bostonian yelled at them 'You black rascals, what have you to do with white man's quarrels?' Boston was not typical in that Black runaway slaves like Attucks could adopt false identities among seamen and sea-based artisans, and the motive for protest may not have been political but simply to take part on mob activity However it suggests a Black presence in protests which are normally seen as 'white man's quarrels'. Attucks became a legend and Martin Luther King referred to his 'moral courage', though his main significance might be in being shot and becoming a symbol of resistance, even being given the honour of being buried in a White-only cemetery in Boston.

However there is evidence of some genuine commitment to the Patriot cause. The Black writer and poet, Phillis Wheatley – an enslaved woman from the Gambia taken up by her owners as a literary prodigy – wrote a somewhat turgid Ode to Washington on appointment as commander of the Continental Army:

Proceed, great chief, with virtue on thy side,
Thy ev'ry action let the Goddess guide.
A crown, a mansion, and a throne that shine,
With gold unfading, WASHINGTON! Be thine.

The great chief acknowledged a somewhat flowery dedication to 'his excellency' but his appreciation did not lead to any great revision of his belief in slavery. Despite being feted in England and corresponding with Voltaire, Wheatley died in poverty.

Despite these interesting examples, standard accounts of the Revolution do not include much on the contribution of Black Americans. Perhaps this is not surprising because relatively so few were in a position to join protests or take a willing part in the armed struggle, simply because they were not free to do so. This was in contrast to the French colony of Saint Domingue where a large population of people of African heritage included many free Black and mixed-race people. This was not true of the English colonies where there were under 50,000 free Black people by 1780 or about 7 per cent of the Black population. Most of these were in the North. Only 4 per cent of Black people in Virginia were free and under 2 per cent in the Carolinas and Georgia. Given this, it is surprising that any contribution was made, but there was participation by Black Americans in the fighting, certainly on both sides in the support for the armed forces.

Given the relatively big proportion of slaves in some areas, the expectation was that slavery would be important in the outcome of the war. In October 1778, Lord North told George III that the rebellion *'was in a perilous position because of the great number of slaves in proportion to whites'*. Logically, this should have had consequences. With farmers and plantation owners away fighting, the production of food and raw materials might be left in the hands of slave labour without the discipline needed. It might have been expected that there would be runaways or even slave revolts which would have weakened supplies to the Continental Armies and kept many Patriots occupied dealing with unrest or desertions. The fear of loss of slave property might have been an incentive to come to terms with the British. Large numbers of potentially disloyal forced labourers might have been a major source of weakness for the colonists.

Alternatively, if Black labour or even military capacity had been utilised then it might have been expected that the role of Black Americans in the war would have been considerable given the relatively high numbers of the Black population.

In the event, neither of these potential developments actually took place. There was no massive slave rising equivalent to the considerable revolution in Saint Domingue (Haiti) in 1791, even when war disrupted normal discipline and slave owning areas were theatres of war. Though there were many instances of slaves either running away or being confiscated, the overall effects on the economy were not large enough to be a decisive factor in the outcome of the war.

Also, though Black Americans did take part in the actual military operations, this was not on a scale which could be seen as decisive. However, it was greater than is suggested by the absence of coverage of this aspect in many standard narratives, in factional depictions and in the way that the war is generally remembered. Unlike the second of America's civil wars, large scale Black units were not formed and Black and White men fought together. There was too limited enthusiasm to make use of armed Black troops on both sides, which prevented a hugely valuable resource being used in a conflict in which both sides faced problems in bringing enough troops to the battlefield.

The different ways in which Black Americans participated will be considered below as it seems wrong that this should be somewhat hidden from history. However, the most usual way that the Black population and the American Revolution is usually considered is in terms of the effects of the war on slavery and the relationship between the races. The impact of the second civil war and two world wars is usually given more attention, but the Revolutionary War did impact significantly on Black Americans in a way unforeseen by the revolutionary elite who propelled the conflict to protect liberty and property.

The Contribution of Black Americans to the Revolutionary War

Given the relatively limited numbers of Black Americans, either free or slaves, in New England compared with the South, it might be surprising to find that some had had military experience in the militias and in the fighting against the French in the Seven Years War (or the French and Indian Wars). Before his defeat the British General Braddock had written of 'numbers of mulattos [men of mixed race] and free negros' in the force he took to humiliating defeat by Native Americans. In the very first fighting at Lexington and Concord in April 1775, general statements give way to some actual names. A slave named Peter Salem was freed by his owners to fight with the militia against the British. Cato Boardman and Cato Stedman are named in the ranks of militia. One of the first casualties of war was Prince Esterbrook.

Prince Esterbrook was the slave of a farmer and miller, Benjamin Esterbrook, of Lexington and was born there around 1740. He went with his master to fight the English troops on 19 April, along with seventy Minutemen to prevent the seizure of arms. Eight colonists were killed, but both Benjamin and Prince escaped, though Prince was wounded in the shoulder. He remained in the colonial army until 1783 when he was rewarded with his freedom for protracted military service. Though free, he remained with his former owner, working on the farm until 1805. Possibly the bond of having fought together was strong and having worked on the farm until the age of 35, it was difficult for Esterbrook to move anywhere else. He died in 1830. Like the example of Salem Poor, it is difficult to judge how typical this experience was. However, the number of Black Americans who fought for masters and former masters is likely to run into thousands.

There were also Black soldiers in the battle of Bunker Hill. One was commended for bravery so his name survives – Salem Poor. Though not a household name, Poor was the subject of a commemorative 10c stamp with his picture on in 1975. He was an American-born slave who took the surname of his owners, John and Rebecca, in 1747 and worked on a farm in Andover, Massachusetts. Somehow, he was able to raise enough money to buy his freedom in 1769. He married a free woman of African and Native American parents in 1771, who worked as a maid to a White family. In 1775, for reasons unknown and possibly to gain money, Poor enlisted. His force was sent to occupy high ground at Charleston, Massachusetts. In the battle he is supposed to have killed two British officer A militia record recommended him

We declare that a Negro man called Salem Poor of Col. Frye's Regiment, Capt. Ames Company in the late Battle of Charleston, behaved like an experienced officer, as well as an excellent officer, to set forth particulars of his conduct would be tedious. We would only beg leave to say in the person of this Negro centres a brave & gallant Soldier.

He was part of Washington's army at Valley Forge and was discharged in 1780. He sadly appeared in legal records as being ordered to leave Providence Rhode Island with his second wife, and he married a White woman after her death; he died a pauper in 1802. His life challenges some stereotypes of racial attitudes, but it is difficult to say how typical he was. However, his service in an army which did not seem to practise segregation, and commendation for bravery give food for thought.

The degree to which these early fighters for independence have been remembered varies. Cato Boardman gained some posthumous fame when a local historian at Cambridge, Massachusetts, found his hitherto unrecognised grave in a local historical churchyard, but information about Cato and his fellow Black volunteer, Neptune Frost, was limited. Cato was apparently the slave of a Captain Stedman, by whose side he is buried. He fought at Bunker Hill and Stedman freed him. Remarkably he continued in service through most of the war, though was given 100 lashes for stealing a cow before eventual discharge. He was given 100 acres of land in Rhode Island in lieu of back pay but he and his wife could not farm well and he moved back to Cambridge. Most of the information about him derives from local research in 1905.

Cuff Whittemore enters the records because he sold a British officer's sword taken at Bunker Hill – a battle with large numbers of British officer casualties. Massachusetts regimental records contain the names of both free Black people and slaves as well as Native Americans. If this were shown in a modern movie, many might consider this woke and anachronistic, and it raises questions about race relations and attitudes. These had hardened by the time of later wars as segregated regiments were the norm until after the Second World War, but the early burst of revolutionary warfare was multi-racial. The same is seen on the British side when Lord Dunmore, the British Governor of Virginia, was determined to wage war on the rebels and issued a proclamation that '*all indentured servants, negroes and others … should join His Majesty's troops in reducing the colony to a proper sense of its duty*'. Possibly 800 Black Americans took up the offer to gain freedom. Even among Black Americans the conflict had the character of a civil war. When Lord Dunmore fought the rebels at Great Bridge, half of his force of 600 loyalists were Black men.

Gradually enslaved men took part in actual fighting. From 1780, groups of slaves were used in combat alongside British forces, mainly in South Carolina and Georgia. Interestingly over a hundred were used as cavalry in 1782. However, larger scale recruitment, though proposed by the enterprising Dunmore, was rejected by the British military establishment.

The fate of slaves who came under British control was varied. The capture of Charleston led to quite large numbers of Black people being available, so much so that a special commissioner was appointed to deal with their use, recording 5000 Black Americans. A special labour corps built the fortifications at Yorktown and many were used as labourers. There were also some more bizarre deployments as in January 1782, when British officers used female slaves to dress up in rich clothes at an exotic 'Ethiopian ball'.

Generally, as in 1775, smallpox took its toll, many deserted and some were given away to loyalists. One William Mills of South Carolina had lost 57 slaves to Patriots who had plantations and in compensation the British gave him 100 slaves in the winter of 1780.

Amid this bleak and heartless approach, there were instances where the war did give Black participants the opportunity, if that is quite the right word, to make a contribution and there were instances of heroism and leadership. The problem is that legend may have overtaken reality, such as in the story of two Black Americans who were credited with accompanying Washington in the crossing of the Delaware. Their names have been given as Prince Whipple and Oliver Cromwell. The famous painting by the artist, Emanuel Leutze, of 1851 shows them. One is shown rowing near a very powerful looking Washington, posed in a sort of Napoleonic way, standing up and leading the crossing. However in a slightly later painting which is rather less heroic, the crew seem to be White. Whipple and Cromwell, if indeed they were there, have disappeared. The film *The Crossing* (2005), has a rather wooden Jeff Daniels as the great man sitting more sedately in a boat crossing the Delaware, and though evocative mists make it hard to pick out individuals, the two Black soldiers of the 1851 picture seem difficult to find.

Like many individuals, they have been the subject of research and subsequent celebration. Prince Whipple was a slave to the famous General Whipple who signed the Declaration of Independence and was an aide to Washington. There is little evidence that he was actually at the crossing on Christmas Eve 1776.

He was born in Africa but brought to America in 1760 where he worked as a major domo in General Whipple's household and took his name. He was literate enough to petition for freedom with others to New Hampshire's assembly in 1779, without success. Despite military service with the General he was not freed until 1784, though his wife gained freedom in 1781. He served in Saratoga and is credited with being at Trenton. However, the only evidence is in a study of 1855 by a writer called William Nell, in a book called *Coloured Patriots of the American Revolution*. The painting by Leutze includes a Black soldier rowing beside Washington but there is little proof that it was Whipple.

The other solider credited with action in the Crossing was called Oliver Cromwell and he was interviewed by a New Jersey newspaper, *The Burlington Gazette*, in 1852 when he claimed to be 100 years old. He told the reporter that he was born in New Jersey, enlisted in a local regiment and fought at Trenton, Brandywine, Monmouth, and Yorktown when he saw the last man killed in the war. '*His eye brightens at the name of Washington, and in all his conversations he exhibits that deep-seated attachment to his illustrious commander for which all soldiers of the Revolution are celebrated.*' However, somewhat disconcertingly he claimed that he never received a pension! When he applied, he was refused, apparently in an act of mean spiritedness.

A postage stamp of 1976 showing the painting had documentation identifying the two men, but this may rely a lot on the book by Nell produced at a period of considerable abolitionist activity and conflict about slavery with the author wishing, rightly, to praise the efforts of Black Americans in the Revolutionary era.

The artist, Leutze, was aware that there had been Black soldiers in Washington's army but the evidence that the two often named were actually Whipple and Cromwell is inconclusive and this may be typical of attempts to separate myth from reality when assessing individuals. Though it is clear that contemporaries did see Black participation, and in some ways this early stage of the rebellion was one of the most remarkable periods in the history of race relations and had it continued the nature and consequences of the war might have been very different. However, fears about race and property were greater than calculations of military advantage.

Of the body of volunteers who responded to Dunmore's offer, less is celebrated in local memorials or antiquarian research. Most died of smallpox, but there is a record of an attack as the Earl and his hastily gathered forces attacked in the Chesapeake area. At Kemps Landing, Virginia, a small encounter between Dunmore's slaves and a group of White people took place in which the latter were driven away, but a Colonel Hitchins recognised one of his former slaves who had fled to join the British and fired at him. The musket ball went astray, and the man struck Hitchins with a sabre and led him into British captivity.

These early encounters were worrying for the Patriots and there were severe warnings issued to slaves thinking of running away. Washington decided that the dangers of slaves with weapons were greater than being undermanned when fighting the British and forbade the enlistment of Black men. General Gates prohibited any 'negro or vagabond' from being recruited or volunteering. Individual colonies issued ordinances prohibiting the enlistment of both slaves and free Black men. In October 1777, Congress held a meeting about this issue, which Washington attended and along with Benjamin Franklin agreed to stop Black enlistment. The slaves who had been taken from British sympathisers were made to pay for the 'sins' of their owners and some were confiscated and put to work in the deadly lead mines of Virginia. Slaves who were captured fighting for the British were to be sold to the West Indies and likely death in the much harsher conditions of the sugar plantations. Armed men were detailed to patrol farms and plantations to stop runaways.

All this sat uneasily with the noble rhetoric of the Declaration of Independence, but what changed the situation was not so much any belief on either side in Enlightenment values of the rights of man but sheer necessity. The laws against Black recruitment remained in place but were increasingly ignored. Of the million men who might have served in the Continental Army, the total under arms never exceeded 50,000. Washington's force had shrunk to 9000 after the first campaigns, when he was in the bitter conditions of Valley Forge, and by

March 1778, 3000 had deserted. Congress used all sorts of inducements of promises of land and even grants of confiscated slaves to persuade White men to enlist. Washington had to change his policy. In 1778, he had sent officers to ask the Rhode Island Assembly to recruit slaves. Other states followed suit and possibly 5000 Black Americans served in the Continental forces.

The policy of substitution led to some being enlisted. It was not considered a particular disgrace for colonists to pay for a substitute to take their place in military service. This produced some strange practices. One man in New Jersey, a certain Casper Bergen, purchased a slave to take his place. This man was called Samuel Sutphin. A deserter from Washington's army who lived in North Carolina called William Kitchen sent his slave, Ned Griffin, to fight in his place.

The northern states were more open to requests to use slaves. South Carolina and Georgia were asked by Congress to raise '3000 able bodied negro troops from slaves' but refused. Virginia would only allow free Black men to serve, and these were a minority in the South. Even when slaves were soldiers, they sometimes faced demands from their owners or more likely the heirs of owners who had died for their return, often leading to quarrels and legal suits as commanders resisted – not for ideological grounds, but for military reasons.

Typically, Black soldiers were enlisted for longer than White draftees or volunteers – often for three years or the duration of the war. They were not generally segregated but mostly were in the infantry. There were few Black cavalrymen or gunners. Often, they did not actually bear arms but were used for foraging – a vital element in a war where supply was haphazard – or in ancillary duties in camp or in building fortifications. On the British side it was predominantly as support workers, not fighters that runaway slavers or volunteers were first used. On both sides captured slaves were seen as spoils of war and allocated to regiments or individuals in a similar way to captured horses.

In some cases, states bought slaves for use as labour in war production or for road making or fortification. Virginia's Board of Trade used purchased Black labour in arms manufacture. At the end of the war, 'public negroes', as such unfortunate people were called, were sold off at public auctions. With the spread of the war to the South, quite large numbers of slaves fell into British hands. Some entered military service. There were Black troops in many of the major battles and their presence was noted by a Hessian officer:

> *The Negro can take the field instead of the master and no regiment is to be seen in which there are negroes in abundance, able bodied, strong and brave fellows.*

There was more concern on the Continental side about Black recruits. It seemed safer to many state authorities to have Black seamen than soldiers. Though few African Americans had been trained soldiers, more had served on ships. Many American ships had a mixed crew and there were instances of slaves taking responsibility. In his memoirs, US Navy Commodore James Barron, who served as a captain in the Virginia Navy during the war, recalled several Black men among the crews who took part in engagements. Caesar, the slave of the Virginian Carter Terront, was an eminent pilot in the Chesapeake area on the vessel *Patriot*, and his services were valued enough for his daughter to be granted 2667 acres of land in Ohio after the war. Remarkably the pilot, Mark Starlin, was virtually in charge and known as 'captain of a ship' which attacked British vessels successfully at Hampton Roads. But Virginia being Virginia, he was reclaimed by his master after the war. One of the most famous Black seamen was James Forten, who had spent time on a British prison barge before being released in a prisoner exchange. Forten went on to become a successful businessman. On the other side, a slave called Thomas plotted a pro-British insurrection in Charleston and was burned to death as a punishment. Many British ships used Black pilots and perhaps a quarter of those who escaped to British lines ended up working on ships, some acting as commerce raiders known as 'banditti'. Most Black seamen were used in lowly capacities, but one picture[1] shows a Black officer with sword and fine uniform. Though this image has been widely used to show that the war did allow Black servicemen to rise in the ranks and take command, it is sadly problematic. *The New York Times* has revealed that the painting has been painted over and was originally of a White officer.

The largest force of Black troops in the war was probably the contingent used by the French general in the siege of Savannah in 1779, when D'Estaing massed 545 Black soldiers from Saint Domingue out of a total of 3600. However, though slavery was not legal in France itself, it certainly was in the West Indies colonies so French officers were as keen as loyalists, Patriots and British commanders to take their share of slaves as plunder of war.

Enslaved people were also used as spies and to gather information as they were often seen as too lowly to be noticed and were almost invisible. Both sides took advantage of this and gained information deriving from prejudice and disdain. In late 1780, there is a record of a British officer, Lord Rawdon, writing to Cornwallis 'a negro asserts that a party of rebel cavalry lay last night twenty five miles from here'. The dashing and unscrupulous Banastre Tarleton made extensive use of Black spies and sometimes spying led to more developed activities. A slave named Tye led a crew of twenty-five men who raided rebel homes in New Jersey, kidnapping and plundering until killed during a raid. On the American side, a slave called Pompey found out the British password and helped colonial forces, under General Wayne, take Stoney Point, New York in 1779. James Armistead was a successful double agent, sent by Lafayette to spy on Cornwallis's camp. The British persuaded him to spy for them and he carried false information to the British.

It is obvious from the above that circumstances did not lend themselves to Black troops having a very decisive effect on the war, and poor organisation, disease and desertion probably lessened the impact of slave workers on supply and fortifications. However, it may well be surprising that the contribution of many individuals is known about, if not particularly celebrated.

It may be more pertinent to look not so much at the effect of Black Americans on the war as to the effect of the war on Black Americans.

On the face of it, there was every expectation that the war would have a profound effect on the situation of Black Americans. Disputes about taxes and land were elevated to a different level by the rhetoric of liberty and rights. If the war was fought on the premise that 'all men were created equal', then surely the outcome might deliver that aspiration. It might make White colonial America reflect that slavery was compatible with the noble ideas that had motivated resistance. In building a new country, would slavery have a place or was it, as Jefferson had said, an imposition by a wicked British king and so be brought to an end when that king no longer ruled? In addition, the noble cause had been adopted by French idealists and even free Black citizens from Haiti, so the new Republic's international standing would surely requite fulfilling its ideas of liberty as seen by foreign nations. The contribution of slaves and free Black men, too, would surely carry weight. Some had taken up the cause of liberty willingly. Some had served for a long period in the Continental Armies. Some had been with Washington at Trenton, had been at Saratoga, and had fought at Yorktown. In addition, even before the war, there had been questioning of the morality of both the slave trade and slavery. Racial stereotypes had been challenged by some eminent Black Americans and there had been some significant legal decisions which had undermined slavery.

Many historical studies have suggested that the war accelerated change. The historian Peter Kolchin[2] makes the point that in the Revolutionary era 'the questioning of slavery … represented a significant departure'. It has been claimed that 'thousands were freed by slaveholders under the spell of the magic of the Declaration of Independence'. Certainly, there were many instances of a direct link. Philp Graham of Maryland freed his slaves in 1787, writing that slavery was not only repugnant to the laws of God but 'to every principle of the late glorious revolution', and it was increasingly common after 1782 for slaves to be freed in wills.

Sometimes there seemed limited appetite for change even when there had been opportunity to flee. Fanny Tucker of Farmville Virginia, reduced to working the farm while her husband was away, was faced with a large British force in the vicinity in 1781 to which her slaves could easily have fled. However, she wrote that none had deserted her. One feature of the war was that many slaves had greater autonomy and closer bonds to their owners, but also flight was dangerous if British forces decided to sell them or use them as forced labour. However, one colonial leader, General Moultrie, recorded that when he returned to his estate in South Carolina in September 1782 '*Everyone took me by the hand and said "God Bless you master". I then possessed two hundred slaves and not one left me*'.

Before too rosy a picture emerges, it is important to note that property owners took considerable pains to prevent slaves leaving with guards, roll calls, searches, and checks on ships on rivers and coasts. In extreme cases, harsh punishments and even executions for runaways were a feature of post-war America in some areas.

However, there was some change. Prior to the war there had been legal cases brought by individuals or groups challenging the right of slave owners to hold them in bondage. These had been mostly in the North and they achieved a surprising amount of success. This continued into the wartime period and a case which might merit the importance given to later legal decisions was the Quock Walker case, bought in 1781 and finally decided in 1783.

This case is much less famous than subsequent legal decisions involving slavery or segregation and may be worth considering as a development of the Revolutionary era. Quock, born in 1753, was a slave of Ghanaian descent. His name was adapted from Kwaku and his parents belonged to a family called Caldwell from Worcester, Massachusetts. The family promised to free him at age 25 but James Caldwell died and his wife remarried. Her husband, Nathaniel Jennison, refused to honour this promise when Mrs Caldwell died in 1772. When Quock was 25 and still a slave, he ran away to a nearby farm owned by James Caldwell's brothers. Jennison found him there and beat him badly. Supported by the Caldwell family, Quock sued Jennison for assault. Jennison argued that the Caldwells had enticed Quock away and deprived him of his rightful property and was awarded damages of £25 by a local court. But Seth and John Caldwell's lawyers, in a later criminal trial, claimed that the Massachusetts Constitution of 1780, followed the US Declaration of Independence in stating that '*All men are born freer and equal and have certain natural, essential and unalienable rights. Among which may be reckoned the right of enjoying and defending their rights and liberty*'. The jury granted Quock freedom and £50. Attorney General Cushing pursued a case of assault against Jennison. His statement virtually ended slavery in Massachusetts and is worth quoting:

> *I think the idea of slavery is inconsistent with our own conduct and Constitution; and there can be no such thing as perpetual servitude of a rational creature, unless his liberty is forfeited by some criminal conduct or given up by personal consent.*

By 1790 there were no slaves in Massachusetts. Unlike the more famous legal cases, like Brown versus Topeka Board of Education in the 1950s, the decision was not imposed on an unwilling population as both public feeling and economic change had led to a consensus against it, but the case deserves greater consideration than it often receives Walker married and had children but the date of his death, sometime before 1810, is not known and after the case he fell into obscurity though is honoured in Massachusetts in a special Quock Walker Day established in 2022.

In addition, the period after the end of the war saw a significant rise in the free Black population – 8 per cent of the Black population to 13 per cent. This was mainly in the North but numbers also rose in Virginia. In 1790 there were roughly 60,000, but by 1810 this had risen to over 186,000. There was a decline in the slave population in the war through flight or disease – South Carolina lost 25,000 or a third of its slave population between 1775 and 1790.

After the war there were moves in the North to end slavery and websites and text books rightly say that by 1817 every northern and western state had committed itself to a life without slavery. In 1787, Congress's North Western ordinance barred slavery from the new territories in that region.

All this feeds into a view of the war as an instrument of change and reform. However, like other reforms fought for idealistic motives and 'liberty' the results were mixed. The second civil war gave slaves emancipation, but for years to come they faced a pseudo slavery in share cropping and unrelieved discrimination and unpunished violence.

So, it is not surprising that there was a gap between the aspirations to liberty of the Revolutionary era and the actual outcome for Black Americans. In the immediate aftermath, the new state had to deal with the considerable disruption caused by war and the movement of slaves. Thousands had fled; thousands had been taken from owners; thousands had become spoils of war. Washington was anxious that Black Americans taken by French or British forces or by American officers should be returned. He made provision for them to be guarded by troops of the Continental Army, not to be freed. Not only was this a likely threat to public order, but it was also a matter of individuals being able to regain their legitimate property. Washington had no intention of relinquishing his own slaves and though he freed them in his will, he kept them for his lifetime. In the event, the British took away large numbers of slaves. In July 1782, for example, 1568 were taken to Jamaica. The evacuations were considerable – 6000 were taken from Charleston; 4000 from New York; 4000 from Savannah. The Black population of Jamaica increased dramatically, and other destinations were St Lucia, East Florida and some to Britain. France took numbers to Saint Dominque and Guadeloupe. There were also migrations to

Canada. The evacuations were mostly able-bodied – older, sicker and helpless people were left behind. Some wanted to go fearing a return of previous masters or reprisals; some were forced. Some ended as slaves, some as indentured labour and some were able to start a new life. James Derham ended up as the property of a British Army surgeon who sold him to a French doctor in New Orleans. He was able to gain his freedom and used his medical knowledge to set up a famous practice in Philadelphia. Others died as smallpox raged on board ship and in crowded accommodation in new destinations. Many ended up in West Indies plantations. Those who went to Canada alongside loyalist exiles tried to settle in Nova Scotia, but little was done to help them and nearly 1200 were part of a repatriation scheme to settle in Sierra Leone. Sixty-five died but the survivors did set up Freetown in 1782. Slaves taken from loyalists were generally freed in New England but not in the South. Virginia sold them alongside the 'public slaves' who had helped with war work. Virginia tried hard to overturn grants of freedom made to Black people who had served the cause of freedom. Washington turned down a plan by his French ally, Lafayette, to settle former slaves on unoccupied frontier land.

What of changes made by individual states in the new constitutions adopted during the struggle for independence? In fact, for all the talk of liberty, only Massachusetts ended slavery outright and that as a result of court decisions by 1783, not by passing a specific act of liberation. Most states in the North followed the example pf Pennsylvania in 1780 and went for gradual emancipation. Pennsylvania passed a law in 1780 that declared all slaves born after its passing to be free. Existing children would be free on their twenty-eighth birthday. Existing slaves were sill property and could be bought and sold. New Hampshire, Connecticut and Rhode Island followed suit in the 1780s. It took New Jersey until 1804 and New York until 1817. New Jersey still had 236 slaves by 1850, though usually seen as a 'free state'. As there were relatively small numbers of slaves in the North and as they were not very economically significant, it was not too difficult to accept the end of slavery which, with the decline in the tobacco trade, had lost much of its economic importance. The South, though, stood resolutely against emancipation and as cotton became increasingly profitable from the late 1790s, worked hard to replenish its stock of slaves and to use its influence to maintain slavery. The war's main effect seemed to be to reinvigorate a belief in slavery for all the contradictions with ideals of liberty, not to weaken it.

It was southern pressure that ensured that there was no official nationwide abolition of the slave trade until 1807 – twenty years after the new United States Constitution was drawn up, and also that slavery was written into the Constitution. The representation of states in Congress was a compromise between the larger and smaller. In the Senate, each state had two members regardless of size, but in the lower house – the House of Representatives —membership depended on population. But what about slaves? In the end it was decided that each slave should count as 3/5 of a free man for the purposes of computing how many representatives would be elected. By doing that, the framers of the Constitution had accepted the legal status of slavery. As cotton as a major cash crop grew, and the territory of the US grew, so did slavery. By 1860 there were four million slaves.

Whatever else the Revolutionary War had bought, it had not brought the universal freedom of the Declaration of Independence throughout the new states.

A popular patriotic song of the 1790s, written by Charlotte Rowson, expresses the pride of the new USA as sailors long for their American home:

> *When tempests howl along the main,*
> *Some object will remind us,*
> *And cheer with hopes to meet again thos friends we've left behind us.*
> *Then under snug sail, we laugh at the gale, and tho' landsmen look pale, never*
>   *heed 'em,*
> *But toss off a glass to a favourite lass, To America, Commerce, and Freedom.*

The problem was that commerce and freedom were not always compatible.

Note

1. https://thefoundingproject.com/who-black-patriots/
2. Peter Kolchin, *American Slavery, 1619–1877*, Penguin Books, 2003.

Chapter 9

The American Revolution and the Native Americans

The story of the involvement of the indigenous peoples in the Revolution is a sad and uninspiring one. However, in the history of the US it is also important and does not get due attention in many accounts of the Revolutionary War. Big books about the Revolution have not always given much consideration to the Indian contribution. A standard work on the Revolution devotes 7 pages out of 685 to this aspect, and even studies of the Indigenous peoples seem more anxious to get onto the nineteenth-century massacres and wars.

The American Declaration of Independence gave short shrift to the indigenous peoples and propagated the idea of them simply as savages. In listing the iniquities of George III, this was included:

He has excited domestic insurrections amongst us, and has endeavoured to bring on the inhabitants of our frontiers, the merciless Indian savages, whose known rule of warfare is an undistinguished destruction of all ages, sexes, and conditions.

Relations with the 'merciless Indian savages' had been far more complex than colonists defending themselves against attacks. In the French and Indian War, the Europeans had negotiated for Indian support with a well-developed confederation of Native Americans. There were important trade links. When the 'savages' came to Philadelphia, rooms were set aside in Independence Hall for them. Since the beginning of British colonisation, there had been all sorts of links established. Disney lovers will know the story of Pocohontas, brought to London as the wife of a leading settler. The pro-British Iroquois leader, Joseph Brant, was educated in English-speaking schools and visited England not as some sort of curiosity but as a friend and ally of Britain. One of the most prominent leaders of the Cherokees was a chief called 'Little Carpenter'. He arranged for his niece, Nanyeh, to marry an American trader called Brian Wade, with whom she had a child. She became known as Nancy Wade. This was a diplomatic marriage to improve relations between the Indians and the settlers. Eventually Wade returned to his English wife, but Nancy visited him on amicable terms.

This incident helped to save the life of a woman called Mrs William Bean who had been captured by a Cherokee raiding party in 1776. Their intention was to burn her to death but Nancy Wade, eager to make peace between Cherokees and colonists, used her standing in the councils of the Cherokee to secure her release. Frontier America was a complex place in the late eighteenth century. The Chickasaw people allied with the British against the Patriots under the influence of a merchant called James Logan Colbert, who had settled among the Indians and married a number of prominent women, by whom he had two sons who were important in the councils of the Indigenous people, even though they were not full Indians. Colbert's father had traded with the Chickasaws and when his wife died, he took his son to live among them. He too traded in weapons and established a farm with slaves. He married three Chickasaw wives, one of whom was prominent in the Chickasaw nation. It was though her that he and his sons exerted authority. Logan persuaded most of the Chickasaws to support Britain, though his kin's influence as the inheritance traditions were through the mother and not the father. The Chickasaws were divided between Logan's pro-British faction, supported by his extended family and by neighbours and allies, and a pro-Spanish group. Spain had joined the war against the British in 1779 and Chickasaw patrols attacked Spanish shipping. The Indian fighters were active along the rivers and harassed Spanish vessels sailing down the Mississippi. Another White man of Scots descent was a British Army officer, Alexander Cameron, who was appointed to negotiate with the Cherokees and lived with them for fifteen years, marrying and having three children. He was a strong influence and a military leader accepted by the Indians whose lifestyle he adopted.

The wars between France and Britain had involved complex diplomacy to win over the Native Americans who had become adept at playing off the rival Europeans. At the heart of the struggle between France and Britain lay the lands of the Iroquois Confederation. They lived in the key Northwest Territory. When the war with Britain broke out they were between British held Canada and New York. In theory, their support was vital. They seemed to be strong because of the unusual alliance between the six major tribes which went back to the sixteenth century. They had a sound economic basis in their farming settlements and towns. They had links with the Europeans in trade. Their fighting abilities were shown in the spectacular defeat of a British force in 1754 with the death of General Braddock, something Washington witnessed firsthand in a battle which he was lucky to have survived.

The Iroquois Confederation was a remarkable example of long-standing, political cooperation comprising the Mohawks, Oneidas, Onondagas, Coyugas, Senecas and from 1722 the Tuscaroras. It dominated its western neighbours, the so-called Delawares and the Shawnees, and had even given away their lands in a treaty of 1768 without their approval. The Iroquois were a mixture of sophisticated diplomats, farmers and hunters; they were a socially advanced people who gave women a say in policy in a way unknown in Europe, and inclusiveness. They accepted leaders from European backgrounds and allowed other people's acceptance into their community.

One of the most remarkable accounts of their life was by a European woman called Mary Jemison who had married into the tribe. From a family of Northern Irish immigrants, she was captured by a party of Seneca Indians and French troops on the Pennsylvania frontier in 1755. Her family were killed and scalped and, in her book *The Narrative of the Life of Mary Jemison*, published in 1824 and the result of giving a description to a clergymen, she describes her arrival at the Indian village.

> *Having put the scalps, yet wet and bloody, upon the hoops, and stretched them to their full extent, they held them to the fire till they were partly dried, and then, with their knives, commenced scraping off the flesh; and in that way they continued to work, alternately drying and scraping them, till they were dry and clean. That being done, they combed the hair in the neatest manner, and then painted it and the edges of the scalps, yet on the hoops, red. Those scalps I knew at the time must have been taken from our poor family, by the color of the hair. My mother's hair was red; and I could easily distinguish my father's and the children's and babies from each other. That sight was most appalling and horrifying; yet I was obliged to endure it without complaining. In the course of the night, they made me to understand that they should not have killed the family, if the whites had not pursued them.*

Mary Jemison lived with the Seneca and married one of the men in the Indian village. When he died on a journey to upper New York she married another native American and had seven children, becoming quite an influential figure. Unlike the young girl kidnapped by Apaches in John Ford's movie *The Searchers*, no John Wayne figure came looking for her and she did not try to escape. One of the features of frontier life was an acceptance of hardship and the necessity of adopting different lifestyles.

A key Iroquois figure, Joseph Brant, of whom more later, was part of the family circle of the British Indian commissioner Sir William Johnson, who married Brant's sister, Mollie. This was not looked on with disapproval by the Mohawks and was part of the social and economic links that the Iroquois had with their European neighbours. So far, so liberal and encouraging. However, a major element in the life of the Iroquois, and to a greater or lesser extent of the other indigenous peoples, was the warrior ethos. There was no contradiction in their outlook and culture between peaceful agriculture, women's rights, accepting Christianity, conducting treaty negotiations and extreme violence. Warriors were trained to attack their enemies fiercely, to rob and scalp victims, to carry off captives who would either be made part of the community or horribly tortured and killed. Their role as military allies was severely limited by this style of warfare. Their troops were relatively lightly armed, moved swiftly and secretly, and attacked quickly and ruthlessly. They were, in military terms, irregular light infantry. However, they had little concept of defensive warfare or the type of ordered group fighting that was needed against larger organised forces. They also could not withstand sustained firepower, nor did they maintain their formations but tended to move away from dangerous situations. Adept as scouts and in ambushes and raids, they were not generally of great military value and could not muster very large forces. They were also, as they themselves made clear, not able to fight in a European manner or be bound by any European conventions about rules of war and treatment of prisoners. More important, perhaps, was the lack of commitment which made loyalty precarious. Many fought for pay, for gifts or because of family links. They also made decisions based on the best way to secure their lands, hunting grounds and sacred sites. In this respect they were not very different from many of their American opponents. Frontiersmen were not moved by tea duties or Lockeian concepts of representative government. They had moved to the frontier area to have the freedom to gain land and live an independent existence. There was probably more affinity between the Indigenous people of the frontier and their settler or militia opponents than between the colonial frontiersmen and the lawyers, merchants, planters and intellectuals of the American Revolution.

It is not surprising that the American War of Independence, which involved the Native Americans, was of a somewhat different nature than the war fought by Washington and the main Continental Army against the British.

The Indian communities had little to gain from the War of Independence and everything to lose. The whole ideology of resistance to foreign rule and freedom from taxes and controls had little relevance. The colonisation of America had seen pressure put on their lands and resources. The westward expansion of colonies was a threat and treaties made with both British and Colonial authorities proved unreliable. Whatever the outcome, the future was uncertain. If British authority had been restored, it would have been unlikely that in the long run the pressure for White expansion could have been resisted. If the Colonists won, then the floodgates would be opened. Commitment to the losing side would bring punishment.

Neutrality was probably the least hazardous option, but there were some who supported the Colonial cause. The most famous examples are the Stockbridge

Indians and the Catawba Nation in South Carolina. Neither was numerous and neither made any very significant contribution to the outcome of the war.

The experience of the Munsee and Mohican fighters sums up the plight of Indians. During the Severn Years' War members of these groups had served as scouts and supporters of the British Army fighting the French. Despite this, they lost rights to their lands in the Hudson Valley after the war. This resentment against the British authorities led them to volunteer for the colonists and some fought at Bunker Hill and Saratoga. By 1778, around sixty soldiers formed a well-thought of light infantry company defending the New York region. They were caught in an ambush by Hessian and loyalist troops in August 1778 and there was a massacre in what is now the Bronx area of New York with the loss of over forty men. There was little reward for the sacrifice and the Munssee people were stripped of their lands and forcibly removed.

The American authorities were more generous to the Catawbas. These people lived in the Piedmont area of the Carolinas and were noted as ferocious warriors, employed by the British during the Seven Years War and in operations against hostile tribes. When the War of Independence broke out there were not many more than 1000 Catawbas because a ferocious smallpox epidemic had killed many. They supported the Colonists, perhaps because they had little choice given the prevailing Patriot allegiance of the areas around them, perhaps for rewards or perhaps out of some loyalty to their neighbours. They were skilled rifleman who fought with the Patriots defending Charleston. They were active in partisan warfare against loyalists and in hunting down escaped slaves, something they excelled in and continued after the war. They did take part in more regular conflicts in Georgia in 1779 and in North Carolina where they fought in the battle of Guilford Courthouse.

Though they kept their settlements until South Carolina took over their lands in 1840, and did get some support when a British expedition in 1780 destroyed much of their homeland, their immediate rewards were limited. One of their soldiers petitioned in 1822:

> *I fought the British for your sake. The British have disappeared, nor have I gained by their defeat. I pursue deer for subsistence; the deer are disappearing, and I must starve.... The hand which fought the British for your liberty is now open for your relief. In my youth I bled in battle that you might be independent; let not my heart in my old age bleed for the want of your commiseration.*

However, this small and militaristic ethnic group showed surprising loyalty to the White South. They fought in the war of 1812, the Mexican War of 1848 and for the Confederacy in the civil war in 1861. Their role as slave hunters and owners is rather passed over in accounts which attempt to show the love of liberty by the Indians who supported the colonial cause. In the long run, those who joined the colonists achieved little more for their efforts than those who were either neutral or took the more logical position of supporting the British. At the end of the war, the British simply handed over all the western lands to the new Republic. But even at the start of the war, Britain did not have the resources in Canada and the west to offer much in the way of support for any Indians who allied with them. In their turn, the Indians could not offer much in the way of military support in sustained campaigns. The way of fighting and the attacks on colonial settlements had an adverse effect on loyalist support and gave the colonists material for propaganda against British cruelty.

The Cherokees in the South, with possibly a population of 10,000, were more numerous than the Catawbas and were initially neutral but they had come under pressure from colonial expansion and were persuaded by emissaries from the Iroquois to support Britain. The Cherokees of the Southeast had been protected from colonial expansion into territories taken from France in 1763 by the so-called proclamation line. But it was difficult to stop incursions and the largest was at Watuga (now Elizabethton, Tennessee). In 1774, a strange incident occurred when a North Carolina businessman named Henderson negotiated a treaty at Sycamore Shoals with a Cherokee noble, who had no right to speak for his people, from which huge areas were ceded making up modern day Kentucky and much of Tennessee. The Watuga settlement was declared illegal by the British colonial authorities, but the settlers remained and naturally supported the cause of independence. The new governments after 1775 supported them, and even as the war against Britain raged, more setters entered Indian territory. There was not a united Cherokee nation, only various settlements, groups and leaders. The most forceful leader was Dragging Canoe who argued for war, rightly foreseeing that the Cherokee 'once so great and formidable will be compelled to seek refuge in some distant wilderness'. The war he supported ran parallel to the War of Independence and continued into the 1790s. Too late the colonists attempted to win over the Cherokees. In May 1776, the British attempted to bring about a confederation of Indian nations, though a concerted strategy did not come about. Dragging Canoe planned attacks on Virginia and North Carolina from one force; another assault on North Carolina and a third on South Carolina and Georgia. The aim was to take colonial forts and attack settlements. These were not major engagements. At a fort called Easton's Station, a force of 170 militia repelled the attack in some ferocious fighting. The response was brutal with the destruction of fifty Cherokee towns, the burning of crops, massacres and enslavement of prisoners.

The leading chief, Little Carpenter, and his niece, Nancy Ward, attempted to end the conflict.

Nancy Ward or Beloved Woman shows a number of interesting aspects of colonial life. First, the links between Native Americans and colonists as her second husband was a White trader. Secondly the role of women in some Indian societies. She was the Head of the Council of Women who were entitled to take part in the decision making of the Council of Chiefs. The opponents of the Americans' struggle for liberty had more equal societies in terms of the rights of women and tolerance for outsiders. They faced, in the freedom-loving colonists, a campaign which was not far off genocide and a land grab of five million acres. Though the war had come to an end by May 1777 officially, the more militant Cherokee faction called Chickamauga continued to fight the colonists in Georgia for twenty years. Nancy Ward had a continued influenced on the Cherokee, whose population and lands were seriously reduced by the war she had opposed. However, one of the innovations was the introduction of slaveholding as well as other aspects of White colonial agriculture.

However, the main theatre of what is often called 'the frontier' war was in the North in the Pennsylvania border area and Upper New York. Here was a war of attacks on homesteads and counter attacks on Indian settlements, or massacres and scorched earth. There was one set piece battle of any significance at Newton and some Indian assistance to the campaign of Burgoyne which ended at Saratoga. It saw one of the best-funded, sustained campaigns by a colonial force in the war which has been described earlier, and which demonstrated a new brutality in the mainstream of the war as opposed to the militia campaigns further south. The crucial decision was that taken by the Iroquois Confederacy

For motives which may be difficult to get to, given the evidence available, an educated and well-travelled leader, Joseph Brant, led a movement to war which resulted in ruthless raiding and largely pointless slaughter, which provoked bitter reaction among the colonial forces. Importantly large numbers of indigenous people found themselves on the losing side and subject to the vengeance of their enemies. The British found their allies more of an encumbrance and they achieved little of military significance. Unable to control the way their allies fought, the reputation of the British was badly affected and both they and their White Tory allies, who fought alongside the Indians, became brutalised and tainted with what we would now call war crimes. The colonists were drawn into racial massacres and wasting resources on unsuccessful, if destructive, scorched earth campaigns. As horrific massacres could be blamed on the British and justified by accounts of torture, scalping and mutilation, the reputational effect on the Americans was more limited. There was also wholesale seizure of land after the war had ended – and the Indian campaigns went on longer than the war with Britain. The war was the prelude to decades of conflict, which has left the expansion of the west – a massive achievement – with an indelible moral stain.

Thus, the decisions made in the early part of the war are a turning point in American history and the key figure of Joseph Brant is worth looking at. The difficulties of separating myth from reality are shown very clearly by attempting to get the truth about this man. Few other Indian leaders were as famous – though he does not always get much consideration. The historian, Robert Harvey, has 568 pages on the war in his widely read study *A Few Bloody Noses* (2004), but Brant does not appear in the index. However, there is a town in Canada named after him; there is a statue in Ottawa; and there are no less than nineteen portraits of him, including one by the famous portraitist George Romney. The documentation of his life is considerable, and he was the subject of a two-volume biography by an American historian in 1838, using a variety of contemporary memoirs. Also, there was a feature film made of part of his life which might be a starting point as it shows that views of the Revolution have moved on. In *Divided Loyalties*, a 1990 movie directed by Mario Azzopardi, Brant is shown first as a leading adviser of the British Indian commissioner Sir William Johnson in 1768. Brant's sister, Molly, was Johnson's wife. The movie shows the Americans as racialist and intolerant. The British are shown as stupid and class ridden when Brant goes to London. Brant is shown as a noble figure, who is driven to support war against the Americans when his home is burnt and colonists seize the home of the Johnson family. He urges the Iroquois leaders to fight but is expelled by those who wish for peace. He gathers a force and ambushes and defeats a colonial army. In another council scene he persuades more leaders to back war but muses on splitting the Confederation. In an attack on Cherry Valley, Brant loses control to a violent and psychopathic Tory officer, Butler, and is horrified when there is a massacre by his fellow Indians. Washington is shown as an unsympathetic figure ordering a punitive expedition by Sullivan, and we see fire and slaughter. Bedraggled Iroquois gather at Fort Niagara in 1781 and Brant faces the anger of his son. When news comes of a British surrender, Brant finds kindness from the British Governor in Canada and the Iroquois exiles establish a new life at Grand River Valley. A scene set in 1792 again shows Washington negatively trying to use Brant to negotiate a peace which will allow for American expansion. Generally, Brant is shown as a noble character eager for the best for his people – driven to violence but recoiling at slaughter. The movie has a rather dour view of the Revolution, and the search for a flawed hero is a long way from the celebratory view taken by many. This is not the vision of the Revolution of the inaugural speech of Donald Trump in January 2025 in his brief vision of American history:

Our American ancestors turned a small group of colonies on the edge of a vast continent into a mighty republic of the most extraordinary citizens on Earth. No one comes close. Americans pushed thousands of miles through a rugged land of untamed wilderness. They crossed deserts, scaled mountains, braved untold dangers, won the Wild West, ended slavery, rescued millions from tyranny.

Contemporary American sources referred to Brant as a 'monster', not the heroic figure, and his first biographer in 1838 takes great care to separate him from the blood-soaked raids which partly provoked Washington's decision to lay waste the Iroquois lands in 1779. There are stories which portray a sort of Robin Hood figure, saving a pregnant mother, sparing a freemason, showing loyalty to the father figures of George III and the Johnson family.

Brant's Mohawk name was Thavenendangea. What the movie does not show is that this ambitious and personable man owed a lot to women. Molly Brant was a key figure in the Wolf Clan as well as having the marriage to the British official, Johnson. His second wife who was part Mohawk and part Irish was an authority in the Turtle Clan. His vanity and ambition are shown in the nineteen portraits that he sat for. The graceful and dignified figure depicted in the movie does not have this personal desire for renown. Brant was not a major chief and he did not have the authority to push the six nations into war. This decision was taken in his absence in a war council in July 1777 which divided the nations and split the Confederation. Initially he commanded a small force and his raids, which caused a considerable amount of damage, were conducted with under 400 men at most. His one direct encounter with colonial forces, as part of the Saratoga campaign, ended with an indecisive result and sixty Iroquois dead – something regarded by the people as a disaster even if colonial losses were higher. He did not take part in the massacre which earned him the name 'Monster Brant' but was present at the Cherry Valley massacre. There is no completely decisive evidence of his being personally bloodthirsty, but the guerrilla warfare he waged on the frontier did involve killing and widespread destruction. The guerrilla activity at German Flatts was considered particularly shocking. And it was partly this that led to punitive action by Washington. (This is described in Chapter 5.) Both sides, therefore, engaged in ruthless economic warfare with limited military results. Brant was raiding again in 1780. No amount of attacks on isolated colonial frontier settlements could ensure British victory in what became a world war.

He gained the confidence of the British commander in Canada who was of Swiss origin, and he did get money and supplies. The results of plunder were the acquisition of a large estate in the region of Fort Niagara and the use of slave labour, including the purchase of a 7-year-old called Sophia Pooley whom he subsequently sold after some years of service. This is not featured in the movie.

It has been argued that he was more influential as a leader after the war. He had been ambitious as a young man, but it was in Canadian exile that he enjoyed influence and an opulent lifestyle, with slave labour and the trappings of an elaborate type of mansion. Again this is not shown. Myths remain persuasive even for those who seek to escape the traditional depiction of a revolution which was a 'glorious cause'.

The Iroquois chief Cornplanter, half Indian and half Dutch, who reluctantly accepted the decision to go to war in 1777, led his forces with the rank of captain in the British Army and then, to avoid further punishment and destruction by Washington's forces, made peace in 1790, is a less celebrated but more typical figure, caught between a reluctance to commit to the war and the demands of other leaders. He did not have the ambition of Brant and did not emerge as either such an object of hatred or as the subsequent folk hero. Like so much about the American Revolution, myth has replaced reality.

The groups of Native Americans known as the Delawares, though more accurately the Lenni Lenape and the Shawnee, lived in the upper Ohio Valley. They had moved to get away from their traditional enemies, the Iroquois. In 1768 the Iroquois had made a treaty with the British in which the six nations had ceded lands which did not actually belong to them to Britain in return for protection from westward White settlement. That land was considered by the Delaware their own, though as with most native Americans there was no actual concept of ownership – it was land that they simply used by custom. The Shawnee objected to losing land on which they traditionally hunted. When the war began, both Britain and the Americans tried to get the support of these disposed peoples. Initially both the Delaware leader, White Eyes, and the Delaware leader, Cornstalk, agreed to stay neutral and live in peace. They had been betrayed by the British in alliance with their enemies the Iroquois, but also resented ongoing encroachments by the colonists. The prospects were not very promising but there was the possibility of using the need of their enemies for support that might have encouraged their leaders to think they might take advantage of their potential bargaining power.

This policy was put under pressure from more radical younger leaders and also from neighbouring peoples who were more anxious to fight against the colonists and hope for a British victory to stop encroachment. The Mingo warriors, the neighbours of the Delawares, had raided colonial settlements in Kentucky in 1776. They were joined by some Shawnee and Delaware fighters in attacking the towns of Wheeling and Boonesborough in 1777. The border violence that was customary seemed likely to lead to a full-scale war as Virginia began preparing for a major campaign against the Mingo. The danger that this would lead to an end to the neutrality of the Delaware led to Congress intervening and requesting that the invasion be held up. However, Congress was not strong enough to control the desire of the 'men on the spot' for a war. Settlers began attacks on the Mingo and a local colonial commander, Edward Hand, gathered a force of some 2000 men for a large-scale attack on them. There was still a desire among the Shawnee to maintain peace and they sent two delegates to negotiate with the Americans at Fort Randolph. The commander there decided to hold them as hostages. Cornstalk himself went to negotiate their release. He and his son were also imprisoned. The violence of the frontier made negotiation impossible. A group of Mingos had ambushed a group of colonists and their friends in revenge and shot and killed the four captives in cold blood.

The murder of Cornstalk has given rise to myths and fantasies. He was buried in the grounds of Fort Pleasant, but his body was moved in 1840 and was again reburied in the 1950s, or what little was left of his remains. He rests in a park in Point Pleasant, West Virginia, but legends talk of a curse he made before his death which was protracted as he was shot multiple times. A mysterious 'mothman' is reputed to haunt the area and there have been an unusually large number of accidents which have been attributed by lovers of paranormal happenings to the curse of the chief. No contemporary evidence exists of his making a curse.

This violent incident pushed the Shawnee to join the Mingos and the western tribes, the Miami, Wyandot, Chippewa, Ottawa and Kickapoo, in fighting against the Americans in alliance with Britain. Groups of Shawnee raided settlements and took prisoners. Irregular forces of volunteers from Virginia hastened to the frontier to retaliate. Edward Hand's expedition finally got under way but achieved little and was notorious for the murder of some Delaware women. This 'squaw campaign' was not enough to move the Delaware from keeping the peace and White Eyes signed a treaty at Fort Pitt in 1778, in which the Americans guaranteed the Indians territorial rights. This had the possibility of a separate Indian state. This was an interesting might have been of history, but it was more a reflection of the naivety of the Delaware leaders than a reality. Congress had no intention of creating a fourteenth state and the colonists began to insist that the warriors become part of the Continental Army. Like Cornplanter, White Eyes was murdered by White settlers and his death covered up,

In 1779, the successor, Killbuck, led a delegation to Philadelphia to meet Congress in search of clothing and supplies as a sign of friendship, but by this time other Indians were mocking the Delaware as cowards and it was clear that the treaty meant little. The Delaware leaders were divided but the war faction won and Killbuck was forced to flee to safety at the American stronghold of Fort Pitt. The Delaware town of Coshocton was attacked by a force of 300

Pennsylvania militia and Delaware dissidents but had been largely evacuated. The troops killed and scalped the fifteen defenders and in an act of racial violence fired on Christian Delawares who were living at a nearby Moravian mission.

Once again this brought reprisals and Delaware and Shawnee warriors raided Christian missions which they thought were spying for the colonists and forcibly removed the Christianised Indians as well as attacking isolated settlements and scalping and kidnapping settlers. Again, reprisals followed in a raid led by Colonel David Williamson, which murdered over ninety men women and children at Gnadenhutten in March 1782. An eyewitness testified:

They made our Indians bring out all their hidden goods and then they took them away… they prayed and sang until the tomahawks struck into their heads. A boy who was scalped got away said blood flowed in streams in their houses. They burned the bodies together with the houses which they set on fire.

Clashes between Americans and Indians had not been uncommon before the war but the struggle for independence intensified the conflict and justified racial violence as part of a wider cause, The numbers involved were not huge. Williamson took 170 men with him. Indian raiding parties seldom exceed a couple of hundred. Compared with the large-scale battles of the war, this was not game changing. However, its importance for future relations was considerable. The failed treaty of Fort Pitt was to have many later precedents, and the legacy of bitterness and betrayal was to have tragic, long-term consequences.

The reality of the tragic involvement of the Native Americans in the Revolution is one of futile violence. The Iroquois peoples who did not join the British side suffered the same dispossession and discrimination as those who waged a pointless campaign of frontier destruction. The Americas gained little from the Indian allies they had and their troops were led into equally pointless scorched earth tactics that proved as militarily futile as those pursued by their successors in the twentieth century.

Chapter 10

Aftermath

The American Revolution is often compared favourably with other revolutions. The French Revolution was started by enlightened middle class reformers but resulted in bizarre scenes of public executions, the emergence of crankish political ideas and a military dictator, Napoleon, who caused millions of deaths in vainglorious wars, The Russian Revolution overthrew one supposed tyranny and replaced it with a one-party state with a brutal dictator, Stalin. Under the Tsars, political opposition was exiled to Siberia. Under the Commissars vast numbers of ordinary people ended in horrific labour camps to fulfil arrest quotas and act as slave labour. The English Revolution was begun by property owners who disliked taxes, pro-Catholic religious fervour and arbitrary power. After a costly civil war, from 1642 to 1646, they ended with higher taxes, religious fervour of a different kind and a military dictator, Oliver Cromwell. The Chinese Revolution which seemed to free the people from a corrupt and foreign-dominated regime in 1949 ended up with the greatest repression and loss of life of any country in the twentieth century, as a dictatorial 'Chairman' Mao Zedong pursued repression and costly economic and social experiments regardless of human costs.

The Patriots in America, however, seemed to have achieved their aims without unlooked-for and tragic consequences. Washington did not take over power as a dictator. Instead, he emulated the Roman general Cincinnatus and retired to his estate. The republic maintained its elected assembly. It kept its independence and achieved what Jefferson called 'the empire of liberty' by expanding over the continent. It developed into the world's greatest economic power and, in political terms, achieved a world influence unforeseen by the men of 1776.

No wonder then that the Revolution is looked back at with such respect and affection. However, did all the American people really benefit from it?

This short study has shown that there were substantial numbers of Americans who were the losers from the conflict. Those who doubted the wisdom of taking resistance to the level of armed conflict and those who were active opponents of the 'noble cause' certainly lost. They suffered from ostracism and physical violence, and thousands faced loss of property and exile. They still face exclusion from the favoured historical narrative, especially that of the later stages of the war but also in the standard accounts of the growing opposition to British policies after 1763. These often give the impression of a much greater consensus for 'liberty' than really existed.

For the native Americans, marginalised in the 'Revolution Story' and not even included in such things as computations of population in the eighteenth century, the Revolution was a disaster. British protection against colonial encroachment had been uneven, but the impetus that Independence gave to westward expansion was disastrous for the Indigenous peoples. Those who hoped for security by helping the Patriot cause achieved little in the long run. Those who were on the 'wrong' side and helped the British, also found little reward and like other loyalists suffered from reprisals, persecution and exile.

The Black Americans who supported the Patriots did not find the new Republic to be grateful or enlightened. The victory of the colonists was a victory for slavery. The new constitution of 1787 enshrined the Institution by deciding that the population requirements, which determined how many representatives each state had in Congress, would include 3/5 of the slave population. Though many states had ended the importation of slaves, there was no official ban until 1 Jan 1808, following an act passed in 1807. Slavery was not only recognised but it spread as the new Republic grew. The invention of a machine to pick the seeds from raw cotton helped to boost plantation profits and to make slavery even more essential in the minds of the property-owners in the southern colonies.

But what of the supposed winners? These included the ideologically motivated White male elites, the volunteers for liberty, the individual states who wanted to be free from restrictions, unpopular taxation and allegiance to an authority that they had little sympathy within a far-off capital city. What of merchant interests who looked for prosperity away from British control?

For many, the main aim was liberty for smaller communities – their families, their communities and their states. There was no consensus to create another overarching authority to impose taxes and trade regulations, a national bank and a standing national army. During the war, the power of Congress had been quite limited, and there had been no national leadership as such. Washington, as Commander-in-Chief, dealt with Congress not an American ruler. The needs of war had led to the Articles of Confederation – a more centralised government – but after the war, the United States remained a loose alliance of independent states. There was no mechanism or authority for central taxation of trade regulation. The Continental Army had been difficult to keep together even during the war, but after the peace it dwindled to a few hundred. State militias remained under the control of elected state assemblies. State government could be supported by local taxes; the independence the patriots had fought for was the independence of each state.

One feature of colonial life, which this study has described, was the ongoing local unrest and dislike of authority. This has often been seen as a precursor to the demands for the end of British rule. However, opposition to authority is not the same as support for the ideology of national independence, and there is a continuity of popular unrest and opposition to authority from before 1776. The 'common sort' did not always draw a distinction between resentment of British authority and resentment of financial imposition by the governments of the new Republic.

By 1787, there were fears among the elite groups that the Republic would go in the direction of classical models. There were fears of social unrest. Support of local authorities and courts for debtors over creditors seemed to threaten stability. There were concerns about unwillingness of state governments to pay for war debts and the failure of states to keep order in the face of popular protests. Well-read American elites had studied in their schools and colleges how plebian unrest had helped to undermine the idealism of the ancient Roman Republic. Would it lead to dictatorship and even a restoration of monarchy and aristocracy in the new American republic, as it had in ancient Rome?

The most famous incident was an episode of social unrest in Massachusetts called Shays Rebellion. Though the achievement of Independence was celebrated, in practice old problems remained in the new Republic. The newly settled areas of rural Massachusetts saw many suffering from problems of debt and, as before 1776, shortage of currency. Far from ending tax burdens on them, the war had increased them. Before 1776 there had been complaints of a remote government imposing taxes and being unresponsive to needs. In rural areas the new state authorities in Boston were as remote as the pre-war authorities in London.

The precedent for protests had been set by the dissidents of the 1760s and once again extra-legal meetings were called and there were assaults on established institutions. As often in the past, courts were attacked in Autumnn 1786 to free debtors from jail. Just as pre-war protestors found leaders, so did the Massachusetts farmers in the form of Captain Daniel Shays, a veteran of the Continental Army.

The rulers of the new Republic found themselves faced with the consequences of their own revolution. The Declaration of Independence made it clear that there was a right of resistance; what was the difference between rebellion based on a dislike of taxes and discontent with government in 1776 and rebellion based on much the same thing in 1786?

The propertied classes were determined to restore order more effectively than Britain had done when they themselves rebelled. The Governor of Massachusetts, Bowdoin, organised a military force that quickly dispensed Shays' malcontents. However, unrest continued in many areas in the north and middle states.

Shays demonstrated to many that a stronger means of social control was necessary in the form of a reorganised central government.

This had many of the features seen in protests in the earlier part of the century and was not the isolated incident which some narratives imply. It highlighted the vulnerability of the new Republic. If a central authority could not ensure order and did not have the means to sustain a strong defence, then the European powers might once again threaten. Spain had supported the colonists but was still in control of substantial areas. Britain still had Canada and bases in the Caribbean.

There were powerful interests who saw the future as a much stronger union with an overall authority headed by a president. There were calls for an executive to be able to raise taxes, regulate trade, organise defence and pursue stronger diplomacy.

A number of meetings were held to promote change and to strengthen the Articles of Confederation, but there was no great popular groundswell of support. A long struggle had ended British authority and there was limited popular appetite for replacing it with another form of control, let alone a permanent and indissoluble union of states which had very different economic needs, religions and societies. One of these meetings at Annapolis, however, gained the somewhat reluctant support of Washington. Once again, he became a key figure.

Visitors to Mount Vernon may get the wrong impression of Washington's position. The house is modest; there is little of the opulence of the 'Gone With the Wind' plantation era. However, Washington owned huge amounts of land in the Ohio Valley and had every incentive for a stronger state to defend it and to allow further expansion and to promote large scale economic projects. He was also a member of the Cincinnati Society, made up of senior ex-officers, concerned about social unrest and the prospect of another war for which the Republic would be unprepared. However, Washington had some doubts about supporting a new convention but was persuaded by more enthusiastic fellow Virginians.

In the end, delegates did meet at Philadelphia in 1787 with the modest aim of simply strengthening the Articles of Confederation. The meeting had some legitimacy because it had been approved by elected state assemblies. However, what followed was of very doubtful legality and is on a par with the irregular assemblies elected or formed in the period before the Revolution. No state had chosen to draw up a completely new and binding constitution or to set up a process whereby special popular assemblies were called to ratify the new constitution. The Philadelphia convention and the so-called Founding Fathers were really instituting a coup without any real authority which is closer to elements of the French, Russian and Chinese Revolutions than is sometimes thought. A relatively small number of elite White male property owners decided to change the whole direction of the Revolution and institute a procedure to have their ideas accepted which was devised according to their own wishes.

This is not the place to give an outline of the Constitution, which is still, with amendments, the basis of US government today. Apparently, a surprising number of Americans have limited knowledge of its complexities, but in 1787 there was quite a widespread discussion of the ins and outs of the provisions. The draft of 1787 was considerably less democratic than the modern system. The president was to be elected indirectly by special electors, not chosen directly by popular vote. The upper house of the Senate, as its Roman name implies, was to be chosen by state assemblies on the basis of two senators per state. The more democratic House of Representatives was to be chosen on the basis of the population of each state, with larger states having more representatives. Each slave was to be seen as three fifths of a person so that the southern colonies with large slave populations who, of course, had no legal or political or even human rights, could still count.

This was a monstrous idea by modern standards and even at the time was criticised. The vast majority of women could not vote or take part in public affairs and the native population was of course excluded.

The president and the government he chose had powers to tax, regulate trade and take all necessary measures, but his power was balanced by Congress (The Senate and the House of Representatives) and the Supreme Court which eventually declared government acts unconstitutional.

Much of this went against what the original revolution had been about. There had been no talk of a sort of elected limited monarch and no talk of a union which would be perpetual and which no state could leave. In fact the Declaration of Independence was formed on the principle that the right to reject government which was oppressive was fundamental. Britain had claimed that the former colonies could not just leave the Empire at will. Now the Republic was saying that the states could not leave the union if they felt they were being oppressed.

In 1861, when the Southern states thought that the election of an opponent of slavery, Abraham Lincoln, would threaten their freedom to oppress human beings, they referred to the Declaration of Independence and the Right to Resist. The great document of liberty was being used to defend a way of life built on the oppression of people of another race. It was also being used by the Federal Government to justify the defence of the union formed as a result of that same Declaration. What a moral maze!

The constitutional proposals were to be put to special Ratification Assemblies – an idea that came somewhat out of the blue. There has been relatively little interest in these assemblies by historians and their deliberations are still difficult to access. The proponents of a stronger Federal state have had the blessing of most historians who thought they were right to bring about a constitution which has been seen as 'a good thing'. This has been rarely challenged, even to the extent of supporters of lax gun laws defending a dangerous situation by reference to a 1791 Constitutional amendment establishing the right to bear arms. The need for arms in an expanding frontier society with no effective police was very different from the need to own multiple deadly weapons in urban areas not threatened by wild animals, groups of bandits or hostile native peoples and defended by strong police forces, but the Constitutional right does not seem to be able to be successfully challenged.

The supporters of a stronger state were known as Federalists and their arguments in the so-called Federalist Papers are often treated with enormous respect. The opponents were known derisively as the 'anti-Federalists', a term of abuse in the late 1780s. The discussions varied from state to state. Georgia was strongly for a stronger government for the practical reasons of its proximity to Spanish territory and concerns for defence. However, nationally there was a strong body of opinion which opposed the proposed constitution.

The situation was not unlike 1776, with some passionate supporters of change, some with reservations and some opposed. The assumption is often made that this widespread discussion was conducted like a sort of national debating society. In fact, the same rancour and intolerance that opponents of independence faced in many cases was suffered by those who opposed the Constitution. Their views were often deliberately omitted from newspaper reports or minutes and once again threats of tarring and feathering or ostracism emerged. The study made by the historian Pauline Maier using records of the discussions is revealing. Once again, as in so many revolutions, 'the people' were evoked by the supporters of what could be seen as a second revolution to justify change. The eminent lawyer John Jay wrote that 'the people would be the only source of just authority'. In other words, assemblies which had no legal authority or general popular support would be the source of establishing a new constitution devised and promoted by an elite. This could be an episode in the French Revolution or a justification for Lenin's seizure of power. It is common in revolutions for 'the people' to be invoked to sanction change but claiming that 'the people' support change is not the same as 'the people' actually doing so.

'The people' could be intimidating. In the course of the Ratification debate in Philadelphia, the leading opponents of the constitution were staying at Boyd's Boarding House. They were attacked by a pro-Constitution crowd who threw heavy stones at their window and threatened them with hanging. Pressure from Federalists forced the owner of the *Pennsylvania Herald* to sack a journalist who had the temerity to publish speeches critical of the new Constitution and only material favourable to the proposed changes was published. Dissenting voices, such as the inhabitants of Paxton, Massachusetts who thought the Constitution 'Subversive of Liberty and Extremely dangerous to the Civil and Religious rights of the People' often found it difficult for their views to be reported.

On the whole, history has favoured the victors. The eloquent critic of the Constitution in the New York debates, Melancthon Smith, faced the leading supporter of a strong government, Alexander Hamilton. There is no rap musical devoted to Smith, but Hamilton's fame remains. Few remember Samuel Spencer of North Carolina who argued that taxation imposed by a remote Federal government was akin to the taxation imposed by a remote British government. His view was that 'The most certain criterion of happiness that any people can have is to be taxed by those representatives who intermix with them, know their circumstances… Our federal representatives will not know our situation'. However, this is not a well-remembered viewpoint.

It is an irony that the richer southern landowners in 1787 and 1788 were won over by a recognition of the existence of slavery and largely supported the constitution as a method of social control. It was this very class that in 1861 revived the anti-Federalist arguments and stood for a dissolution of the indissoluble union that their ancestors had supported.

Distrust of Federal government persisted and still exists. But the elites were once again able to mobilise support and opposition was made, as in the Revolution, to appear unpatriotic. The struggle against the interference of one government ended with a vote for interference by another.

And did the Revolution bring about the hoped-for prosperity? It seemed as if the colonies had broken free from the controls on manufacture imposed by the British navigation laws. However, in practice it had been impracticable to restrict the mainly small-scale manufacturing undertaken in colonial workshops. There is little evidence of actual limitations of larger scale manufacturing under British rule. In 1750, restrictions were placed on iron manufacturing in the colonies to protect British exporters but some twenty-five factories were set up in Pennsylvania and Delaware alone. British authorities rarely enforced restrictions, and the Revolution made little difference in practice. The British were mostly concerned with profits from trade, The Navigation acts required colonial exporters to route their sales through Britain. However, with limited regulation of direct trade it is unlikely that extra costs amounted to more than 3 per cent of colonial GDP before 1775. In addition, subsidies from Britain and the benefits of Britain meeting defence costs made the economic relationship favourable and well worth the modest attempts of Britain to recoup military costs. A recent economic study by AD Yel in the *Journal of Economics* of the University of Michigan concluded that by comparing economic costs and benefits the colonists stood to increase their per capita income by 0.4 per cent by becoming independent. The disruptions to trade and the damage caused by war and economic dislocation meant that per capita income may have fallen from $74.02 to $59.19. In addition, as Congress lacked authority to tax and had limited credit as a new institution, it had to resort to borrowing to pay for the war. This caused a depreciation of the value of currency and a rise in prices. Inflation eroded real income for at least twenty years after the war. The war disrupted trade and, though there was a recovery of possibly 37 per cent by 1790. this was more domestically based and more a result of rising population than exports. The French Revolution, partly brought about by the financial problems of France as a result of its involvement in the American war, led to sustained war in Europe which had a major disruptive effect on US overseas trade after 1793

A factor not often considered is the loss of manpower as a result of the exile of so many loyalists. In many areas, there was a shortage of skilled labour and a manpower shortage as a result of the losses of war and the disruption caused by the departure of substantial numbers of people. There is evidence of decline in urban centres and the economic effects of the movement of loyalists to Canada were marked.

Given modern calculations of a loss of per capita income greater than the costs of being part of the Empire, it is probable that the Revolution brought about few immediate economic benefits.

Figures for human losses vary, but there may have been 6800 colonial deaths in actual fighting. The death toll from disease was much higher at perhaps 17,000 and substantial numbers dying in captivity, between 8000 and 12,000. Given the much smaller population, the human costs were proportionally higher than in the much greater bloodletting of the second civil war (1861–5) and the subsequent World Wars. The war did not bring a lasting peace. Casualties in the war between Britain and the US from 1812–1815 were actually higher than those in the war for independence. In the two decades following 1783, the economic costs were still being felt. The war did not bring the whole of America into the control of the new Republic as Spain and Britain continued to control very large areas and the colonial powers were still established in the Caribbean. The colonists who had disliked central taxation and interference from government found themselves with a sort of elected monarch and taxes, and institutions such as a national bank, which they had not fought to establish. Unfree labour persisted, as did considerable concentration of wealth. Democracy in the sense of universal male suffrage was decades away. Democracy in terms of all White people, including women, voting was over a century away. Democracy in terms of all Americans, regardless of race, voting and participating in public life, was even further away. The right to resist governments that was so clearly stated in the Declaration of Independence was restricted by the establishment of a perpetual union. Against all this was a sense of freedom and opportunity which made the USA a refuge for so many from poverty or oppression in Europe. The energies which sustained a costly and divisive struggle saw one of the great movements in world history as the West was explored, settled and transformed. The optimism of a new land found voice in the poetry of Walt Whitman, and for all its faults the American Revolution did lead to idealism, Whitman's oft quoted and much-loved poem of 1860, *I Hear America Singing*, celebrates the community of a democratic new world. However, it may be best if it is not too closely analysed – the glorious singing is done mainly by men working heroically while women pursue their domestic tasks. Native Americans do not share in the musical celebration and there are no enslaved voices from the plantations. The poem was written when the Republic was on the brink of civil war, based on intense disunion and disagreement about the results of the Revolution:

> *I hear America singing, the varied carols I hear,*
> *Those of mechanics, each one singing his as it should be blithe and strong,*
> *The carpenter singing his as he measures his plank or beam,*
> *The mason singing his as he makes ready for work, or leaves off work,*
> *The boatman singing what belongs to him in his boat, the deckhand singing on the*
> *steamboat deck,*
> *The shoemaker singing as he sits on his bench, the hatter singing as he stands,*
> *The wood-cutter's song, the ploughboy's on his way in the morning, or at noon*
> *intermission or at sundown,*
> *The delicious singing of the mother, or of the young wife at work, or of the girl*
> *sewing or washing,*
> *Each singing what belongs to him or her and to no-one else,*
> *The day what belongs to the day – at night the party of young fellows, robust, friendly,*
> *Singing with open mouths their strong melodious songs.*

But the Revolution was never blamed for failing to resolve issues. Lincoln made one of the most famous speeches in US history in the aftermath of a horrific battle at Gettysburg in 1863. This tragic encounter between Americans saw blood literally flow down the streets of the small Pennsylvania town in streams, and amputated limbs fill whole rooms – as the guides to the town relate to tourists. The Gettysburg Address offers this view of the founding of the American union:

> *Four score and seven years ago our fathers brought forth on this continent a new*
> *nation, conceived in liberty, and dedicated to the proposition that all men are*
> *created equal.*

There was certainly a 'new nation', but it still does not occur to many that if the other statements had equally been the case, then 600,000 Americans would not have died in a dispute about the nature of that liberty and a fundamental disagreement whether or not 'all men' included millions of enslaved men and women of a different race.

George Washington deserves the last word. In his farewell address as president in 1796 he reflected on power:

> *It is important, likewise, that the habits of thinking in a free country should inspire caution in those entrusted with its administration, to confine themselves within their respective constitutional spheres, avoiding in the exercise of the powers of one department to encroach upon another. The spirit of encroachment tends to consolidate the powers of all the departments in one, and thus to create, whatever the form of government, a real despotism. A just estimate of that love of power, and proneness to abuse it, which predominates in the human heart, is sufficient to satisfy us of the truth of this position.*

How successful he and his fellow revolutionaries were in the very long term of avoiding the dangers he raised must await the judgement of future historians.

Dear Reader,

We hope you have enjoyed this book, but why not share your views on social media? You can also follow our pages to see more about our other products: facebook.com/penandswordbooks or follow us on X @penswordbooks

You can also view our products at www.pen-and-sword.co.uk (UK and ROW) or www.penandswordbooks.com (North America).

To keep up to date with our latest releases and online catalogues, please sign up to our newsletter at: www.pen-and-sword.co.uk/newsletter

If you would like a printed catalogue with our latest books, then please email: enquiries@pen-and-sword.co.uk or telephone: 01226 734555 (UK and ROW) or email: uspen-and-sword@casematepublishers.com or telephone: (610) 853-9131 (North America).

We respect your privacy and we will only use personal information to send you information about our products.

Thank you!